FIRST & ONLY
WOMEN

History's female
trailblazers

LYNN SANTA LUCIA

PIER 9

Contents

Introduction

In a world of fighter pilots, physicians, four-star generals and Supreme Court justices who define themselves first and foremost as women, it cannot be forgotten that until recently women had a measly menu of options for authentic self-expression. Marriage was their main calling (if they weren't forced into some form of prostitution), meekness their virtue. If a woman was stirred to study, or to speak out, or to celebrate her artistry or athleticism, she usually found herself facing, at best, impossible odds and obstacles and, at worst, the harshest of criticism that sometimes would lead to her death.

For every woman today who makes great strides in academia, gets to use her voice and her vote, and has a playing field of her own, there was a first in the field who dared to be different and blazed the trail she now walks.

The women whose stories are presented in these pages performed extraordinary feats for their time. Some defiantly broke with tradition and publicly challenged their male counterparts, come what may. Christine de Pisan of France could not bear to read another page of misogynist writing from her medieval library and, with controlled fury, penned a slew of letters to renowned male scholars and to her majesty Queen Isabeau in a daring defence of her sex. Equally feisty, Elizabeth Blackwell became the first woman in the United States to earn the degree of MD, at a time when an education in medicine was considered a distasteful, even dangerous, pursuit for a woman. Her entrance into medical school came after years of dogged persistence, her interest in such an eccentric goal soaring after more than a few well-wishers declared it an utterly impossible dream.

Other female firsts shook off the chokehold of convention more subtly, like the decorous Isabella Bird, who often excused herself from Victorian society for 'a change of air' to combat a growing list of life-long ailments, not least a serious case of wanderlust. While globetrotting was nothing to boast about for a proper Victorian lady, Isabella's vividly written accounts of her far-flung travels earned her not only a respectable income and a considerable following of eager readers, but the honour of becoming the first woman Fellow of the prestigious Royal Geographical Society. Social advocate Lucy Stone, who refused to take her husband's name as an assertion of her individual rights, stirred interest in the women's rights movement among obstinate male opinion leaders and galvanised other female leaders, like Susan B. Anthony and Elizabeth Cady Stanton, to take up the cause. And she managed to do so with a soft, but firm, touch. She fought when she had to; when agitation served no purpose she retreated.

Whether possessing a disdain for injustice or a desire to escape poverty, an insatiable curiosity or an aggravating streak of perfectionism, the women here all had one trait in common: blazing spirit. Not surprisingly, from one decade to the next one woman's spirited achievements often sparked another to go still a step further. In 1909, Frenchwoman 'Baroness' Raymonde de Laroche playfully took up the challenge from a flirtatious aviator to learn how to fly, and became the world's first fully qualified woman pilot. Ten years later, twenty-seven-year-old African American Bessie Coleman was still looking for a way to make something of herself when her brother ribbed her that French women were superior because they were making careers as airplane pilots, and unwittingly ignited Bessie's interest in aviation; she would become a barnstorming media sensation, the first 'full-fledged aviatrix' of her race, and use her celebrity whenever she could to effect change for her race and her gender. Then, in 1928, a new heroine was born when Amelia Earhart became the first woman to cross the Atlantic Ocean by air. When the plane touched down safely in the harbor at Burry Port, Wales, Amelia was an instant international celebrity—much to her embarrassment; she didn't think her role as passenger warranted such fanfare. So she took it upon herself to *really* earn her reputation, and in 1932 became the first woman to fly the Atlantic Ocean solo. She accomplished the daring feat not only by herself, but faster than anyone on record, and was the only person to fly it twice.

Some of the first women in this book didn't fly at all during their lifetimes, but rather fell severely from grace. Pearl Hart, a well-brought-up young lady seduced by the legend of the Wild West, ended up in jail as the first woman ever to be convicted for robbing a stagecoach. And then there is Civil War-era Southern sympathiser Mary Surratt, who would be sentenced to death by hanging, becoming the first woman ever to be executed by the United States government, and the only woman in the history of the republic to hang by official execution.

These are women—noblewomen and 'nobodies', mystics and the matter-of-fact, daredevils and despots—who landed their number one positions against seemingly impossible odds, sometimes by defying the establishment, sometimes through sheer force of an unshakable belief and unstoppable will. Decorously or defiantly, they opened the way to new ways of thinking, new ways of acting, and fresh frontiers.

PHARAOH HATSHEPSUT (c. 1508–1458 BC)

His majesty, herself, ruled Egypt famously

Deep in a valley basin surrounded by steep cliffs, on the west bank of the Nile River, sits a splendid collection of ancient temples. The most magnificent of all is Djeser-Djeseru ('the Holy of Holies'), dedicated to the god Amun, but also built as the resting place for one of Egypt's most unusual pharaohs.

The temple rests atop a series of colonnaded terraces, reached by long ramps that once were graced with gardens. Inside, the walls are carved and painted with scenes that recite the tale of the life of this pharaoh: a birth overseen by gods, a triumphant coronation, an offering to the deity Horus, and an expedition to the exotic Land of Punt on the east African coast. The pharaoh wears a beard, a collar, a kilt, and the very ceremonial crowns fit for a king. Some of the 200 statues that once stood along the pathways have been pieced together by archeologists, a number of them lifelike images of a king with feminine features, others stone portraits of a woman leader. And on each and every inscription, the royal name has been erased and carved over. But, after many millennia, it is now clear: the king's name was Hatshepsut—a ruler whose biggest claim to fame is that she was ancient Egypt's only full-on female pharaoh.

Pharaoh Hatshepsut ruled Egypt in defiance of tradition for twenty years.

Hatshepsut lived 1000 years after the pyramids were first built and seventeen centuries after the Egyptians had begun writing their language in hieroglyphs. For a little more than two decades, from c. 1479 BC to 1458 BC, Hatshepsut ruled Egypt. During her relatively peaceful and prosperous reign at the beginning of the New Kingdom, she built a vast number of magnificent monuments, masterminded a highly profitable trading mission to the resource-rich Land of Punt, protected Egypt's borders, and promoted remarkable innovations in the decorative arts and architecture. Although less familiar to the modern world than the much later Cleopatra VII (with her fleeting ill-fated reign), Hatshepsut's successes were far greater and her achievements far more significant. In fact, she is considered one of the most successful of the 18th Dynasty kings.

Hatshepsut went to a great deal of trouble to appear as a typical pharaoh, taking on the five titles of a king, the male clothes, even the paraphernalia—including the false 'beard of wisdom' a pharaoh characteristically wore. Even more impressive, the first woman to proclaim herself Pharaoh of Egypt took the unprecedented action of usurping her stepson's throne. In fact, Hatshepsut had a career path that from the get-go was impossible to beat.

Her Majesty was a maiden

Hatshepsut, royal daughter of the much-beloved Pharaoh Tuthmosis I and his Great Wife Ahmose, grew up under the 18th Dynasty to rule Egypt, a period when Egypt was peaceful, prosperous and respected throughout the known world. Though she may have been the only one of Tuthmosis' five known children who was fully royal, she would not be trained to succeed her father as ruler; that training was only for her three half-brothers, born to women in her father's harem. Instead, like her sister Neferubity, Hatshepsut was prepared for a life as a queen, the royal wife of a pharaoh. She learned to read and write, manage the household servants, and take part in the myriad religious rituals a pharaoh and his queen had to conduct to preserve *maat*—ancient Egypt's sense of cosmic order.

When Tuthmosis died at the relatively old age of fifty, he had outlived all but two of his children: Hatshepsut and Tuthmosis II, son of the pharaoh and a harem woman named Moutnofrit. Seventy days after his death, Tuthmosis I would be laid with solemn ceremony in a tomb filled with all the accoutrements he could possibly want and need in the afterlife, and Tuthmosis II would choose a wife. If the young

Tuthmosis wanted to bolster his right to be crowned pharaoh, his queen would have to be of the royal blood. That meant his twelve-year-old half-sister Hatshepsut. As the sole child of Tuthmosis I and the Great Wife, Hatshepsut was her dynasty's last hope of keeping the royal bloodlines of Egypt intact.

CLEOPATRA VII

(69–30 BC), from the Ptolemaic dynasty, was the Egyptian civilisation's last pharaoh. Originally sharing power with her brothers, Cleopatra ruled with supreme political savvy, allying herself and forming relationships with the Roman powerhouses Julius Caesar (with whom she had a son who became co-regent) and, later, Marc Antony. When her plans to establish an empire with Marc Antony were crushed, Cleopatra committed suicide and her son was executed, ending 3000 years of pharaonic rule in Egypt.

❦

But Hatshepsut would not settle as mere queen to her half-brother's king. She had other goals. For probably three years of 'tandem' rule, she held the reins. The only time the duo may have genuinely teamed up was with the conception of their daughter Neferure, although it's possible the child was the daughter of Hatshepsut's lover Senenmut. Around 1479 BC Tuthmosis II died—perhaps to a sigh of relief from Hatshepsut, who sprang into action as official regent to the very young heir, Tuthmosis III (her husband's only son, by a harem girl named Isis).

It was a job Hatshepsut, perhaps just fifteen years old, had been training for since her earliest days by her father's side. Who other than the royal daughter of Tuthmosis I and the royal widow of Tuthmosis II, after all, knew more about palace life and protocol, was familiar with officiating at the rites in the temples, and was comfortable around royal advisers and visiting dignitaries from other lands? Women had acted as regents for infants and children at other times in Egypt's history, until the rightful heirs were old enough to be crowned pharaoh. So, until Tuthmosis III was mature enough to wield power, the acting ruler of Egypt would be his stepmother and aunt, Hatshepsut.

For a general notion of Hatshepsut's appearance at this early stage of her career, one only has to refer to a wall inscription still visible at her resting place, Djeser-Djeseru. It states that 'to look upon her was more beautiful than anything; her splendour and her form were divine'. It's more than likely that the praise came from Hatshepsut herself. All ancient Egyptians prepared for their own burial and the construction of their burial places. And the pharaohs customarily used their temples and tombs to aggrandise their unique achievements and virtues. Hatshepsut, who would come

Fanciful interpretation of the coronation of Hatshepsut by a nineteenth century artist.

to execute more building projects during her reign than any of her predecessors, had plenty of opportunities to laud herself to the hills. In fact, she has been called the most accomplished pharaoh of all at promoting her accomplishments. 'She was a maiden, beautiful and blooming', the hieroglyphics run, and regardless who ordered the inscription, there is probably no reason to doubt it.

As the blooming maiden settled into her role as dowager, she gradually took on more responsibilities and guided more of the royal decision making. She appointed officials and advisers, dealt with the priests, and eventually put herself front and centre when she and the young heir appeared in public ceremonies. After seven years, with zero bloodshed or fuss, the regent made a bold and unprecedented move: she had herself formally proclaimed His Majesty, Female King of Egypt. But taking on the five titles of a pharaoh wasn't enough. Upon her coronation, Hatshepsut donned an outfit fit for a king—wearing a man's short kilt instead of a woman's long dress, as well as a king's broad collar—and had herself crowned with the red-and-white double crown of the two Egypts (north and south). And just as any pharaoh would, she assumed a throne name: hers would be Maatkare (from the root word *maat*), to signify a pharaoh strong enough to ensure cosmic order, even if that pharaoh was, indeed, a woman.

Cementing her position

Hatshepsut was a masterful politician and an elegant stateswoman with enough charisma to keep control of an entire country for more than twenty years. Early on, however, she was smart enough to understand that her charm and experience could carry her only so far. So she used two devices to clinch her smooth coup d'état. The first was to claim that she was her father's intended successor. Later, to support her argument, she would order an inscription on the walls of her mortuary temple to read:

> *Then his majesty said to them: 'This daughter of mine, Khnumetamun Hatshepsut—may she live!—I have appointed as my successor upon my throne … she shall direct the people in every sphere of the palace; it is she indeed who shall lead you. Obey her words, unite yourselves at her command'. The royal nobles, the dignitaries, and the leaders of the people heard this proclamation of the promotion of his daughter, the King of Upper and Lower Egypt, Maatkare— may she live eternally.*

Just in case not everyone bought it, Hatshepsut went one step further to strengthen her position as rightful heir to the throne. She swore that she had been chosen as pharaoh by the gods themselves, even before her birth. According to the story told on the walls of Djeser-Djeseru, the Oracle of the god Amun proclaimed, on behalf of the deity: 'Welcome my sweet daughter, my favourite, the King of Upper and Lower Egypt, Maatkare, Hatshepsut. Thou art the Pharaoh, taking possession of the Two Lands'.

Hatshepsut managed, next, to gain the support of key officials, including her highest-ranking man, Senenmut, who tripled as steward, architect, and tutor to her daughter Neferure … and maybe was even her lover. To keep the pro-Tuthmosis III faction calm, Hatshepsut agreed, on paper, that it was a dual reign, that she and her stepson would be acting as co-rulers of Egypt. Tuthmosis III, however, did not forget that it was his birthright to become Egypt's sole ruler. As he came nearer to his coming of age, Tuthmosis III had his own story ready to prove his divine claim to the throne. On an important feast day, the young heir arranged to have a procession carrying the statue of the god Amun come to a stop in front of him, and then lead him through the temple at Karnak to the 'Station of the King', the spot where only the pharaoh normally stood during a ceremony. From all appearances, the god Amun had chosen Tuthmosis to be king. But it would be years before this prophecy was fulfilled.

Eventually, Hatshepsut would have her stepson married to her daughter. It was the perfect arrangement for keeping a close eye on Tuthmosis III, and cutting off at the pass any stirrings of revolt. Poor Neferure was really caught between a rock and a hard place: not only did she have the thankless task of marrying her restless half-brother, but she had to inform her mother of his every move. As compensation, Hatshepsut, the wifeless pharaoh, handed over to her daughter the role of Great Wife, which included officiating at religious ceremonies and administering huge estates. In due course, Neferure, Tuthmosis III, the royal court and everyone else would recognise Hatshepsut as the pharaoh on the throne until she died.

A glorious reign

Hatshepsut's reign, in comparison to that of most other pharaohs, was long and peaceful, with the exception of a few successful military campaigns against Nubia, the Levant and Syria early on in her career. Her focus for more than twenty years was to grow Egypt's prosperity and power through exploration, trade and building.

A shrewd businesswoman, Hatshepsut organised a daring trade expedition that sailed from the Gulf of Aqaba, through the Red Sea and south along the coast of Africa to the land of Punt (a region that can probably be pinpointed around Somalia or Ethiopia). Her mission, most of all, was to acquire frankincense and myrrh—the two most rare perfumes of the ancient world. Made from the resin of a small bush and a tree that grew only in faraway Punt, frankincense and myrrh played an important role in Egyptian religious ceremonies and in embalming the bodies of the pharaohs. When Hatshepsut's five-ship fleet returned to Egypt, after two long years away, with a tangy cargo of cinnamon, myrrh, ebony, ivory, panther skins, ostrich eggs and live baboons, the finest treasure of all was thirty-one live frankincense trees, their roots bound in balls of their indigenous soil. For Hatshepsut, this expedition was a highlight of her reign. It was the sort of accomplishment she wanted memorialised forever in her mortuary temple. When the exotic trees were planted across a fragrant terrace at Djeser-Djeseru, it would become the first known attempt to transplant foreign vegetation.

JADWIGA OF POLAND

(1373–1399), also known as St Hedwig, became Europe's first and only female 'king' in 1384, when she came to the throne in Poland at the age of ten. Her official title, *Rex Poloniae* (King of Poland), rather than *Regina Poloniae* (Queen of Poland), emphasised that she ruled in her own right and was not a consort. She spent much of her short life supporting the poor, giving away much of her personal wealth, and funding educational institutions. In 1997 she was canonised by the Catholic Church.

Her policies, administration and, not in the least, her success at re-establishing trading relationships lost during a foreign occupation before her reign brought tremendous wealth to Egypt, and enabled Hatshepsut to initiate massive building projects. She commissioned grander and more numerous monuments, statues, temples and shrines throughout Upper and Lower Egypt than any of her Middle Kingdom predecessors. During her reign, so much statuary was produced that almost every major museum in the world today possesses some Hatshepsut-influenced pieces among their collections. And because her output was so great that it was almost unbelievable, later pharaohs tried to claim some of her projects as their own.

Following the tradition of most pharaohs, Hatshepsut had a medley of monuments constructed at the Temple of Karnak in Thebes (modern-day Luxor).

Following pages: painted relief of Hatshepsut as pharaoh with the god Amun.

At Karnak, she also took on an impressive restoration and enlargement of the original Precinct of Mut (Queen of the Gods, wife of Amun) which had been ravaged by foreign interlopers during the Hyksos occupation. According to ancient Egyptian tradition, a king who respects the monuments of his ancestors will in turn have his own buildings respected; a king who deliberately demolishes an earlier monument is storing up trouble for himself. Even so, respecting monuments was one thing, restoring them quite another; no pharaoh was obligated to bring any ancient ruin back to its former glory. Hatshepsut's gesture, she hoped, would be taken as a sign of bringing order to chaos—part of the role of the pharaoh as the upholder of *maat*.

LADY JANE GREY, THE 'NINE DAYS' QUEEN'

(c. 1536–1554), is claimant to the shortest rule in England's history as well as being its first Queen Regnant. The niece of Henry VIII, she took the throne in accordance with her cousin Edward VI's deathbed wish to recognise her, a Protestant, as his heir ahead of his two sisters, the first of whom, Mary, was a Catholic. Mary soon mustered the support in Parliament to have the sixteen-year-old Jane's accession revoked and ordered her execution, along with that of the Duke of Northumberland, the mastermind behind the appointment.

The masterpiece of all her building projects was her magnificent terraced temple set against the sheer coral cliffs at the site known today as Deir el-Bahri. It is on the West Bank of the Nile River, near the entrance to what has come to be called the Valley of the Kings because so many of her successors chose to match their complexes with the grandeur of hers. Hatshepsut's temple was to serve in honour of Amun—the god who was supposed to be the divine father of every pharaoh—and as a dedication to Egypt's first female pharaoh once she had passed to the otherworld. Designed and realised by her royal steward-consort Senenmut, Djeser-Djeseru is made up of a series of colonnaded terraces, reached by long ramps that once were graced with gardens. It is a structure of perfect symmetry whose likeness was not to be seen for another 1000 years with the Parthenon. Needless to say, its architectural design was far ahead of its time.

When Hatshepsut had been on the throne for fifteen years, she declared a jubilee, a year of special celebration. Most pharaohs held a jubilee in the thirtieth year of their reign; maybe this pharaoh felt she had accomplished enough in half that time to deserve a celebration. Or perhaps she was celebrating her thirtieth birthday. To mark the event, she ordered two obelisks to be built and erected in her father's temple at Karnak. The successful planning, cutting, transportation and erection of a pair of obelisks in just seven months was a remarkable feat of engineering. The monuments were hewn whole from pink granite in a quarry many miles from Thebes, each weighing well over 300 tonnes. They were manoeuvred on wooden rollers to the river bank and loaded onto barges. It took twenty-seven boats rowed by 850 strong men to guide the barges down the Nile to Karnak. In the end, the roof and pillars of the temple hall had to be removed to fit them. One still stands here, nearly 30 metres high. It remains the tallest ancient monument in Egypt and, after the Lateran obelisk in Rome, is the tallest standing obelisk in the world. Hatshepsut's inscriptions, carved on the shaft and base, follow the same old themes: praise for the gods, and praise for herself.

Resurfacing from history

On 16 January 1458 BC, in the twenty-second year of her reign, Hatshepsut died. Unfortunately, no detailed record of her passing has been preserved, but today it's assumed that she died a natural death. The once-popular idea that Tuthmosis III finally snapped and had the female pharaoh killed now seems unlikely. At the time of her death, Hatshepsut was in her fifties and had reigned for a very long time without any sign of rebellion from her stepson. Impatient as Tuthmosis III must have been for his co-ruler to be out of the ring, he probably waited until after she had died naturally to get his revenge.

At some point following Hatshepsut's death a serious attempt was made to wipe out all traces of her memory from the historical record. Hatshepsut was omitted from the king lists of Abdos and Sakkara, where the succession was recorded as passing from Tuthmosis I to Tuthmosis II and then directly to Tuthmosis III. Similarly, she was excluded from scenes on the wall of the Ramesseum, where again the procession of royal ancestors shows Tuthmosis I, II and II in sequence. But elsewhere Hatshepsut's elimination was carried out in the crudest manner possible. Her cartouches and images were chiselled off stone walls and monuments, leaving very obvious gaps. At Karnak a wall was erected in an attempt to conceal her towering obelisks. At Djeser-Djeseru her statues and sphinxes were torn down, smashed and flung into rubbish pits. Seemingly, this assault was motivated by more than hatred; by removing every trace of Hatshepsut it was actually possible to rewrite Egyptian history, this time without the female pharaoh. Interestingly, the defacements were sporadic and haphazard, with only the more visible and accessible images removed. Millennia later, statues with inscriptions of her name were uncovered in obscure places—with Hatshepsut identified as queen, however, not as pharaoh.

Still, the female pharaoh's name was to be lost for thousands of years. As the centuries passed and all knowledge of hieroglyphic writing faded, Hatshepsut sank deep into obscurity. But during the 1800s, Djeser-Djeseru, ruined and almost completely buried under sand dunes and piles of rocks, started to attract attention: the first to come and poke around were Western tourists, increasingly fascinated by Egypt's ancient past, and then the archeologists. Jean-François Champollion had just decoded the writing on the Rosetta Stone, opening up the world of ancient languages; now at Djeser-Djeseru he deciphered some cartouches of a king named Maatkare Hatshepsut. But he was confused, for while the wall illustrations were apparently of a king, the texts made reference to a female ruler. Archeologists would become more and more aware of Hatshepsut's contradictory identity. By the late nineteenth century, however, much of the confusion had been cleared away. Hatshepsut's name, titles and principal monuments were known, and she even had her own entry in a dictionary of Egyptian archeology published in 1875.

> ## QUEEN VICTORIA
>
> (1819–1901), the longest-serving monarch of Great Britain, and the longest-serving female monarch in history, reigned for sixty-three years, and was the first monarch to live in Buckingham Palace. She ruled over the largest empire the world had ever seen and commanded the most powerful nation of the era. The Victorian Age, spanning much of the nineteenth century, was a time of great cultural, scientific, industrial, and military advancement.

In June 2007, a group of Egyptologists announced they had identified Hatshepsut's mummy. A single tooth and some DNA clues appeared to have solved the mystery of the missing pharaoh. The mummy had been unearthed in the Valley of the Kings in 1903, when it was found to have a missing tooth with only one root left behind. One hundred and four years later, orthodontics professor Galal El-Beheri from Cairo University matched up to it a molar, with a root attached, that had been found in 1881 in a small wooden box inscribed with Hatshepsut's name and cartouche, among a cache of royal mummies in a simple tomb about 915 metres distant from Hatshepsut's empty royal tomb. The tooth fit perfectly into the socket in the mummy's jaw. Case solved. Maybe. A number of Egyptologists not involved in the project have reservations; they will not accept the identification until it is confirmed by further testing. But if this recent discovery is correct, it would appear that Hatshepsut died of septicemia in her fifties, and probably suffered from arthritis and diabetes—not to mention bad teeth.

It is not surprising that the mummy of the first female pharaoh would have been hidden in a humble tomb. After her death, and in the wake of her stepson's attempt to destroy every trace of her and her reign, *somebody* who recognised her historic contribution hid her preserved body away for very safekeeping.

————⇒◈⇐————

Hatshepsut was the first great woman in recorded history. Her rise to power went against all the conventions of her time. As a pharaoh she was definitely different—she was a woman. And her contributions were significant, even if it was her successor, her stepson-nephew Tuthmosis III, who would become the greatest of all pharaohs, 'the Napoleon of ancient Egypt'. Nevertheless, the fact that Hatshepsut was able to contain the ambitions of this crafty and charismatic fellow for so many years hints at the qualities of her character. After 3500 years hidden in the dark, Hatshepsut has regained her rightful place in history.

Hatshepsut's fabulous mortuary temple at Deir el-Bahri in the Valley of the Kings.

LILIUOKALANI

(1838–1917)

*First Hawaiian queen and last Hawaiian monarch,
celebrated for her musical farewell*

Queen Liliuokalani looked down from her balcony as boatloads of US Marines landed on the shores of Honolulu, capital of the independent Kingdom of Hawaii, marched through the streets, and took up their positions around her palace. On 17 January 1893, the queen surrendered at gunpoint, yielding her authority to the government of the United States. The first queen of Hawaii had held the crown for only two short years. There would never be another queen, nor for that matter a throne to be occupied, in Hawaii again.

Liliuokalani was born in Honolulu to a high chief and high chieftess, who already had nine children (one of whom was to become King Kalakaua), and so decided to turn their daughter's care over to another couple at birth. Her adopted parents sent her, from the age of four, to the Royal School, where she mastered the English language and immersed herself in Western studies. But she was a Hawaiian through and through, never forgetting her native tongue and traditions.

She started out a princess, in the literal sense, and in 1874 unexpectedly became heir to her brother David Kalakaua, after King Lunalilo died and Kalakaua was elected to succeed him. Thus it was that in 1881, when Kalakaua left Hawaii on a trip around the world, forty-three-year-old 'Crown Princess' Liliuokalani was left in charge. She had absolutely no experience in ruling a kingdom. But that didn't stop her from acting decisively in the interests of her people, and proving that she was no pushover. When a serious outbreak of smallpox was attributed to the Chinese labourers being brought to the islands to work the sugarcane plantations, Liliuokalani closed Honolulu's port. The result: a fall-off in smallpox cases, and an outraged business community—meaning wealthy European and American sugarcane growers—protesting vehemently and pitting her as the enemy. Liliuokalani refused to budge.

Liliuokalani inherited the throne from her brother Kalakaua on 29 January 1891. She moved immediately to draft a new constitution that would restore veto power to the monarchy and voting rights to economically disenfranchised Native Hawaiians and Asians—but her efforts were fruitless. The Kingdom of Hawaii was on the brink of economic collapse, and the sugar growers were pushing for

Left: Queen Liliuokalani wearing the insignia of Hawaiian monarchy.

annexation to the United States as a means of economic survival. A Committee of Public Safety, headed up by the less and less prosperous plantation owners, was formed in opposition to the queen, essentially because their best interests were not being met. The clash of interests between plantation owners, Native Hawaiians, the US government and the Queen's cabinet would not be resolved. And so, US troops were transferred to Hawaii's shores, ostensibly to ensure peace and enforce neutrality.

When she relinquished her authority, Liliuokalani had hoped the US, like Great Britain earlier, would eventually restore Hawaii's independence. But when the queen lost her throne, the Hawaiian people lost their kingdom. A provisional government, composed of European and American businessmen, was instituted until annexation with the US could be achieved.

On 7 February 1895, ex-Queen Liliuokalani formally renounced her rights to the throne of Hawaii, declared the monarchy ended forever, and took the Oath of Allegiance to the Republic. Three weeks earlier, she had been arrested when firearms were found in the gardens of her home (several days after a failed rebellion by Robert Wilcox), of which she denied any knowledge. She was charged with encouraging an uprising, fined $5000 and sentenced to five years of hard labour by a military tribunal, but the sentence was commuted to imprisonment for eight months in Iolani Palace. Eventually, the Republic of Hawaii gave her a full pardon and restored her civil rights.

Hawaii officially became an incorporated US territory in July 1898, when President McKinley signed the resolution for annexation. Up until then, Liliuokalani fought tirelessly for Hawaii's right to self-govern. She made several trips to the US to protest against annexation, and even attended McKinley's inauguration holding a Republic of Hawaii passport that was personally issued to 'Liliuokalani of Hawaii' by President Dole.

Ironically, the last monarch of Hawaii is remembered just as much for a poignant farewell song she composed while under house arrest, even today one of the best known of all Hawaiian melodies. By the time Elvis Presley recorded 'Aloha 'Oe' ('Farewell to Thee'), it had long been a staple of every Hawaiian musician's repertoire.

Liliuokalani died at the age of seventy-nine, at Washington Place, her private Honolulu estate, which was to become the Executive Mansion for twelve governors *and today is a National Historic Landmark. She proved herself passionate about her past and loyal to her people, a woman in conflict with her times who managed to weather the storm with the utmost dignity and grace. Even—maybe especially—in her music (she composed some 150 songs in her life, sang alto, and is said to have played guitar, piano, organ, ukelele and zither), Liliuokalani is celebrated for preserving Hawaii's inimitable aloha spirit.*

This c. 1901 collage of members of Hawaiian royalty includes Liliuokalani at centre right.

HYPATIA OF ALEXANDRIA (c. 355–415)

Mathematics whiz didn't add up for murdering mob

Wrapping up her lecture to an enraptured crowd of admiring scholars, Hypatia spoke in the self-possessed, unabashed voice for which she was celebrated: 'Reserve your right to think, for even to think wrongly is better than not to think at all', she instructed. Then, flinging her man's cloak around her shoulders, she descended the steps of the Alexandrian Museum, stepped into her chariot and took the reins.

No sooner had she set out than a mass of God-fearing citizens, murder in their hearts, surged around the chariot and threw Hypatia onto the roadway. The mob stripped her naked and forced her into the nearby church, pushing and prodding her along the nave and up the chancel steps to the altar. Shaking herself free from her tormentors, Hypatia opened her lips to utter one final thought, but not a word came out. For in that moment, the leader of the pack struck her down, and the throng closed over her bare body. In a frenzy, her attackers dragged her back outside, savagely scraping flesh from bone with sharp roof tiles and broken pottery, tearing her body apart limb by limb, and tossing the remains into a fire.

Fifth century terracotta statue of Hypatia of Alexandria.

Philosopher, teacher, first known woman mathematician, and the single most brilliant mind of her time, Hypatia dominated the cultural life of Alexandria during the final decades of the fourth century and the early part of the fifth century. Ironically, she owes her fame in history more to the violent and politically contentious nature of her death in 415 AD than to her lifetime achievements.

She cut a brilliant—and purportedly beautiful—figure at a time when Alexandria was considered the preeminent cosmopolitan centre of the time, although it was also a city as turbulent and troubled as modern Gaza. The Roman Empire had gained control of Alexandria in 30 BC, and during Hypatia's lifetime, the Romans were gradually converting to Christianity. By the late fourth century, Alexandria was officially Christian, but beleaguered by tensions between Christians and the rest of the population: Jews, heretical sects, diverse schools of Neoplatonists, and an assortment of pagans, whose beliefs and practices were still tolerated, albeit begrudgingly. The empire's most valuable city was also its most volatile. And the situation was declining precipitously in 412 AD, under the Patriarch of Alexandria, Archbishop Cyril.

With Cyril celebrating his rise to power by a series of oppressions—not in the least expelling the Novatianist heretics from their churches and seizing the contents of their treasuries, levelling synagogues to the ground, and eventually driving the Jews out of the city—it was not a good time to be a champion of any non-orthodox Christian faith, or any other faith; nor, for that matter, was it a good time to be a mathematician. As a believer in Greek scientific rational thought, and an esteemed teacher among pagans, Jews and Christians alike, Hypatia—in the eyes of Cyril—was much too great a threat. Gradually, this rational-minded career woman of influence moved to the top of the patriarch's enemies' list.

Books, brains and beauty

Hypatia grew up in an atmosphere rich in learning and inquiry. Her hometown was Alexandria, in Egypt, a Greek state at the time of her birth sometime around 355 AD, and the cultural and intellectual hub of the known world. She was a privileged child, the cosseted only progeny of Theon Alexandricus, a mathematician famed for his commentaries on the works of Ptolemy and Euclid, and a gifted and distinguished professor of mathematics and astronomy at the renowned institute for higher learning, the Museum of Alexandria. For a Greek girl of her time, when only one-half of the population—the male half—went to school and held jobs, Hypatia was raised in an unusual manner. Her father was determined to cultivate a perfect specimen in his daughter. And so he set about schooling Hypatia not only in mathematics and physics, astronomy and astrology, literature and logic, but also developing an exercise program of swimming, horseback riding, and mountain climbing to transform her body into the perfect vessel to carry her impressive, well-trained mind.

Leaving no stone unturned, Theon focused, too, on his daughter's social skills. She was trained in speech, persuasion, debate, acting and rhetoric. She also learned enough of all religions from her father to turn her from the lot. Theon is said to have declared, 'All formal dogmatic religions are fallacious and must never be accepted by self-respecting persons as final. Reserve your right to think'. Hypatia took this to heart, and came up with her own conclusions: 'Fable should be taught as fable, myth as myth, and miracles as poetic fancies. To teach superstitions as truth is horrifying. The mind of a child accepts them and only through great pain, perhaps tragedy, can the child be relieved of them. Men will fight for superstition as quickly as for the living truth—even more so, since a superstition is intangible you can't get at it to refute it, but truth is a point of view, and so is changeable'. Later, she would hold sway over many with her beliefs.

At the museum, with its extensive facilities for research and teaching, Hypatia worked as a librarian and snapped up knowledge from the half-million book scrolls in the most celebrated library of the ancient world. Here, where dedicated scholars from across the Roman Empire lived and studied, she joined in discussion with some of the greatest intellectuals in the history of humankind.

Hypatia not only soaked up knowledge like a sponge, but also formulated new ideas and theorems in the fields of philosophy, mathematics, mechanics and astronomy with impressive creativity and imagination. It is thought that, at the age of

---

GABRIELLE ÉMILIE LE TONNELIER DE BRETEUIL, MARQUISE DU CHÂTELET

(1706–1749) was a mathematician and physicist of the Enlightenment whose translation and critique of Isaac Newton's *Principia Mathematica* became, and remains, a defining work. Excluded from many of the forums where scientists of the day discussed their ideas, Gabrielle was largely self-taught. She frequently disguised herself as a man to attend the Parisian coffee houses where the great minds of the age mingled. In 1737 the first of her many works, *Dissertation sur la nature et la propagation du feu*, was published by the French Academy of Sciences.

nineteen, she assisted her father in writing his eleven-part commentary on Ptolemy's *Almagest*, and that with him she co-produced a new version of Euclid's *Elements* to make it more palatable for Theon's pupils; the new and improved version was, indeed, approved by Alexandrian students, as well as by later Greeks who referred to it almost exclusively. But Hypatia did not live in the shadow of her learned father. Her single-handed attainments in mathematics were later widely praised. Influential contemporaries, including the Byzantine ecclesiastic Philostorgius, and the lawyer Socrates Scholasticus, lauded her impressive commentary on Diophantus's *Arithmetica*, a thirteen-volume definitive study that included alternative solutions to problems and new problems concerning first-degree and quadratic equations. Another of her commentaries, on Apollonius's *Conics*, addressed a discipline that after Hypatia's day would be largely neglected until the seventeenth century.

> ## MARIA GAETANI AGNESI
>
> (1718–1799) was an Italian mathematician, and the first woman to be appointed as a university professor—although it is not certain that she accepted the post. Her greatest work, *Instituzioni Analitiche ad uso Della Gioventù Italiana* (*Analytical Institutions for the Use of Italian Youth*) began as a book to help teach her brothers calculus, but became a universal text, published in many languages.
>
> ᴄᴏᴗᴗᴏ

Her contributions to science are reputed to include the charting of the sun, stars and planets with the pane astrolabe, a device used to measure the positions of celestial bodies and one that Hypatia perfected to the point where it could accurately solve problems in spherical astronomy. She is also credited with the invention of the hydrometer, a sealed tube about the size of a flute, weighted at one end, used to determine the relative density and gravity of liquids.

As a young adult, Hypatia did the almost unthinkable for a lady of her day: she left Alexandria and toured the ancient world, landing in Athens to study at Plutarch's school of mathematics. Here she firmly established her skill as a mathematician. But philosophy did not take a back seat. It was at Plutarch's school that she really started to shape her beliefs in the Platonic system of thought—in the laws of rational nature, and the capacities of the human mind free of imposed dogmas. Word got out about this intense and brilliant young woman; by the time Hypatia returned home, a celebrity of sorts with a reputation for having 'the mind of Plato in the body of Aphrodite', the museum had a teaching job waiting.

The philosopher in the public eye

Hypatia was as remarkable a teacher as she was researcher, inventor and writer. By all accounts she was also a great beauty. Her youth and exceptional looks, as much as her erudition and eloquence, soon attracted vast crowds of students and admirers from near and far, including Syria, Cyrene and Constantinople. From her home in Alexandria, Hypatia formed an intellectual circle made up of virtual disciples who came to study privately, some of them for many years. Her followers came from wealthy, high-ranking families in both religious and political circles. Among them were two of the most powerful men of the day: Orestes, Prefect of Alexandria, and Synesius of Cyrene (who would later become Bishop of Ptolemais). By some accounts, Synesius all but worshipped her. He went so far as to write a letter defending her as the inventor of the astrolabe, although earlier astrolabes predate Hypatia's model by at least a century, and Theon had already gained fame for his treatise on the subject.

> ## ADA LOVELACE
>
> (1815–1852), daughter of poet Lord Byron, was raised as a mathematician and scientist and became the world's first computer programmer, in 1833, working with inventor Charles Babbage on his calculating 'analytical engine'. A software language developed by the US Department of Defense over one hundred years after her death was named 'Ada' in her honour.
>
> ❧

Nevertheless, while Synesius misplaced credit where credit was due for this ancient astronomical computer, he let his opinion of his teacher blatantly reveal itself when he addressed letters to her as 'The Muse' and 'The Philosopher'.

Around their teacher, Hypatia's students formed a community based on the Platonic system of thought. What Hypatia was talking about was the redemptive powers of reason, but also the search for the 'divine' through religious revelation. They called the knowledge passed on to them by their revered teacher 'mysteries', and kept it secret from people of lower social classes, whom they regarded as unequipped to comprehend divine and cosmic matters. Besides, the path on which Hypatia led them to reunion with the divine was indescribable; following the path required tremendous mental effort and will, ethical strength and a deep desire for the infinite. The ultimate goal was to achieve religious experience as the essential ideal of philosophy.

Hypatia supposedly never married because 'she was wedded to the truth'. It has been suggested (post-mortem, by her enemies) that she had a number of lovers. It's more commonly accepted that she remained a virgin to the end of her life. One story sets the stage this way: she was so alluring that one of her students couldn't help but fall in love with her and openly display his infatuation. Hypatia is said to have cured him of his affliction by gathering her menstrual rags stained with blood and saying, 'This is what you love, young man, and it isn't beautiful!' The student was so affected by shame and amazement at the sight that he experienced a change of heart and went away a better man. Whether or not this incident ever took place, Hypatia was, indeed, as renowned for her chastity and virtue as she was for her intellectual prowess, and consistently displayed a dignified manner toward her students, as well as to men in power. Nicephorus and Philostorgius, church historians at odds with Hypatia's beliefs, even praised her for her upstanding character, as well as her scholarship.

All sources agree that Hypatia was a model of ethical courage, righteousness, and civic devotion. Some of her lectures took place in the city's lecture halls. Occasionally she participated in the activities of the polis, serving as an esteemed adviser on current issues to both municipal and visiting imperial officials. She undoubtedly kept company with Alexandria's movers and shakers, including Orestes, civil prefect and number one nemesis of the patriarch Cyril. Unfortunately, her powerful connections not only could not protect her, but more likely than not helped do her in, at a point when Alexandria was on the cusp of momentous change.

Climactic change

Much of Alexandria's population in Hypatia's time was in no mood to acquiesce to the political ascendancy of the Christians. The civil prefect, Orestes, was particularly annoyed. Orestes stubbornly fought against Cyril's growing encroachments on the sovereignty of civil power; and even when Cyril tried to make peace, Orestes remained intransigent.

It was no secret that Hypatia was a friend of Orestes. In Hypatia, the church authorities realised they faced a woman endowed with considerable moral authority who was determined in defence of her convictions and exerted a great deal of influence. They feared that through her own influential students she might win support for Orestes among those close to the emperor. Feeling threatened, Cyril decided he had no choice but to launch a propaganda campaign against Alexandria's most revered teacher.

Hypatia was stripped naked before the altar in the church called Caesareum.

His first attempt to discredit Hypatia would be to call her a pagan. This would be a challenge. It was too obvious that, although she was not an orthodox church follower, she strongly sympathised with Christianity. In her lectures, Hypatia often said that 'the person of Christ' was holy to her, but that she also felt affinity with 'the gods enrobed in the eternal fabrics of the cosmos'. To Hypatia, the deities revealed themselves in the beauty of nature, in the intelligence of the astral bodies, in the wonder of art. Moved by her impassioned elucidations, pagan and Christian students

The murder of Hypatia, last scientist of the Golden Age of Pericles.

alike flocked to her lectures. Her favourite student, Synesius, understood that through his teacher's guidance he could achieve spiritual and religious integrity; he went on to become a Christian bishop.

But while Hypatia held sway over her disciples, it was a whole other story convincing the stern patriarch that, when it came to Neoplatonism and Christianity, 'the words are slightly different, the sense is very much the same'. Cyril pronounced: 'Your gods are reduced to dust, at the feet of the victorious Christ'. This elicited from Hypatia a passionate response:

> *You're mistaken, Cyril. They live in my heart.*
> *Not as you see them—clad in transient forms,*
> *Subject to human passions even in heaven,*
> *Worshipped by the rabble and worthy of scorn —*
> *But as sublime minds have seen them*
> *In the starry expanse that has no dwellings:*
> *Forces of the universe, interior virtues,*
> *Harmonious union of earth and heaven*
> *That delights the mind and the ear and the eye,*
> *That offers an attainable ideal to all wise men*
> *And a visible splendour to the beauty of the soul.*
> *Such are my Gods!*

Cyril decided he needed to take a different tack: he set out to discredit Hypatia as a witch who, through Satanic wiles, had beguiled not only the prefect (the only explanation Cyril could come up with for Orestes' challenging behaviour), but also 'God's people', and the entire city. This accusation seemed to stick, at least with a fanatical sect of Christians from Nitria that backed the patriarch. One early evening, in 415 AD, some 500 zealous Nitrian monks descended on the city in support of Cyril. They confronted Orestes and stoned him nearly to death, accusing him of paganism and idolatry, over the prefect's loud protestations that he was a baptised and believing Christian. And, once they were through with Orestes, they fell on Hypatia, 'dragging her from her carriage', and taking her to the church called Caesareum, where they completely stripped her and then murdered her with oyster shells (or roofing tiles). After tearing her body in pieces, they took her mangled limbs to a place called Cinaron, and there burnt them.

AMALIE EMMY NOETHER

(1882–1935) was a celebrated German mathematician. She revolutionised the fields of algebra and physics, and was described by Albert Einstein as 'the most significant creative mathematical genius thus far produced since the higher education of women began'. When Nazi Germany ordered in 1933 that all Jews be dismissed from their university positions, Noether took up a position at Bryn Mawr in the United States.

The demise of Alexandria's woman of great scholarship and influence was precisely what Cyril needed to secure his position. Once Orestes' powerful supporter was eliminated, the prefect gave up his struggle against the patriarch and left Alexandria for good. Not long after that, hordes of scholars packed up, following close behind him. Church authorities swooped in on the city and paralysed the prefect's supporters with fear and intimidation. A few city councillors attempted to intervene with the emperor, but their efforts were futile. Cyril's supporters surrounded the patriarch and, according to his greatest fan, the Coptic bishop John of Nikiu, 'named him "the new Theophilus"; for he had destroyed the last remains of idolatry in the city'. Alexandria would be, henceforward, under an ecclesiastical thumb. And the symbol of 'idolatry'—really that great model of scholarship and wisdom, beauty and persuasion—would be nothing more than a memory, but a memory refusing to fade.

Hypatia's beauty, her chaste life as a follower of neoplatonism, and her cruel death at the hands of an angry mob, provided all the drama needed for later embellishment. From the moment she died, her story came alive in countless versions, each with its own underlying message suited to the messenger. Many writers and influencers (like the philosophers Voltaire and John Toland) exploited the figure of Hypatia as an innocent victim of a fanatical, nascent Christianity fearful of her way of reasoning. Others lament Hypatia as the 'last of the Hellenes', and maintain that her murder marked the demise of the Greek notion of a harmonious cosmos and freedom of inquiry—even though recent historians can illustrate how paganism did not die with Hypatia, nor for that matter did mathematics or Greek philosophy.

What is more than certain is that Hypatia fell at the hands of Cyril's supporters. Roman Catholic commentators normally stoutly defend the archbishop; anti-clericals gleefully denounce him. Whether or not the mob was given orders or was acting on its own behalf, and whether the murderers were religiously or politically motivated, are questions still up for debate. Perhaps the view most telling and balanced comes from the Anglican historian Canon Bright, who wrote: 'Cyril was no party to this hideous deed, but it was the work of men whose passions he had originally called out. Had there been no [earlier such episodes], there would doubtless have been no murder of Hypatia'.

Woman of Alexandria, scholar and philosopher whose life and spiritual individuality have sustained interest in her for many centuries, Hypatia leaves us with this thought: 'Life is an unfoldment, and the further we travel the more truth we can comprehend. To understand the things that are at our door is the best preparation for understanding those that lie beyond'.

ELENA LUCREZIA CORNARO PISCOPIA

(1646–1684)

Venetian paragon of learning

For most of her life, all she really wanted to do was study. Elena Lucrezia Cornaro Piscopia was the first woman in the world to earn a doctoral degree when she received a doctorate in philosophy from the University of Padua in 1678.

She was the quiet, pious daughter of a noble Venetian family. Undoubtedly gifted in her own right, nonetheless as a product of Venice's highest nobility she was set on her course with not just a few advantages. By the time of her birth in 1646, Venetian aristocrats—notably among them the Cornaro Piscopia family—had been participating for two and a half centuries in the flowering of Italian Renaissance culture in the areas of art, music, and literature. Among the Cornaro Piscopia family's ancestors was a plethora of intellectuals and patrons of the arts and letters. Elena's own grandfather had amassed a magnificent library of close to 2000 carefully catalogued volumes, which he directed in his will was to 'remain in the house equally accessible to all my children and their legitimate descendants as perpetual caretakers' as his cultural legacy.

When Elena was seven years old, a well-educated parish priest recognised her as a child prodigy. From that point her father, Giovanni Battista Cornaro Piscopia, was determined to give her the best possible education. From the age of seven until she was twenty-two, Elena studied Latin and Greek with the priest, followed by classical and modern Greek with a priest of the Greek Orthodox Church in Venice. Her studies in mathematics, the sciences, and modern languages were made under the tutelage of a Jesuit scholar who had studied in Paris with the free-thinking intellectual Pierre Gassendi; philosophy under the Paduan professor Carlo Rinaldini; theology under the Franciscan friar and Paduan professor Felice Rotondi; and Hebrew with the leading Jewish rabbi in Venice, Shemuel Aboaf. But she didn't focus her energies exclusively on her books. By the time she was seventeen, she could sing admirably, compose music, and was adept at playing the violin, harp, clavichord, and harpsichord.

Elena's achievements attracted the attention of not just her tutors and the clerics, but other intellectuals, astronomers, and scientists. Many came to Venice explicitly to spend time in her company. She was not only brilliant she was also

---

Left: Antonio Molinari painted Elena surrounded by allegorical beings.

beautiful, and she had a number of suitors. But marriage was the furthest thing from the young scholar's mind. When she came of age, Elena wanted to enter the Benedictine Order. She turned down marriage proposals, took a vow of chastity, and secretly practiced the disciplines of the order, spending time serving the sick and the poor when she wasn't buried in her books, even wearing a habit under her elaborate silk gowns. Her father, however, refused to allow her to enter the order, and had her apply for a degree from the University of Padua, instead.

Elena was awarded her doctorate by the University of Padua.

Giovanni Battista had a mission: to make of his brilliant daughter a paragon, a living monument to the Cornaro Piscopia.

Although she had never experienced university life, because no school at the time admitted women for advanced studies, Elena's preparation in the highest disciplines of philosophy and theology was comparable to that of any man schooled at a university. The members of the university board, the Reformers of the University of Padua, were in complete agreement, and recommended that she receive a doctorate in both fields. Cardinal Gregorio Barbarigo, chancellor of the university, vetoed the degree in theology, as it would have granted Elena the right to teach theology, something a woman was not allowed to do. But on 26 June 1678, at the age of thirty-two, Elena Lucrezia Cornaro Piscopia was awarded a doctorate in philosophy by the University of Padua after successfully completing her oral examination on Aristotle's Posterior Analytics *and* Physics, *thus becoming the first woman university laureate in the world. In addition to her doctorate, Elena received the doctor's ring, the teacher's ermine cape, and the poet's laurel crown, because her examiners agreed that her accomplishments far exceeded the doctoral requirements. Some sources say that she became a lecturer in mathematics at the university.*

The University of Padua did not offer another degree to a woman for another seventy years. And not until the nineteenth century would women begin to be admitted to universities in other European countries outside of Italy, and to undergraduate institutions founded exclusively for women in the United States. Among these women-only US universities was Vassar College, founded in 1861, where in 1904 a stained-glass window was mounted in the Thompson Memorial Library depicting Elena Lucrezia Cornaro Piscopia surrounded by professors, in receipt of her university degree, to inspire the generations that followed.

WU ZETIAN (c. 625–705)

China's only reigning Empress was 'a treacherous fox'

In the winter of 654 AD, Emperor Gaozong's first-rank concubine, and his open favourite, Wu, gave birth to a daughter. Palace protocol required that Empress Wang, as the overseer of the inner palace and lead wife of the emperor, should pay her a visit and check on the baby princess. When the empress came to Wu's bedchamber, the consort was not there. The empress cradled the infant in her arms and pressed her cheek against the baby's face, before laying her gently back in her crib. Then the empress left the room.

Shortly thereafter, Gaozong came to see the new princess; by now Wu was back in her chambers. They found the baby cold and dead. Wu shrieked and burst into tears—and demanded that her attendants tell her what had happened. Meekly, they answered, 'The empress was just here'. Instantly Wu cried out, 'The empress has murdered the emperor's daughter!'

For the emperor it was the final straw, and he resolved to have Empress Wang deposed; Lady Wu would take her place. Within a year, Wu would hold all the strings of power, manipulating the emperor like a puppet.

Wu Zetian ruled her country for half a century.

Wu Zetian, the only woman in the history of China to assume the title of Empress Regnant, came to the throne using her looks, cunning and connections to rule one of the largest empires of the world. She ruled in all but name for more than three decades (from 655 to 690) before breaking all precedent by founding her own dynasty and reigning as emperor for another fifteen years. With ruthless determination she wielded her power and influence, subjecting China to a reign of unprecedented terror. Yet, at the same time, she was an able administrator, introduced some positive programs and, some say, helped bring more equality between the sexes. Her mere presence on the throne was an infuriating challenge to Chinese orthodoxy, which insisted that no woman could or should ever meddle in politics, much less take on the role of imperial ruler. Even when she was long gone, the complex figure of Wu would be equally maddening to historical commentators to come.

Fair Flatterer Wu

Born a commoner during the Tang Dynasty, in the seventh century AD, Wu Zetian lived during an era when Chinese women enjoyed increasing power. Under the Tang aristocrats, women disregarded Chinese tradition and scandalously refused to remain hidden from sight, rode horses, sported trousers and wore short veils or none at all, like the freer, more independent women of the Turkic tribes. Even so, no woman would ever be considered for the role of ruler under the title of emperor. Before Wu was born, it was prophesied that the coming baby would become emperor, but the prediction was seen as ridiculous when the baby turned out to be a girl.

Even as a young girl, however, Wu displayed a steely determination to succeed. At the age of thirteen or fourteen, she caught the eye of middle-aged Emperor Taizong and was summoned to the palace to become a royal concubine. This was regarded as a great honour, equivalent to winning a beauty contest among the most desirable women of the medieval world. It's true that Wu's family had good connections, which may well have helped smooth her path to the palace, but even so she must have been quite lovely—at least in the looks department. Her mother Lady Yang wept bitterly as she farewelled her daughter, but Wu responded, 'How do you know that it is not my fortune to meet the Son of Heaven? Why are you crying like a young child?' Suddenly Lady Yang understood the intensity of her daughter's ambitions.

By the time the pretty young virgin arrived at the palace, Emperor Taizong—once a great soldier who supposedly had single-handedly engineered a revolution, a civil war and the foundation of a new imperial dynasty—was taking life decidedly more easily. He was mourning the death of his chief wife, and seeking solace among the younger handmaidens around him. Wu found herself at the bottom of the totem pole, probably acting more as maid than consort, but apparently came to the emperor's notice enough for him to give her the nickname 'Fair Flatterer'. And early on she stood out for more than just her looks, by Wu's own account, anyway. Years later, she would recount a moment of teenage bravado: once she broadcast to the emperor himself what she would do to control his unruly horse, declaring, 'I will whip him … I will strike his neck with the stick and … I will cut his throat with the dagger'. In Wu's words, 'Taizong admired my spirit'.

Taizong wasn't the only one who admired Wu. His adolescent son, Gaozong, who was to be selected as the new heir apparent, may have had something of a crush on Fair Flatterer Wu. With Taizong's death in 649, Wu, along with the other childless concubines, was sent to Ganye Temple and became a Buddhist nun. As luck would have it, her retirement was short-lived: the new Emperor Gaozong, still a teenager, remembered the charming, feisty and fabulous beauty and included her in his selection of palace concubines. Now twenty-four, Wu would not be content to play second fiddle to anyone and, wasting no time, she took the first steps on her path to power.

Wu systematically lied and murdered her way to the top. First, she won over Gaozong—being in the prime of her beauty, she did this in the most obvious of ways—quickly replacing his openly favourite consort of many years, Consort Xiao. Empress Wang and Consort Xiao, former romantic rivals, now joined forces against Consort Wu, but to no avail. Wu was well aware of what they were up to and made sure she garnered favour with all the people the supposedly haughty empress had ever offended. By the time the empress and Consort Xiao started bringing complaints

CATHERINE DE' MEDICI

(1519–1589), was one of the most influential people in Renaissance Europe and a key player in the French Catholic–Huguenot wars. She acted as regent on behalf of her sons after the death of her husband, King Henry II of France. Her reign is one of contrasts —on the one hand she was one of the greatest patrons of the arts of the times, on the other she was a ruthless ruler, responsible for the St Bartholomew Day massacre in 1572, when religious tensions came to a head and thousands of Protestants were killed in Paris.

against Wu to the emperor, there were many influential people ready to defend her. Once the emperor's favouritism was firmly secured, the throne became Wu's next goal.

During the years 652 to 654, Wu gave birth to two sons and a daughter. When the newborn daughter was found dead in her crib, the wily Wu seized the opportunity to incriminate Empress Wang, accusing her of murder (though there is debate over whether or not the baby died naturally or was smothered or strangled by Wu as a way to trap her rival, all historians agree that Wu used the baby's death to cast doubt on the empress's virtue). Persistent in her attacks and insinuations, Wu eventually managed to convince Gaozong that maybe the empress did the child in out of jealousy. With no help from the palace courtiers, Empress Wang was unable to clear herself in Gaozong's eyes.

Wu framed her opponent once and for all when she accused the empress of sorcery and of plotting to kill the emperor. With that, Gaozong considered deposing his wife. But before he made any definitive move, he sought out ministerial approval; he would give as a reason for deposing Empress Wang the fact that his chief wife had failed to bear him a son— sufficient grounds for divorce under Tang law.

His proposal to replace the empress with Consort Wu was met with almost unanimous opposition from his six highest-ranking ministers, still wincing at Gaozong's unsavory move in acquiring his deceased father's concubine, an act considered incest in Confucian thought. Any accusation of incest, they asserted, must inevitably blacken the emperor's reputation. Only one did not demur, saying to the emperor, 'This is a household affair of Your Majesty. Why do you need to inquire from outsiders?' That settled the matter for the emperor; he deposed both Empress Wang and Consort Xiao and put them under arrest, and in 656 AD Wu Zetian became his empress, beginning a climb that would scale heights greater than any other woman in China would ever scale.

ELIZABETH I

(1533–1603) was the last Tudor monarch of England, one of its greatest leaders, ruling during the country's 'Golden Age'. She oversaw her fleet's victory against the Spanish Armada off England's southern shores, beginning England's ascendancy in the maritime world and securing Protestantism as the state religion. She is the only English monarch who has chosen never to marry, thus maintaining complete control, but denying herself the chance to secure an heir.

Court ladies: portion of a mural in the tomb of Princess Yongtai, Wu Zetian's granddaughter.

The Empress Consort digs in her heels

One of Wu's first moves as Empress Consort was to order Empress Wang and Consort Xiao killed after Gaozong showed signs of wanting to release them. On Wu's secret instructions, the former empress allegedly was given a ferocious flogging, her hands and feet were cut off and she was left to drown in a vat of wine. Over the next thirty-five years, sometimes as policy and, according to some historians, always with pleasure, Lady Wu murdered five of the emperor's sons (including two of her own), two of her brothers, one of her sisters, the sister's daughter and several hundred of her husband's relatives.

It was easy to allow Wu to start taking the reins. The emperor was ailing (some historians think his illness was the result of slow poisoning by the Empress Consort), and by 675 he was so unwell he considered having Empress Wu formally rule as regent. Chancellor Hao Chujun and an important official named Li Yiyan strongly opposed the idea, so the emperor held back. But Wu would not be deterred. She began gathering the support of palace insiders—specifically, a number of mid-level officials who would write a selection of works on her behalf, including the *Biographies of Notable Women*, and *Guidelines for Imperial Subjects* —and then called on these 'North Gate Scholars' for advice to divert power from the chancellors.

As early as 675, a number of persons were to fall victim to Empress Wu's ire, one of them her strong-willed eldest son Li Hong, the Crown Prince. First, he annoyed her by urging her not to exercise so much influence on Gaozong's governance. Then, he outright offended her by requesting that his two half-sisters, the daughters of the late Consort Xiao, be allowed to marry, even though Wu had them under house arrest. Then Li Hong suddenly died. Some historians believe that Wu poisoned him. In 680, Wu accused her middle son, Li Xian, of treason and had him deposed and exiled. Li Xian's more malleable younger brother, Li Xian (by now renamed Li Zhan), was made the new Crown Prince.

In late 683, Emperor Gaozong peacefully passed away. Li Zhan, at twenty-seven years old, took the throne as Emperor Zhongzong, but Wu would retain actual authority as dowager empress and regent. It was no time to sit back and relax. She is reported to have extended her killing ways to Zhongzong's daughter, the incredibly beautiful Yongtai, who officially died in childbirth in 701 at the age of seventeen.

Wu declares herself China's first female emperor

When Emperor Gaozong died, and Lady Wu assumed the regnancy, she quickly transformed government by murder into government by massacre. Facing serious opposition, Wu's first strike would be against her son, Emperor Zhongzong, who early on showed signs of discontent and disobedience. Dowager Empress Wu deposed him in February 684, only a few months after his accession, reduced his title to Prince of Luling, and sent him into exile. Wu replaced Zhongzong with her youngest son, twenty-two-year-old Li Dan, who she would name Emperor Ruizong. And, just in case there would be no surprise attack from the far corners of the empire, Wu sent one of her generals to Li Xian's place in exile and had him force her allegedly treasonous eldest son to commit suicide. Ruizong would hold the title of emperor, on paper, but in practice Dowager Empress Wu held all the power. Officials were not allowed to meet with Emperor Ruizong, nor was he allowed to rule on matters of state. Suspicious of just about everybody, Wu demoted, exiled, and executed hundreds of officials. Others died every day in the torture chambers operated by her secret police.

In 686, most probably to test his loyalty, Wu offered to hand over the reins of power to young Ruizong; fortunately, he knew his mother too well and declined. Wu continued to exercise imperial authority and Ruizong's life was spared. In this period the Dowager Empress had impregnable copper mailboxes set up to encourage the people of the realm to secretly report on anyone suspected of opposing her. In this atmosphere of suspicion and terror, whole villages came to be wiped out by ambitious commanders, who could use the mailboxes to 'prove' a case of sedition whenever they wanted promotion.

When all possible opposition was crushed, Lady Wu created her own dynasty, the Zhou, and in August of 690 had herself crowned as the first Zhou emperor, becoming the first and only woman ever to reign over China as emperor (or in her case, Empress

---

MARIA THERESA, HOLY ROMAN EMPRESS

(1717–1780), was the only woman to rule the 650-year-old Holy Roman Empire, which she did after the death of her husband, Francis I. Her titles also included Archduchess of Austria and Queen of Hungary and Bohemia, and she was the last ruler of the Habsburg Dynasty—her son succeeding to the House of Lorraine. During her reign she did much to actively reform the empire, overseeing a number of civil, judicial, educational and military reforms.

Regnant). She made the former Emperor Ruizong the crown prince, and bestowed on him the name of Wu. Eight years later, Wu recalled her second-youngest son Li Zhan (ex-Emperor Zhongzong) from exile, and Li Dan offered to yield the position of Crown Prince to him.

To general amazement, Wu proved in most respects a model ruler. Once she took the throne, she largely demolished the apparatus of terror and installed a cabinet of honest civil servants who ruled the country well. Despite the ruthlessness of her climb to power, her reign as first female emperor of China proved to be benign. After her troops defeated Korean forces in war, Wu negotiated with Korea to become China's ally and abolished the special tax that paid for border troops, thus generating goodwill from the population. She decreased the imperial government's military budget, replaced military leaders with scholarly bureaucrats, enforced civil exams for government positions, reformed taxes, increased agricultural production, constructed magnificent buildings in the capital, and promoted art and culture.

Wu also began a campaign to elevate the position of women. This challenged Chinese tradition, which had long held that a woman's place was quiet seclusion, far from any political playing field. She had scholars write biographies of famous women, and raised the position of her mother's clan by giving her relatives high political posts. Having created her new dynasty, she would come to say that the ideal ruler was one who rules like a mother does over her children (apparently, not referring to the kind of murdering, banishing matriarch with whom she must have been most familiar).

During her reign, Wu fostered a resurgence in the exotic import that had come to China along the Silk Road: Buddhism, and its far more egalitarian worldview than that of Confucian orthodoxy. While Confucianism placed a high value on knowing one's rightful place in society—and underscored a woman's role as one of subordination to men—Buddhism could serve as the perfect support for Wu in her radical move to elevate herself to full sovereign powers, as the monarch of all under Heaven. Wu

CIXI

(1835–1908) was the last Dowager Empress of China, and the de facto ruler of the nation for nearly fifty years. Born into a middle-class Manchu family, she was chosen by Emperor Xianfeng as one of his concubines and began her ascent to power when she gave birth to his only son. After both the emperor and her son died she orchestrated her nephew Guangxu's accession, but in reality ran the country herself, implementing a number of reforms and supporting the Boxer Rebellion—the beginning of the end of imperial China.

used Buddhism to her own ends in her stand against the traditional argument that no woman could, or should, be permitted to rule the empire.

After fifteen years of rule as Sacred and Divine Empress Regnant, on the evening of 20 February 705, the ageing Wu was overthrown. Her son Zhongzong had known that a plan was afoot, and had tacitly approved of it, but on that fateful night he got cold feet. The agents of the insurgency arrived at the imperial heir's house first, to let him know that several hundred men were ready to move in on Wu's residence. Weakly, Zhongzong inquired if it were possible to put off action to another day. 'Her Majesty is not well', he said ineffectually, 'and we should not alarm her'. But with a throng of military men already en route to the palace, it was too late to change course. Lying through his teeth, a fast thinker assured Zhongzong that the only way to stop the coup was to ride to the palace himself and order everyone to halt. To the nervous Zhongzong this seemed the perfect plan; he could play the roles of rebel *and* Wu's defender, should any of his enemies survive. What Zhongzong didn't realise was that his presence was the signal for action—many of the conspirators had agreed to get involved only on condition that they could be sure they were acting for the imperial heir, not just participating in a random takeover.

On Zhongzong's arrival, the soldiers sprang into action, smashing the gates of the compound and rushing through the palace. Wu emerged from her chambers, woozy from sleep and weak from illness. Among the faces of her ministers in the crowd, she saw her eldest surviving son in the torchlight.

'The raiders have done their killing', she said. 'Now you can get back to the Eastern Palace.'

She had no idea that her very son was supposed to proclaim that her reign was over. In the awkward moment precipitated by Zhongzong's silence, a minister had to step in. No, he told Wu, Zhongzong would not be returning to the residence of the imperial heir—just as his late father Gaozong had always intended, Zhongzong was taking over the throne.

Pardoning all the people

On 24 February, the former Sacred and Divine Empress Regnant left her imperial residence, marking the end of more than five decades under her influence. On 3 March, the Tang Dynasty was restored. Nearly eighty years old, feeble but still formidable,

Wu was purportedly persuaded to relinquish her male harem and maneuvered into luxurious retirement. She knew the time left to her in this life wouldn't be long. But she attempted no comeback, only planning for the inevitable approach of death. Wu began to put her house in order and wrote a will in which, just in case it did her any good in the afterlife, she 'pardoned' all the people who had forced her to kill them. She also revoked her divine status, wanting to be remembered not as Wu the living goddess, or even as Wu the female emperor, but simply as Gaozong's loyal wife, and recorded that her wish was to be buried with her beloved. On 16 December 705, Wu Zetian died.

—»·•·«—

Evil, self-serving, ruthless, ambitious, a callous despot, a usurper. For centuries, Wu Zetian was condemned by Chinese historians and held up as a model for what to expect when a woman rules. Much later, in the twentieth century, she was rehabilitated by the Communists when Jang Quing, Madame Mao, praised her as a revolutionary and women's libber. It's true that Wu was wily, hardhearted, and took a no-holds-barred approach to gaining the throne, not to mention she was a torturer and a murderer. But some would point out that she didn't behave all that differently from her predecessors, among them Taizong and Gaozong, who are regarded as heroes. Nobody will ever know exactly how her rise to reigning empress played out. But what we do know is that she refused to remain hidden from sight. Thirteen centuries after her death she is still tantalising—showing up in the pages of novels, in detective stories, in a slew of television series, and on the silver screen. Apparently we just can't get enough of her.

Right: Pope Joan and her child—woodcut from Hartmannus Schedel's Nuremburg Chronicle, *1493.*

POPE JOAN

(C. 814–UNKNOWN)

*She may have broken
the papal line*

The story has it that Pope Leo IV's successor was riding in a papal procession in Rome, around the year 858, when the unthinkable happened. On horseback she—yes, she—went into labour and delivered a baby on the spot. The papal mama in question was allegedly one Pope Joan, born in 814 in Germany to English missionary parents, and eventually making her way to Rome, in male guise, to become first a cardinal's secretary, then everybody's choice for pope—as Pope John Anglicus—at a time when the status of women was little better than that of cattle.

Her name at birth, according to some accounts, was Agnes; others call her Gilberta or Jutta. Long after her death—assuming she ever lived—scribes began calling her Joan. Countless chronicles of a reigning 'popess' materialised during the Middle Ages, but apparently none were written before then. It's possible, but highly unlikely, that this historical gap was deliberately created by clerics of the day taking great pains to destroy any records of this most unholy of events. Either way, it was some 400 years after Pope Joan's alleged existence that a widely accepted account, purportedly written in 1265 by a Polish Dominican friar, established the particulars of her history and set the papal deception in the ninth century. In the Chronicle of Roman Popes and Emperors, *Martin of Troppau, who was a close adviser to Pope Clement IV (1265–68), wrote about a young woman from Mainz who learned Greek and Latin and became 'proficient in a diversity of branches of knowledge'. As Troppau tells it, this bright woman served as Pope from 855 till 858.*

Once the story was entrenched in medieval imagination, two camps formed: those, like the fourteenth century poet Petrarch, who scorned her, and those who celebrated her. In the 1400s a bust of the supposed popess, bearing the inscription 'John VIII, a woman from England', was placed in the Cathedral of Siena along with those of the other popes. The statue occupied this position for two centuries, until Clement VIII, in 1601, had it transformed into the bust of Pope Zacharias. At the Basilica in St Peter's Square, among the carvings by the seventeenth century artist Bernini, are eight images of a woman wearing a papal crown that seem to tell the story of a woman giving birth.

Then there are the outright sceptics, led by the Catholic Church that insists the papal line, dating back to St Peter, is an unbroken string of men. Pope Joan believers ask how one can explain, then, an unusual marble bench at the Vatican with a hole in the seat said to have been used for intimate investigations to ensure that a gender-bending imposter could never (again?) claim the papal throne. In fact, the seat is of much earlier origin than Joan's supposed existence.

The second part of the tale, of a Pope Joan publicly in the throes of contractions, gets very confused. Some sources say that both she and her child died during labour. Others indicate that a furious crowd tied her feet to the horse's tail and she was dragged along the street to her death, or that she was stoned to death by outraged onlookers. There is another which records that she was banished to a convent and that her son grew up to become Bishop of Ostia. But in most tellings, Pope Joan perished that day. One thing is for sure, Pope Joan is a compelling story, filled with all kinds of embellishments and lively lore.

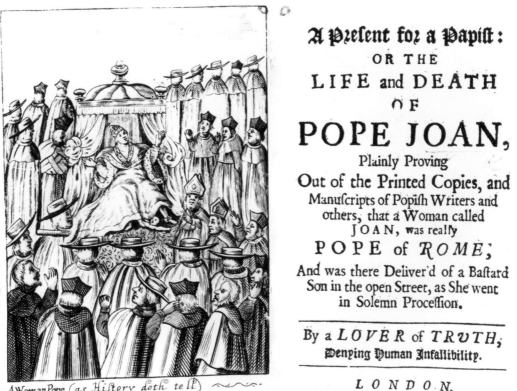

Frontispiece and title page of a Protestant polemic published in England in 1675.

RAZIA SULTAN (1205–1240)

Warrior queen of India

A light rain was misting the early evening air. A dark shape slipped through the shadows, beneath an elaborately carved stone archway and into the mausoleum. Inside, the flickering light of oil lamps highlighted the downcast face of a young woman, the Muslim princess Razia, possibly the next person to take the throne.

Razia approached the huge red sandstone cenotaph in the center of the domed chamber. Her father, Shams-ud-din Iltutmish, had built this edifice himself near the Shamsi Tabab, where he had seen the footprints of the Holy Prophet's horse Buraq. She sat down on the edge of his tomb and laid her hand on the cold stone and bowing her head.

'What would you have me do, Father?' she said. 'It has been but two days since your funeral and already the governors and nobles have refused to honour my ascent to the throne.'

She waited in silence.

The answer did not come from the grave, but from deep within her heart. As a tear ran down her cheek, she rose and made her way to the first of three mehrabs on the west side of the chamber. In each of the three alcoves she placed a silver coin that bore her image. It was a prayer offering.

As she turned to leave she said softly, 'Insha'Allah'. 'If the Almighty is willing', she thought, 'I will rule from my father's throne'.

Architectural detail at the Qutb Minar
complex near Delhi.

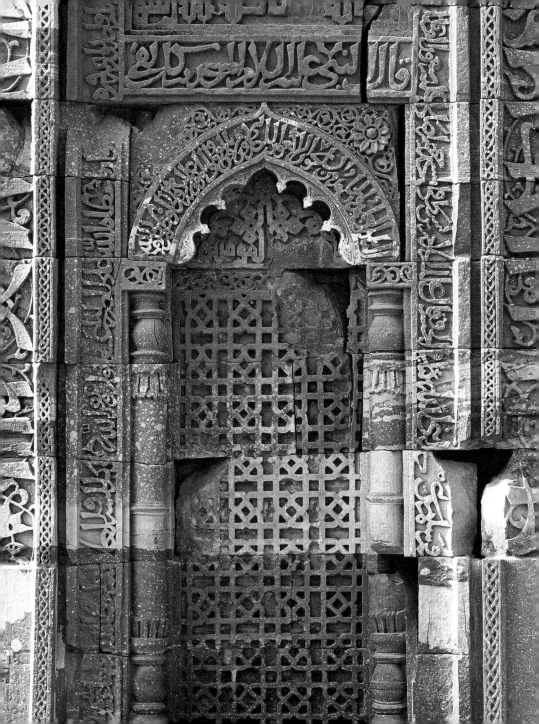

A descendant of the Turkish Muslims who invaded India in the eleventh century, Razia al-Din was the only woman ever crowned in the Delhi Sultanate, which ruled parts of India from 1210 to 1526. Reigning as the fifth Mamluk Sultan in Delhi from 1236 to 1240, she was the first woman ruler in Muslim and Turkish history. Her reign was short, but its impact grand: during that time she established schools, academies, and libraries that housed the works of ancient philosophers along with the Qur'an and the Traditions of the Prophet. She also worked to bridge the chasm that separated Hindus and Muslims.

Historians and biographers have said that Razia Sultan was a 'great sovereign, sagacious, just, beneficent, the patron of the learned, dispenser of justice, the cherisher of her subjects, of warlike talent, and endowed with all the admirable attributes and qualifications necessary for kings'.

The story of her stormy reign is filled with intrigue, battles and even a possible love affair— but her legacy is only now beginning to be realised, recently immortalised in books, movies and songs. The battle queen of India is charging into the twenty-first century on her armoured war elephant.

The beginning of the Delhi Sultanate

The volatile history of India and Pakistan can, in part, be traced back to 1192, when the Turkish leader Muhammad of Ghur defeated the Rajputs at the second battle of Tarain and took control of the Kingdom of Delhi.

After establishing his reign, Ghur returned to Afghanistan, leaving the kingdom in the hands of his trusted slave Qutb-ud-din Aibak. When Ghur died in 1206 without an heir, Qutb-ud-din declared himself Sultan of Delhi. This marked the beginning of the Slave Dynasty, so named because many of the sultans were former slaves. Razia's father, Shams-ud-din Iltutmish, a member of the slave clan, ruled the sultanate from 1210 to 1236.

Iltutmish transformed the sultanate from a tribal alliance into a monarchy, instituting governors and a ruling class. He further 'civilised' the kingdom by creating a currency, building a massive complex of governmental and religious buildings in Delhi, and becoming a huge patron of the arts. Supposedly he groomed his eldest son to be his successor, but in 1229 the son died before he had a chance to wear the crown. What Iltutmish saw in the son next in line, Rukn-ud-din Feroze Shah, was utter incompetence, a man who lived simply for his own pleasure and hardly dependable enough to rule a kingdom. So the sultan turned to his remarkable daughter Razia. The Muslim princess was talented, wise and responsible. Iltutmish recognised her abilities in interpreting the Qur'an and her sharp mind when it came to her studies in the sciences. When he needed to travel abroad, he entrusted his daughter with affairs in Delhi, coaching her in economic administration as well as in diplomacy, in how to keep the nobles in check, and in techniques for garnering support from the army and the people. She learned her lessons well.

But Razia was more than a bookworm and a tactician. She trained hard, along with her brothers, led armies into battle, and became an accomplished warrior herself, mastering both spear and saber. She accompanied her father on many of his campaigns and often rode into battle at his side. Her unconventionality stretched to the way she dressed. She abandoned women's traditional dress and donned a man's loose tunic and pants. She seldom covered her face in public. While we know little about her deeper motivations, it becomes clear in the accounts of scribes and historians that Razia did everything she could to be seen as an equal to any man. And, by all accounts, her strategy worked. The sixteenth century Persian historian Firishta commented that 'men of discernment could find no defect in her except that she was created in the form of a woman'. Razia systematically did everything she could to move beyond the traditional role of women in her culture and take control of her own destiny, and that of her country.

BOUDICA

(c. 25–60 AD), Queen of the Iceni in southeastern Britannia, was the first and only known woman to have led an uprising against Roman rule. When her husband Prasutagus died, leaving half of his lands to the Romans and the rest to his people, the Roman authorities ignored his will—annexing the entire kingdom, flogging Boudica and raping her daughters. Incensed by the violence, oppression and corruption of Roman occupation, Boudica organised a revolt and led her people into battle. The uprising was finally defeated, but Boudica's legend remains.

As soon as Razia came of age, the sultan, disregarding tradition, named his daughter as his successor. She was fully capable, and surely the most competent of the lot to assume the throne. The Turkish nobility would have none of it. Iltutmish overruled the opposition, however, and as part of a celebration to mark Razia's eventual accession he placed her image on the *tanka*, the silver rupee of that time. Nonetheless, when Iltutmish died on 29 April 1236, Razia's brother Rukn-ud-din was elevated to the throne.

Razia's first battle … on the home front

Installed with the aid of several powerful governors and his mother, Rukn-ud-din reigned for only six short months. This power grab went largely unchallenged because the governors knew that Rukn-ud-din was weak and that they could keep, even consolidate, their tribal powers with little resistance. To say that the young ruler did not take his responsibilities seriously would be an understatement. He left governing to his scheming mother Shah Turkaan, and reportedly whiled away his time in the harem smoking opium, or riding the streets of Delhi on an elephant, scattering coins to his subjects. And while Rukn-ud-din was cavorting, his mother was using her position to avenge real and imagined insults she had received while she was a handmaiden in the royal household. She persecuted co-wives with whom she had competed in the past, and banished others who displeased her. She plotted against Razia, whom she rightly saw as a threat. Discontent quickly grew up on all sides. The people were not pleased.

In the meantime Razia, who understood what makes a powerful leader, was smoothly and patiently engaging the citizens in all the right ways. She took every opportunity to appear in public. And, when she did, she showed up in men's clothing—in *kaba* and *kulla*—and often carried a bow or saber as a symbol of power. Every Friday, just before prayers, she presented herself on a balcony near the great Qutub Minar minaret in red robes, the symbol of revolution. She made direct appeals to the disgruntled citizens for justice and support. She exploited the people's outrage over Shah Turkaan's treachery and Rukn-ud-din's debauchery. Possibly holding the silver rupee that bore her image in the air, she reminded the people of her father's decree, that she was the rightful heir to the throne. Her persistent pleas enabled her to garner mass support. This clever woman made a 'deal' with the citizens, essentially asking for a chance to prove her worthiness to rule. This strategy proved successful.

JOAN OF ARC, THE MAID OF ORLEANS

(1412–1431), led a resistance to the English invasion of France during the Hundred Years' War. As a young girl Joan claimed to hear the voices of saints and grew up convinced that the saints were urging her to free France of English rule. Cutting her hair and adopting male armour, she managed to rally an army through the strength of her convictions. She was successful in many battles against the English but was finally captured, condemned as a heretic, and burned at the stake. In 1920 she was recognised as a martyr by the Catholic Church and was made a saint herself.

An illustration of the Qutub Minar minaret from the nineteenth century.

With the mandate of the people, Razia could enlist the army's support and ready herself to make her move. She did not have to wait long.

Soon after Rukn-ud-din grabbed the throne, his brother Ghias-ud-din, Governor of Oudh, openly rebelled, seizing a great convoy of treasure destined for Delhi and invading the capital from the north. Forced to respond, Rukn-ud-din gathered up his own army and marched out of Delhi to engage his unruly sibling in battle. Razia seized the opportunity. With the army backing her, she took the throne and had her mother banished to prison. Not long after, a battle-scarred Rukn-ud-din returned to Delhi and received a surprise welcome: he was thrown into a dungeon and, on 9 November 1236, was taken out of the picture for good, when he and Shah Turkaan were put to their deaths.

With some reluctance, and fearing the army, the governors grudgingly agreed to let Razia reign. She knew that their patronage was tenuous and she would have to earn their trust and respect.

Razia's reign: a brief period of peace and prosperity

Almost from the moment Razia landed on the throne, plots against her were hatched. The governors of Budaun, Multan, Lahore, and Hansi joined forces with Rukn-ud-din's wazir and conspired to overthrow the sultana. Instead of calling on her army to launch a bloody purge, Razia practised her own unique form of 'East Asian aikido'. She quietly sowed the seeds of dissension among her detractors, pitting one against another in ways that forced them to reveal their own selfish motives. It worked. The disloyal governors had a falling out, and in their disarray she marched a small contingent of soldiers into nearby rebel states to capture, kill or run off the few remaining challengers.

This skilful two-pronged victory, using sagacity and force, earned her new respect and prestige, and allowed her to secure her throne. Having engineered a fragile peace, she went about making changes that would maintain political stability. She made fresh appointments and reconfigured the governmental structure in an attempt to ensure that no one nobleman or governor had enough power or resources to rise up against her. To keep her citizens' favour, she made domestic welfare, not warfare, a top priority. During her reign, she used the army to protect the people and keep the peace, not to expand the borders of her kingdom.

Razia instituted an open court; improved her kingdom's infrastructure by building roads, digging wells and planting trees; constructed schools, libraries and theatres; and supported the arts. She continued to make sunny public appearances on holy days and festivals. And finally, she pronounced that she would be called sultan—not 'sultana' meaning wife or mistress of the sultan—but sultan.

Though indisputably accomplished on the battlefield, Razia Sultan's greatest fight may have been for justice and racial tolerance. She attempted to abolish the unjust tax imposed on non-Muslims. Resistant noblemen got huffy, pointing to the Qur'an to justify it; the Holy Book, they would say, commands that non-Muslims be 'conquered, humiliated and subjugated' through the payment of *jizya*, a tribute poll tax that Muslims were not obligated to pay. Razia declared that the *spirit* of Islam teaches that love of one's nation is part of the love of God; that peace with one's neighbours is part of peace with oneself, and the true Muslim spirit is not to destroy, but to build. Razia practised this belief. Records show that, at least on one occasion, she attempted to appoint a recent Hindu convert to Islam to an official position. This incremental campaign for racial equality was part of a broader strategy to garner the loyalty and support of the non-Turkish nobles and population. Aware that the Turkish nobility were fickle at best, untrustworthy at worst, she endeavoured to create a broader power base from which to govern. Ironically, her championship of non-Muslims was, in part, what led to her downfall.

HANNAH SNELL

(1723–1792) is Britain's most famous female soldier, disguising herself as a man and serving first in the Duke of Northumberland's army against Bonnie Prince Charlie in 1746 and later in the Royal Marines. She served in India, joining combat in the siege of Pondicherry. In 1750 she returned to London, and after revealing her true identity published her memoirs, receiving instant fame. Hannah received an honourable discharge from the Marines, her service was recognised and she became the first woman to be granted a military pension.

Jealously, envy and innuendo: the ultimate weapons of destruction

Despite consistent resistance from the Turkish nobles, Razia continued to integrate the government, make new appointments and consolidate power. Within a short time, the entire Hindustan region, including Bengal, submitted to her authority. Razia's authority as sultan was unquestioned, but as a woman her autonomy was limited by cultural mores and jealousy.

In hindsight, it appears that nothing could have stopped Razia from becoming one of the most accomplished, long-standing rulers of the Delhi Sultanate. Except love. What undid her was her relationship with an Abyssinian slave, Jamal-ud-din Yaqut. Publicly, the relationship was all business: Razia appointed Yaqut to the relatively important post of Master of the Horse in the royal stables. This alone upset the insular Turkish nobility, who were determined to maintain a monopoly on the powerful political positions. What made this perceived threat even more unpalatable was that, over time, Yaqut became the sultan's trusted adviser—or, some even say, her lover. Rumours of their supposed affair spread in hushed whispers and jokes among the courtiers. But whether he was playing the role of lover or strictly adviser, Yaqut represented more than just a political threat to the Turkish noblemen. They could not, and would not, stand for a Turkish woman— and a noblewoman, at that—being entangled with a black slave.

> ## CATHERINE II
>
> (1729–1796), known as Catherine the Great, was Empress of Russia, assuming power when her husband, Peter III, was deposed in 1762. She was a patron of the arts, literature, and education. Under her rule Russia was revitalised, and recognised as one of the great powers of Europe. During her reign the borders of the Russian Empire were extended east, west and southwards, adding some 520,000 square kilometres of territory.
>
> ❧❧❧

The Governor of Lahore was the first to react— raising his objections not at the royal court, but on the battlefield in 1239. Razia was expecting such an attack and sharply put him in his place. Atop her massive armoured war elephant, Razia led her troops to a quick victory, scattering his army. The governor fled for his life and later returned, on bended knee, to seek forgiveness. Razia gave it.

But hot on this governor's heels came a more serious threat, in the form of Malik Ikhtiar-ud-din Altunia, Governor of Bhatinda. Altunia challenged Razia's appointment of Yaqut to a high political post, pointing to it as proof that she was unfit to rule. Unlike the Governor of Lahore, he did not run away when her army approached: he defeated her forces, killed Yaqut and threw Razia into a dungeon.

Supposedly, Altunia and Razia went way back; they were cousins and childhood friends and, over time, boy fell in love with girl. Razia, in true storybook fashion, rebuffed his advances. Historians believe that Altunia's rebellion was his personal revenge, made all the more urgent by jealous thoughts of Razia cavorting with a slave.

Essentially to escape death, Razia agreed to marry Altunia. But there was no time for a honeymoon. For, while Razia was held powerless in Altunia's dungeon, another of her calculating brothers, Mui-ud-din Braham, with the help of malcontent army officers and an unfaithful lord chamberlain, usurped the throne—just as she had feared.

Razia and her husband became a united front (maybe not sharing affection, but certainly joined together in their cause), marching to Delhi to retake the throne. Razia and Altunia raised an army to do battle with Braham. It would be easy to imagine the warrior Razia and her warrior husband riding side by side on massive war elephants, the beasts trumpeting and scattering Braham's troops in all directions as they relentlessly marched into battle. But in the heat of their second major battle, on 14 October 1240, Razia and her spouse were killed. Historians disagree over the details pertaining to her death, but if Razia Sultan were true to her nature, she would have died with a saber in her hand and Allah's name on her last breath.

Razia Sultan's legacy

Razia's inconspicuous tomb lies in a courtyard on a narrow lane in Bulbul-i-khana, Shahjahanabad, near the Turkman Gate entrance to Old Delhi. Crumbling and covered in dust and grime, it is surrounded on all sides by apartments. Most passers-by do not know that the remains of one of India's most extraordinary rulers lie there.

Elsewhere during the period of Razia's reign, in 1237 the grandson of Genghis Khan was leading the Mongols into the heartland of Russia; the Holy Roman Emperor Frederick II was defeating the independent city-states of northern Italy; and in Africa the Malian Empire was expanding its reach as far west as the Atlantic, and east beyond the great bend of the Niger River. While all this was happening, a noblewoman in India was ruling, hated by the nobility yet embraced by the masses.

Razia Sultan's reign was short by most standards—a mere three and a half years—but that does not diminish her standing as one of the great monarchs in history. There are her obvious tangible accomplishments, battles to be sure, and also the many public works projects that she initiated and saw to fruition. And then there is the way she ruled. As a leader, Razia set herself apart from her male predecessors. She didn't isolate herself on her pedestal, but maximised contact with her citizens. She balanced the use of force with diplomacy and coalition building. She seems to have operated using a broad and, if it's safe to say, female-oriented strategy. We live in an age when what have traditionally been considered female traits—strong communication skills, a collaborative instinct, a gift for juggling, emotional intelligence—are hailed (and some would say, 'finally', with a sigh of relief) as desirable leadership qualities. Razia possessed these traits in abundance. Unlike the situation for most women in her day, and for centuries to come, marriage was not to be her calling (until it was thrust on her) and meekness not her virtue. She managed a playing field of her own. She was a model leader. And for this, she must be remembered.

Right: An ornamental plate from Cyprus depicting a Muslim noblewoman during the Crusades.

SHAGRAT AL-DURR
(UNKNOWN–1259)

From slave to slaying sultana

Power behind the throne, power on the throne, and back again, Shagrat al-Durr changed her public persona again and again during her lifetime, yet her ability to wield power never waned.

She emerged from the shadows as a Turkoman slave of Egypt's Sultan Salih Ayyub, rising to the rank of mistress and, eventually, wife. Though this advancement was commendable in itself, Shagrat was much more than a mere plaything or humble consort. When the sultan was absent, his wife acted as his regent. In 1249, the French Crusader army under King Louis IX landed at Damietta, at the mouth of the Nile River. With Salih Ayyub attending to business in Damascus, Shagrat organised the defence of the realm. Salih hustled back but, just as the crusading armies were ramping up their threats against

Battle between the Crusaders and Muslims from a medieval manuscript.

Egypt, he died. Shagrat cunningly covered up his sudden passing, pretending he was sick and bedridden. She forged Salih's signature and managed to regroup and lead the Egyptian army in the sultan's name.

Before long Ayyub's son, Turan, appeared on the scene. Shagrat decided there was nothing else to do but announce her husband's death and hand the reins of power to her stepson. Nevertheless, she effectively continued to rule, rendering a crushing defeat on the Crusaders, reclaiming Damietta for Egypt, and orchestrating the capture of Louis IX. The Turkish army leaders, who saw Shagrat as one of them, wanted their female leader to retain control of the realm, so they had Turan murdered, making Shagrat the first and only female Sultan of Egypt. Coins were struck in her name and praise was lobbed her way during weekly prayers at the mosques. But her official reign would last only three months.

The Caliph of Baghdad disapproved of a woman holding the title of sultan, so he sent a celebrated Mamluk soldier named Aibak to replace her. Shagrat stepped down from her post, though she was hardly ready to surrender power. Whether for lust, love or political leverage—probably a combination of all three—Shagrat succeeded in seducing Aibak and convincing him to divorce his wife and marry her. For seven years, she ruled Egypt through her husband, and dared to demand that she be addressed as sultana. Ultimately, in a fit of jealousy over Aibak's desire to take another wife, Shagrat plotted his murder. In retaliation, slaves of the harem, spurred by Aibak's former wife, beat Shagrat to death with their wooden clogs and dumped her body into the moat of the citadel.

CHRISTINE DE PISAN (c. 1364–c. 1429)

A flick of fortune's hand turns one woman into 'an honorary man'

Setting out parchment, quill and inkwell, Christine impatiently took a seat at her desk in her book-lined study, smoothed down the tight sleeves of her cotehardie and prepared to do what she loved and did best: write.

Ever since her husband's death, a grief-stricken Christine had been churning out lyric poems, not only for her own comfort, but also for the lords and ladies in the royal household—who would accept her verses as gifts and reward her with a small jewel, a few yards of cloth, and, more recently, sizable sums of cash. But this time, she wasn't planning to craft an artful love ballad for the Duke of Berry, or the Duchess of Bourbon. On this afternoon, she was spurred to action not by a commission, but by conviction.

Christine's eyes, again, fell on the document before her: scholar Jean de Montreuil's zealous praise for poet Jean de Meun's bawdy verses attacking all women as vain, deceptive, and lewd. She felt her blood boil.

Taking up her quill, Christine let loose with a flurry of words boldly attacking de Meun's misogynist lore. Caught up in a powerful desire to defend the honour of women, Christine de Pisan had launched the most famous epistolary debate of the ages.

Illumination showing Christine de Pisan at her desk, from Collected Works, *1407.*

ENHEDUANA

(c. 2285–2250 BC) is the world's oldest known author, whose works were written in cuneiform approximately 4300 years ago. The daughter of the Akkadian ruler Sargon, she became a high priestess of the moon god Nanna, and a gifted theologian and writer. She was the first writer to use the first person and wrote numerous hymns and poems. Her hymn 'Nin-me-sara' was revered as a sacred document for hundreds of years, and many copies still exist.

At a time when a woman's 'rightful place' was thought to be the private sphere of home and family, Christine de Pisan managed not only to tackle the role of professional writer, but doubly dared to defy convention by engaging in a major public debate in which she held her own against prominent male adversaries (whose reactions to her ranged from patronising condescension to outright hostility). As the most prolific woman writer of the Middle Ages, equally adept in poetry and prose, and author of some 300 poems and twenty books, Christine certainly earned the accolade of Europe's first woman writer known to have earned a livelihood by the pen.

But Christine's is a story of a woman who, had a twist of fate not left her at misfortune's gate, having to fend for herself and her family, perhaps would have willingly remained in the roles that conventions of the day had dictated—obedient daughter, dedicated wife, devoted mother. Christine de Pisan was a reformer, but no rebel. She wasn't looking to change the codes of society. Rather, she had an immensely strong sense of truth. 'No matter which way I looked at it and no matter how much I turned the matter over in my mind, I could find no evidence from my own experience to bear out such a negative view of female nature and habits', she wrote, at the age of forty-one, reacting to the widely misogynist texts of the day. She grabbed onto truth as she knew it, found her voice, and made it known. A medieval woman who would rise up in defence of her sex against the sort of attack that was a large part of clerical tradition was unheard of.

A charmed life crumbles

Christine de Pisan was born in Venice, but as a small child moved with her family to Paris where, early on, she had ample opportunity for study and the youthful conviction that everything good would last forever.

Charles V was ruling France, and the country was experiencing a period of peace. The king's love for learning, and his search for meaning behind the mysteries of the universe, put him on a quest for an academic adviser. He ruled out anyone from the clerically influenced faculty at the University of Paris, instead setting his sights on the University of Bologna, whose students and lay faculty were exposed to some of the most progressive thought of the day. Thus, Christine's father—Tommaso di Benvenuto da Pizzano, a doctor of medical studies from the University of Bologna, and a professor of astrology—was welcomed at the French court in 1368, and quickly became a favoured counsellor.

At a time when most schools and universities were closed to women, Christine had easy access to the royal library, reputedly the finest in all of Western Europe with its collection of no less than 900 volumes. This was an era before the printing press, when books were masterful works of art painstakingly inscribed, laden with gold leaf and bound in silk, and the richest man might be lucky to own fifty in a lifetime. So the library of Charles V at the Louvre was a remarkable accomplishment—and, for those who had an open door to it, an extraordinary privilege. Here, Christine could easily follow her inquisitive mind. Encouraged by a liberal father who pushed for his daughter's education, Christine learned Latin as well as French, and with this knowledge she explored books on philosophy, science, and geometry. As it turned out, she had less time for studies than she would have liked. Her mother embraced the conventional belief that intellectual pursuits were unladylike, and kept Christine busy 'with spinning and silly girlishness'.

But Christine wasn't one to object to following the social codes of the day. When she was fifteen, she married Etienne du Castel, an ambitious twenty-five-year-old scholar who had landed the position of royal court secretary. Christine felt it was a good match. She was unconcerned that he lacked worldly goods. She loved his strong character and sharp mind, and she looked to him as an intellectual role model. Ten happy years and three children later, she never doubted that her position was insecure. Destiny, however, was about to deal a surprise hand to Christine, one far removed from her dreams of domestic bliss.

ANNA COMNENA

(1083–1153), the daughter of Byzantine emperor Alexius I, was a scholar during the Middle Ages. Encouraged by her parents, Anna was one of the most educated women of the period, being taught history, mathematics, science and philosophy from an early age. After the death of her husband, Anna entered a monastery where she continued to study and wrote a fifteen-volume history of her father's reign. The *Alexiad*, published around 1148, makes Anna the world's first recognised female historian.

Without any warning, Christine's beloved husband died of the plague. At the age of twenty-five, she was left a widow with three children and her own recently widowed mother to support. By this time she had lost three important sources of psychological, emotional, and financial support: first, Charles V, who had died just after she married, leaving the throne to his twelve-year-old son; next, her father, whose once prosperous position in the court declined under the new king, and who died impoverished in 1387; and finally, her husband, gone at the age of thirty-five.

Late at night, as her children slept, Christine found comfort in her simple study, her little white dog by her side, her quill etching its way across the page, beginning:

> *Alone and in great suffering in this*
> *deserted world full of sadness has my*
> *sweet lover left me …*

Winning acceptance to write

For a time, Christine seriously doubted her abilities. She found herself in relative poverty, mired in misfortunes and legal technicalities over her husband's estate, and suffering at the hands of corrupt officials. Eventually, she would receive a settlement that could keep her family together—but not before her problems had worn her down so far that she fell ill. In *Le Livre de la Mutacion de Fortune* (*The Book of Fortune's Transformation*) she described this period as a kind of shipwreck. Under the command of her husband, her household, like a ship, had been safe. Then, without warning, 'a sudden and powerful wind started up; the whirlwind was twisted like a corkscrew, and it struck against the ship'. With her 'good master' dead, Christine too wished to die. Then, Fortune came to her. Looking up at the ship's broken mast, she mustered the courage to repair and take command of the ship. 'Thus I became a true man (this is no fable)'.

It would be through her writing that Christine would support herself and her family, and assure her fame. She first turned to writing as a means of comfort, crafting ballads, rondeaux and other poems that would help lift her out of her grief.

> *It's only right that I should be dismayed,*
> *Full of hot tears and with tongue of lead,*
> *I am a widow lone, in black arrayed.*

She sent her verses to various members of the court and, as was the custom, they began to send her gifts, then money, in return. Since Christine was really very good at her craft, she quickly gained a word-of-mouth reputation. Her ability to write for specific audiences helped build her popularity with her patrons (mainly nobles and wealthy bureaucrats) and commissions poured in—and not just for her gifts as a poet, but for her skills as scribe, translator, essayist, historian, and political analyst. Over the course of two decades, she would write allegories, instructional texts, even a manuscript on military strategy. By 1404, she had attracted such a name for herself as a woman of letters that Philip the Bold, Duke of Burgundy, commissioned her to write a biography of his dead brother, Charles V. This was success indeed. Taking the courageous course of earning a living as a professional writer, Christine had become, in her words, 'an honorary man'.

Literary debate

In 1401, this now-renowned scholar questioned why so many learned men had 'devilish and wicked thoughts about women', and that inquiry led her on a new mission. 'I could hardly find a book on morals', Christine wrote, 'where I did not find several chapters or certain selections attacking women, no matter who the author was'. Early that year, the scholar Jean de Montreuil wrote a treatise (now lost) praising Jean de Meun's part of the allegorical poem *Le Roman de la Rose* (c. 1280); he sent Christine a copy of his essay, and she responded with a letter, telling him she deplored de Meun's unfair depiction of women. She dared to assert that women were just as capable of moral worth and heroic conduct as men. In turn, the poem's defenders either dismissed her as incompetent, or demanded she retract her commentaries. One begged her, as 'a woman of great ingenuity', not to exceed her talents; 'if you have been praised because you have shot a bullet over the towers of Notre Dame, don't try to hit the moon'. Another asked her to simply lay off Jean de Meun, 'whom you so horribly dare to reprimand and criticise', to which Christine replied: 'You insult me still further because I am a woman, which according to you makes me fickle, mad, and pretentious, for daring to correct and reprimand such a reputable scholar as you claim this author to be'.

Christine sent the first debate documents to Queen Isabeau in February 1402, accompanied by a letter in which she said: 'I ... wish to send you these epistles, in which, my venerated Lady, … you will see the diligence, desire, and will with which I defend myself as much as I can against dishonourable opinions, and where I defend the honour and praise of women (which many clerics and others make a point of diminishing in their works; this ought not to be tolerated, nor is it sustainable)'. And, 'as weak as my position may be in pronouncing such accusations against such skilled masters', Christine explains her purpose: 'I am motivated by truth'.

The City of Ladies

For Christine, it was not enough simply to defend the reputation of women. Next, she would present a positive model, to balance the literary record. And so, in 1405, she wrote a book, her longest and most ambitious in scope yet: *Le Livre de la Cité des Dames* (*The Book of the City of Ladies*). Throughout its pages, she would present the stories of remarkable women from every source she could find, and set out to put her gender in good standing. And in it, the author would cast herself as the main character.

The story begins with Christine, the character—a scholar engaged in 'the devoted study of literature'—reading a volume of classical poetry and wondering why, once again, women are portrayed in such a negative light. 'Could it be that God made such a vile creature when he created woman?' she asks. Feeling completely demoralised, the protagonist cries out, 'Why couldn't I have been born male?' Then, at her lowest moment of despair, she receives a vision: three ladies personifying Reason, Rectitude and Justice. Lady Reason, holding up the mirror of self-knowledge, speaks first: 'Come back to yourself, recover your senses, and do not trouble yourself any more over such absurdities'. Lady Reason goes on to tell Christine, who by now has wiped her tears and is starting to feel emboldened, that she and her two companions have come to help her build a 'city of ladies', where good women would be safeguarded against cruel assailants. Together they would restore the

---

VIRGINIA WOOLF

(1882–1941), an English novelist and essayist, is regarded as one of the greatest writers of the twentieth century, pioneering the 'stream of consciousness' approach to language and imagery. In 1929 she published *A Room of One's Own*, based on a series of lectures she had given at Cambridge University, in which she contemplated whether or not history could have produced a female Shakespeare. She concluded that 'a woman must have money and a room of her own if she is to write fiction'—making the link between financial independence and freedom (which women traditionally lacked) and creativity and achievement.

An illumination from Le Livre de la Cité des Dames, 1405.

MONA VAN DUYN

(1921–2004) was an American poet who wrote about love, daily life and the power of art, and in the process won every major American prize for poetry, including the 1991 Pulitzer Prize for Poetry with *Near Changes*. In 1992 she became the first female American Poet Laureate. More than 150 years after William Wordsworth landed the post of British Poet Laureate, the United Kingdom is still waiting for their first female laureate.

reputations of those unjustly accused, and remind the world that good women were the rule.

Cleverly posing as an innocent inquirer, Christine speaks through her guides by allowing them to answer her questions: why do men speak disparagingly of women? Have women ever been successful rulers? Are women capable of learning? The three virtues, or ladies, answer her character by telling the stories of the noblest and most accomplished women the world has known. Queens, princesses, warriors, poets, inventors, weavers of tapestries, wives, mothers, sibyls and saints are all brought to light, their stories demonstrating both the power and the piety of women. The city's inhabitants include Blanche, the Queen of France, an effective ruler after the death of her husband, and Dido, who built and ruled the 'marvellously beautiful, large and strong city' of Carthage where she 'lived a long time in glory'. The philosophers and poets Proba and Sappho inhabit Christine's city too, as do warriors like the Amazons and Zenobia. Even long-suffering wives (in effect, saints) like Griselda, who allowed her own children to be killed rather than disobey a despotic husband, have a place in the 'city of ladies'.

Finally, Christine reserves the highest place for her patron saint, Saint Christine—a virgin whose father shut her up in a tower and allowed her to be tortured because she would not worship his pagan gods. Saint Christine's story comes alive: the virgin is chained, beaten, deprived of food, covered with boiling oil and poisonous snakes, and finally her tongue is cut out. In a final act of defiance, she spits her severed tongue in her torturer's face, blinding him. In this celebration of her patron's sacred tongue, Christine—author, advocate of the power of speech—would validate her very role as literary defender of women.

Taking up her pen one last time

Le Livre de la Cité des Dames was but a sliver of a massive scholarly output. In a little over a decade, Christine de Pisan wrote fifteen major works. But following the outbreak of civil war in 1411, and then the English victory over much larger French forces at Agincourt in 1415 during the Hundred Years' War, she was forced to flee Paris and take refuge in the Dominican convent at Poissy, where her daughter was a nun. Christine was silent for eleven years; then something happened that propelled her out of her retirement 'with a resounding paean of joy': in 1429, a young peasant girl from Domrémy donned armor, rallied French troops against the English, and turned the tide of a war in stalemate in favour of the French. Two weeks after the coronation of King Charles VII, in July 1429, Christine again took up her quill, and composed her last work, the *Hymn to Joan of Arc*, part of which reads:

> *But as for us, we've never heard*
> *About a marvel quite so great,*
> *For all the heroes who have lived*
> *In history can't measure up*
> *In bravery against the Maid,*
> *Who strives to rout our enemies.*
> *It's God does that, who's guiding her*
> *Whose courage passes that of men.*

Joan had rescued a wasted kingdom—something 100,000 men could not do. And the imaginary world Christine had dreamed up as a young and hopeful writer, in which women held power and sway, was now manifest. In her excitement, Christine could not contain herself. In one line, she exclaims: 'Ha! What an honour for the feminine sex!'

An honour surely it is, not just for visionary warrior saint and heroine, but for the self-taught scholar and author addressing her. In her final work, 'Je, Christine' greets and congratulates 'Tu, Jehanne'—eminent woman to eminent woman—an event unprecedented in the whole of Europe (but not undreamed of) up to that day.

———◆———

In 1442, French poet Martin Le Franc wrote, in *Le Champion des Dames* (*The Champion of Ladies*), 'For the sake of strangers, let us celebrate the valiant Christine—Although death has snatched away her body, her name will live forever'. The date of Christine's death is unknown. But six centuries after her last words were etched onto parchment, she is recognised as the first consciously feminist voice of modern Europe.

LADY MURASAKI SHIKIBU

(C. 973–C. 1014 OR 1025)

World's first novelist
still evokes awe

In Japan, centuries before Christine de Pisan's time, Murasaki Shikibu authored Enji-monogatari *(*The Tale of Genji*), marking the birth of the novel. And still, after more than a millennium, this seminal literary work about the life and loves of the fictional 'Shining Prince Genji' continues to enchant readers throughout the world.*

The astoundingly gifted Japanese writer is known merely by a nickname. She was born in Kyoto, the daughter of a Chinese classical scholar and minor noble who was at the lower end of the food chain in the powerful Fujiwara family. At the royal court, where she was lady-in-waiting, the writer was nicknamed 'Murasaki' ('purple wisteria blossom') after her tale's main heroine; 'Shikibu' refers to a post her father once held at the Bureau of Ceremony.

The pseudonymous 'Lady Murasaki' lived during Japan's Heian period (950–1050), when the royal court—emperor and empress, princes and consorts, monks and maids—adhered to an exquisitely choreographed dance of deeply embedded ceremony. Called to serve the young Empress Shoshi— purportedly because of her gift for writing and storytelling—she kept a diary describing life at the Japanese imperial palace, loosely basing her novel on her experiences among the privileged lives of drunken courtiers, cutthroat consorts to the emperor, and all their preoccupations and trappings.

Murasaki very early showed a natural talent for languages. In a period when Chinese was Japan's official state language, formally taught only to men for the purpose of keeping participation in politics limited to few, and women were taught to read or write only Japanese, she learned Chinese by listening in on her brother's lessons.

Soon, she was able to translate the passages her brother found too difficult. Her father praised her intelligence and ability, and let her read the Chinese classics in secret, while lamenting she was born a female. She was married in her early twenties and had one child, Daini no Sanmi, who became a poet in her own right. Some time after her husband died, just two years into the marriage, Murasaki answered the call to the imperial court.

Left: 'Truth, Sincerity': Imagined portrait of Lady Murasaki by a famed eighteenth century Japanese printmaker.

No one knows just when Murasaki began The Tale of Genji *or when she finished it, but we do know that around 1000 years ago this lady of the Japanese court wrote a prose narrative that was nothing like the historical accounts and poetry that her contemporaries were reading. 'It was something new: an imaginative re-creation of human entanglements meant to feel more real than reality itself—a novel, as we define it today'. In the fifty-four shining chapters of a novel twice as long as* War and Peace, *Murasaki provides drama and romance and plot twists galore. And all the while, the many layers and nuances*

of human psychology are expressed in microscopic portrayals of the prince and in electric exchanges among the cloistered women of the court.

Called 'the scholar of moods', Murasaki is considered one of the greatest writers of Japanese literature. Statues have been erected in her honour, and her celebrated tale is a staple of every school in Japan. To many, there is no other literary work on earth quite like The Tale of Genji.

Illustration for The Tale of Genji *by an anonymous nineteenth century artist.*

HILDEGARD OF BINGEN (1098–1179)

Renaissance woman of the Middle Ages

Suffering nausea, a low-grade fever, and a general feeling of malaise, Hildegard lay down on the simple bed in the bare cell she had shared with the abbess Jutta for thirty years. At this moment, she wanted nothing more than to rest. Her shoes off, her eyelids drooping, Hildegard took a deep breath and relaxed. Suddenly she saw before her falling stars, spinning circles, flashes of yellow sunbursts. The heavens opened to her mind. A light of blinding brilliance flowed through her brain and ignited her heart, so that all sorrow and pain lifted from her. She felt like an innocent girl, no longer a middle-aged woman. And at once she understood—so clearly—the meanings of the psalms, the Gospels, all the books of the Old and New Testaments.

Hildegard was very much afraid, but at that moment she made up her mind: the time had come to confide what she had been keeping secret for so long.

Hildegard dictating to Volmar, her secretary and scribe, as she receives a vision and simultaneously sketches it on a wax tablet.

MAHAPAJAPATI GOTAMI

(c. 500s–400s BC) was the first woman to be ordained by Buddha and join the Sangha (Buddhist group of disciples). The aunt of the Buddha, Gotami had to work hard to convince him that women should be accepted into the Sangha, asking him three times before he agreed. The Buddha laid down a set of rules for holy women and Gotami established the order of nuns, Bhikkuni —making Buddhism the first religion to create an active role for women.

❧

Hildegard of Bingen experienced 'visual disturbances' from the time she was a young child. But it wouldn't be until the age of forty that she would privately confide this to a monk who was her teacher, and with his encouragement begin to write of her experiences. During her lifetime, Hildegard wrote profusely, not just as a prophet but as a poet, dramatist, musician, physician, and political moralist. She would have been an extraordinary person in any age, but for a woman of the twelfth century her achievements go beyond measure.

She is a woman of many firsts who made countless contributions to religious, cultural, and intellectual life of the Middle Ages. Due in part to her mystical visions, Hildegard was the only woman of her age accepted as an authoritative voice on Christian doctrine, and the first woman permitted by the pope to write theological books. She was the most prolific chant composer of her era and the first woman to write extensively on natural science and medicine. Right up until her death at the age of eighty-one she remained deeply modest, always stressing her lack of formal education, and attributing all her achievements to the glory to God.

A life turned over to God

Hildegard was destined for religious life from birth. However, for a long time no one knew about her extraordinary gift—the visions she had been having, and hiding, from the time she was three years old.

Hildegard was the tenth child of a well-to-do Christian couple from Bermersheim in Germany. When she was born, her parents made the decision to follow the custom of giving the tenth child over to the service of God when she reached a suitable age. A sickly child, and destined to live a cloistered life rather than marry and have children, Hildegard was provided with little education or other training. In 1106 her parents made good on their commitment to tithe their daughter to the Church, and the frail eight-year-old was delivered into the care of the anchoress Jutta von Spanheim, who served as abbess of a cloistered community of nuns associated with a thriving Benedictine monastery at Disibodenberg. Hildegard was enclosed with Jutta in a cell attached to the church, their only communication with the outside world through one window. While Jutta's goal was to provide young Hildegard with a solid religious education, the child's frequent helplessness prevented her from acquiring more than a rudimentary education during her first years at Disibodenberg. Still, the abbess managed to teach Hildegard how to read and to instill in her a thirst for knowledge and a profound love of music, the Latin psalms, and the Holy Scriptures.

Hildegard must have become a quick study, given the breadth and depth of her later intellectual interests. Word got out about the abbess-serving-as-teacher and her clever pupil, and soon their cell, now provided with a door, became a hub for young nuns eager to learn. Hildegard took her vows and became a Benedictine nun when she was fifteen, and continued her studies in natural history, German folk medicine and the ancient Greek cosmologies. And all this time she was experiencing inexplicable, periodic visions of 'the living light'.

These strange episodes—the first one, when she 'saw such a great brilliance that my soul trembled', when she was only three—exhausted her body and drained her strength. Keeping this secret was extremely wearing, but she dared not tell a soul about what was happening to her, fearful that she would be singled out as crazy or 'different'. Eventually, however, Jutta persuaded her pupil to tell her exactly what was going on. Hildegard described a pattern in which a period of illness would be followed by visual disturbances in the form of moving, flickering, dazzling, light in geometric shapes or sometimes a blinding flash. More than one modern-day scholar has attributed such visions to migraine attacks. Whatever the cause, Hildegard would explain that they left her with an extraordinary sense of wellbeing, insight and power.

Soon after Hildegard's disclosure, Jutta died and the nuns elected Hildegard as their new abbess. She was thirty-eight years old. For several years she remained silent

SAINT WIBORADA OF ST GALL

(c. 800s–926 AD) was a Swiss Benedictine nun and ascetic, believed to have the gift of prophecy. In her most profound vision she predicted an invasion by Hungarian forces and her martyrdom at their hands. The prophecy proved true—most of the monks of the monastery at St Gall escaped thanks to her warning, but Wiborada remained and was killed when she was discovered praying in her cell. In 1047 she was venerated by Pope Clement II, becoming the first woman to be formally canonised by the Vatican.

❧

'Universal Man', *from Liber divinorum operum, completed about five years before Hildegard's death.*

about her unique inner visions. Although she was certain by now that they were God-given, it would have been risky to say so. At best, it would be unseemly for a woman of the Middle Ages to presume she was a vessel for God's divine revelations and, even more so, to write about them. At worst, she could be denounced as a heretic and persecuted by the Church. There was always the chance that anyone who knew about her experiences might conclude that they came from the Devil.

But when she was forty-two years and seven months old, Hildegard had an experience that affected her more profoundly than any other: before her appeared an image, and the voice of God, commanding her to write down her visions. 'Forced by a great pressure of pains to reveal what I had seen and heard', Hildegard privately confided her extraordinary experience to a monk named Volmar. He was deeply impressed, convinced that her visions had a divine and not a diabolical source. Volmar not only encouraged her to immediately write down what she saw, but also gained the approval of the Abbot of Disibodenberg for Hildegard to continue writing about her visions; eventually Volmar became her long-serving secretary.

Over the next ten years, Hildegard was to complete her greatest work, *Scivias* (*Know the Ways of the Lord*). Of it she said:

> *What I write is what I see and hear in the vision. I compose no other words than those I hear, and I set them forth in unpolished Latin just as I hear them in the vision, for I am not taught in this vision to write as philosophers do. And the words of the vision are not like words uttered by the mouth of many but like a shimmering flame or a cloud floating in a clear sky.*

God's will

For someone with no formal education, *Scivias* is an extraordinary achievement. Completed in 1151, the book is divided into three parts, covering a total of twenty-six visions. The visions cover a whole gamut of subjects, but essentially they provide everything the individual soul needs to know to attain salvation. Hildegard shares her views on sin, virtues and vices, the work of the Holy Spirit, the meaning of the Trinity, the sacraments, Christ's passion, resurrection and ascension into heaven, and even includes a collection of her songs. Most importantly, her idea of God's love for his children was radical; she saw this love and the power of creation as feminine, tender, and nurturing. Before she even completed her work, Hildegard's writings were creating a stir.

Sometime in 1147 or 1148, Pope Eugenius III sent a commission to Disibodenberg to investigate Hildegard and collect copies of her completed pages. So impressed was Eugenius that he read her work aloud to an assembly of archbishops and cardinals, before sending a letter to Hildegard with his endorsement of her prophetic role, his blessings, and the command to continue writing. With this stamp of approval, Hildegard not only became the first woman to receive papal permission to write on theological issues, but her divine authority was sealed; anyone who opposed her would be thwarting the will of God.

Scivias made Hildegard something of a celebrity. As her fame grew, she was consulted on many ecclesiastical and political matters by popes, bishops, and civil servants. She even embarked on a preaching tour, unprecedented for a woman and actually forbidden by canon law. Even before she had completed *Scivias*, with her writings in circulation, Hildegard was attracting patrons and new members to the ever-growing monastery.

> ### ANNE HUTCHINSON
>
> (1591–1643) was an early American settler who came into conflict with the Puritan leaders in Massachusetts Bay Colony for her liberal views. Originally meeting with other women settlers to discuss her theological beliefs and becoming popular with the wider community, she was seen as a threat to the clergy by promoting religious diversity, the right to free assembly, and the empowerment of women. Banished from the Massachusetts Bay Colony, she became one of the founders of Rhode Island.
>
> ✧

In 1148, after the famous papal seal of approval, Hildegard's timidity went out the window; suddenly she announced that God had ordered her to move herself and her nuns to a new location at Rupertsberg near Bingen. Letting nothing and no one stand in the way, Hildegard browbeat Disibodenberg's Abbot Kuno into submission and had her new nunnery built and populated with her little community by 1150. Moreover, she made sure that she gained control of the property and income that belonged to her nuns. Later, she would explain, 'It was clearly God's will that all this should be legally fixed in writing'.

This gives us only an inkling of her accomplishments. Hildegard's demanding full-time job as abbess of the new foundation entailed holding prayers and services, disciplining and advising her nuns, managing the staff, administering the distribution of food and clothing supplies, receiving visitors, attending to legal affairs, and supervising work on the convent land. All that aside, she spent the next decades of her long life writing prolifically; composing music; and corresponding with the public (everyone from princes and prelates to troubled wives who wrote to her asking for her advice and predictions on the outcome of future events). She became practically the voice of conscience for the influencers of her day, addressing the monastic community, three popes, a host of bishops and scholars, even the Holy Roman Emperor himself. Famously, Hildegard denounced the mighty Archbishop of Cologne as a predatory hawk. And to the emperor, Barbarossa, she sent a warning that he stop acting so childish and appointing anti-popes, lest he be struck down by God. Some 300 of Hildegard's letters are preserved today.

Investigating the natural world

During Hildegard's time, there was no such thing as a medical practice as we know it today. People went to the monasteries for help with their ailments.

Hildegard believed that everything God created, from herbs to stones, was for the benefit of humankind. She wrote two works on natural history and the medicinal properties of just about everything in the natural world, from minerals and metals to birds and bats; together they are known as *Liber Subtilatum* (*Subtleties of the Diverse Nature of Created Things*). These works were uncharacteristic of Hildegard's writings, including her personal correspondences; for the first time, she did not present her material in visionary form and did not make any references to divine source or revelation. However, like all her other writings they did reflect her religious philosophy—that everything was put in the world for the use of God's children. Her deductions were based on strictly her own observations.

It is indicative of Hildegard's unflagging curiosity, and evolving courage, that she also wrote extensively

MOTHER TERESA

(1910–1997) was an Albanian Roman Catholic nun who founded the order of the Missionaries of Charity, dedicated to helping the poor. She worked mainly in India, where she is especially known for her support of people in the slums of Calcutta. She was recognised for her humanitarian efforts with the award of the Nobel Peace Prize in 1979 and of India's highest honour, the Bharat Ratna, in 1980. Mother Teresa was the first non-Indian to receive this award, and only the second woman (Indira Gandhi was the first).

on human sexuality. At a time when medical opinion held women to be more lustful than men, and less likely to control their lust, Hildegard took a different stance:

> *A man's love ... is a blazing heat, like a fire on a blazing mountain, which*
> *can hardly be quenched, while hers is more like a wood-fire that is easy to*
> *quench: but a woman's love, in comparison with a man's, is like a sweet warmth*
> *coming from the sun, which brings forth fruit.*

And she may very well have been the first person to write about orgasms from the female perspective:

> *When a woman is making love with a man, a sense of heat in her brain, which*
> *brings with it sensual delight, communicates the taste of that delight during the*
> *act and summons forth the emission of the man's seed. And when the seed has*
> *fallen into its place, that vehement heat descending from her brain draws the*
> *seed to itself and holds it, and soon the woman's sexual organs contract, and all*
> *the parts that are ready to open up during the time of menstruation now close,*
> *in the same way as a strong man can hold something enclosed in his fist.*

Hildegard was not interested in harping on about the sinfulness of sexual relations. But, she did share her thoughts on the misuse of carnal pleasures:

> *God united man and woman, thus joining the strong to the weak, that each*
> *might sustain the other. But these perverted adulterers change their virile*
> *strength into ... a woman who takes up devilish ways and plays a male role*
> *in coupling with another woman is most vile in My sight, and so is she who*
> *subjects herself to such a one in this evil deed ... And men who touch their*
> *own genital organ and emit their semen seriously imperil their souls, for*
> *they excite themselves to distraction; they appear to me as impure animals*
> *devouring their own whelps, for they wickedly produce their semen only for*
> *abusive pollution.*

She also shared her views on gender and disposition. The way Hildegard saw things, what determined a baby's gender was the strength of the semen, and what determined the baby's disposition was the amount of love and passion involved in sexual relations. The worst case, according to Hildegard, was when the seed was weak *and* parents felt no love, the result being a bitter daughter.

Composer of divine harmonies

Music held an important place in Hildegard's life. She describes it as the means of recapturing the original joy and beauty of paradise. According to her, before the Fall, Adam had a pure voice and joined angels in singing praises to God. After the Fall, music was invented and musical instruments created to worship God appropriately. In between her other projects, Hildegard found time to compose a cycle of seventy-seven songs—a collection of religious music the composer referred to as the 'symphony of the harmony of heavenly revelations'. Freer and more inventive than most Gregorian chant, Hildegard's songs are uncharacteristically joyful for the Middle Ages. She wrote hymns and sequences in honour of saints, the Virgin Mary, John the Baptist and the Holy Spirit. She gave thanks and celebrated the wonderfulness of divine love. And in her passion to praise God with the most beautiful music she could create, she introduced magical harmony. Over the last few decades, her music has been undergoing a revival and enjoying huge public success. The recording by the group Sequentia, the *Canticles of Ecstasy*, captures the unfathomable spiritual depth of her music. As a testament to her talent, Hildegard is the first composer, of either sex, about whom a biography was written.

Her last anthem

At the age of eighty, Hildegard took one last heroic stand as a matter of God's will. At issue was the burial of a local nobleman in her convent cemetery. The Archbishop of Mainz claimed the man had died excommunicate, and ordered Hildegard to have his body dug up and thrown out of the cemetery. But Hildegard was satisfied that before his death the man had confessed his sins and reconciled with the Church. The archbishop, nonetheless made it clear: if she didn't comply with his orders, she and her nuns would suffer the most serious punishment that the Church could impose—they would not be allowed to celebrate mass, receive the sacraments, or sing the divine office. In the end, Hildegard refused the mandate of the ecclesiastics and bore the interdict imposed upon the convent, putting first in her conscience her obedience to God. In perhaps the most important letter she ever wrote, Hildegard protested against the punishment of depriving her convent of their sung office, the music of 'God's intended celestial harmonies', which was central to their spiritual life. Shortly before her death, the excommunication would be lifted.

On September 17, 1179 Hildegard died, loved and revered, among her beloved nuns. To everyone whose life she had touched, she was a saint. But she would not be considered as such according to Rome. The process for her canonisation officially began in 1227 and a document of the evidence for her sanctity submitted in 1233; but this was rejected and returned to the commission of inquiry for amendment. Another letter from Pope Innocent IV in 1243 requests the clergy of Mainz to re-submit the document, but they seem not to have done so.

———————

Hildegard of Bingen was sickly from the day of her birth, and yet she lived to be an octogenarian whose accomplishments were as significant and as varied as perhaps none other than that titan Leonardo da Vinci. Despite founding and serving as abbess of a Benedictine monastery; despite her widely diverse and deep writings on innumerable topics; despite being sought out for advice from popes, bishops, and political leaders in a male-dominated world; despite her ethereal music; and most of all perhaps, despite her defiance of male ecclesiastical authority in order to listen to what she believed to be the true will of God, Hildegard remained largely forgotten for some time after her death. Beatified but still not canonised, the formidable abbess abrogated to herself a place in the Church's calendar; her feast day is on the day she died. Many people today refer to her as St Hildegard, a fitting epitaph for an outstanding woman.

Right: Sculpture of Julian of Norwich commissioned by Norwich Cathedral to celebrate the new millennium.

JULIAN OF NORWICH

(c. 1342–c. 1416)

*Mystic scribe who put desire
for God into prose*

Fourteenth century mystic turned theologian, and the first woman known to have written in the English language, Julian of Norwich has inspired generations of Christians with her revelations and reflections on divine love.

She was born in Norwich, England just five years before the first wave of one of the worst plagues in history, the Black Death, swept over Europe, wiping out populations, ravaging cities, and damaging the standing and spiritual authority of the Christian Church. When priests and bishops couldn't come up with explanations or cures for the recurring plague—deeming it 'God's will'— villagers started to take their frustrations out against the Church. The climax of the social and religious unrest was the Peasants' Revolt in 1381. It was into the wake of these calamitous circumstances that the woman we know as Julian of Norwich brought her message of 'our Lord's meaning' and hope.

In 1373, at the age of thirty, gravely ill and practically on her deathbed, Julian had a series of intense visions of Jesus Christ suffering on the cross. When she recovered, she wrote down a brief account of her visionary experience, which had convinced her that she should devote her life totally to God. She decided not to live in a convent as a nun, but to become an anchoress—a person called to a solitary life who was not cut off from the world but anchored in it. Her home was a small cell attached to the Church of St Julian, Bishop of Le Mans, just off one of the main streets of Norwich. The next decades of Julian's life were made up of prayer, contemplation and counseling, and she became well known throughout England as a spiritual authority.

For another fifteen years Julian contemplated her visions, eventually achieving an understanding that galvanised her to elaborate on her original written account. A Book of Showings *(c. 1393), titled in modern times* Revelations of Divine Love, *was the first book to be written in English by a woman. This lengthy, brilliant text spells out Julian's impressions in the vernacular of her day, not the customary Latin, and shows such literary skill that she has been ranked with Chaucer as a pioneering genius of English prose.*

Where and how Julian—highly intelligent, educated, and especially well versed in scriptural traditions—learned to write so masterfully nobody really knows. There was no shortage of religious stimulation and literature in Norwich, a flourishing centre for religious life and a distinguished centre of learning. But the whole trend of medieval thought was against the education of women, and even in those convents where some study of Latin was encouraged it was considered beyond a woman's reach to involve herself in writing. While monks composed chronicles, nuns embroidered copes. Julian had too sharp an intellect to settle herself in a convent where the order of the day may have been to perfect one's needlepoint. Many male religious orders had houses and centres of scholarship with libraries in Norwich, and once Julian seriously embarked on her life of prayer and meditation, she may have had access to their books.

Revelations of Divine Love covers the most profound mysteries of the Christian faith, and is generally considered one of the most remarkable documents of medieval religious experience. The subject is love, and the text offers up a new twist on the punishing God held in public view at the time. Julian's God is compassionate and loving. In exquisite words, she writes about God's love—all powerful and embracing, unconditional, and unfailing even in hard times, with no place for anger or wrath. In the last chapter, she writes:

> I desired in many ways to know what was our Lord's meaning. And fifteen years after and more, I was answered in spiritual understanding, and it was said: Know it well, love was his meaning. Who reveals it to you? Love. What did he reveal to you? Love. Why does he reveal it to you? For love. Remain in this, and you will know more of the same. But you will never know different, without end.

Simply and sincerely, Julian assures us, 'All shall be well, and all shall be well, and all manner of thing shall be well', a line that perfectly sums up her theology. It is also one of the most individually famous lines in all of Catholic theological writing, and one of the best-known phrases of the literature of her era.

One of the world's most eloquent and profound visionaries spent the latter part of her life as a recluse in an anchoress's cell, but her message has travelled far and wide, spanning centuries. A modern chapel in the Church of St Julian has been dedicated to her memory. Her cell (reconstructed along with the church after the bombing of Norwich in World War II) is a popular site with visitors.

SOFONISBA ANGUISSOLA (c. 1532–1625)

Renaissance painter does more than pass muster

King Philip II cut a striking figure in his gold-embroidered suit of white silk. On his arm was his fourteen-year-old French bride, smiling and joyous, the picture of loveliness in her gold and purple silk dupion gown. But all eyes were fixed on the young Italian lady whom Ferrante Gonzaga was asking gallantly to dance. At the Spanish king's wedding ball, the galliard would begin with Sofonisba.

The lavish festivities went on through the night. Finally the last dance was called, and a torch was passed around. Sofonisba received the torch from the queen's cousin, Prince de La Roche, and chose the Duke of Infantado as her next partner. Quick steps, a glide, and then a perfectly executed lavolta landed Sofonisba right before the king. She reached out confidently, passing the torch to the sovereign himself. Charmed and amused, King Philip allowed a grin to spread across his face, and honoured Sofonisba with a very deep bow. With that, her position at the imperial court was established.

Sofonisba Anguissola, self-portrait.

Sofonisba Anguissola was the first woman artist of the Renaissance to achieve international recognition and legendary praise in her lifetime. A pioneer in portraiture and genre painting, she spent nearly twenty years as a painter for the Spanish Court in Madrid and was the lady-in-waiting and painting instructor for Elisabeth of Valois, the third wife of Philip II. While Sofonisba was still an adolescent, her drawings were critiqued and praised by the mighty Michelangelo and 'the father of art history', Italian art critic and biographer Giorgio Vasari. In the twilight of her long life, she was hailed by Anthony Van Dyck, who made a pilgrimage to visit the last remaining Renaissance artist, and memorialised his visit in his *Italian Sketchbook*.

It has been said that, in an era when the highest level of praise for a woman in the arts was the ability to copy, Sofonisba was the only artist of her time credited with the remarkable gift of infusing an image with life. For this reason, she was frequently called a 'marvel'. Despite all odds, Sofonisba excelled in the all-male field of painting, where no woman artist had even begun to pave the way. Sofonisba set the precedent.

A 'miracle of nature'

Sofonisba was the eldest child in a prestigious noble family from Cremona, a provincial northern Italian city wrapped in the Renaissance spirit. Her ambitious and progressive father, Amilcare Anguissola, gave his six daughters a humanist education equal to that of his son, having them tutored in Latin, literature, history, philosophy, mathematics, and the sciences, but also trained in the arts of the court—music, writing, drawing, and painting. Products of an era when women, even noblewomen, were not accorded the same privileges as men, the Anguissola sisters and their multitudinous talents created quite a sensation. So much so that painter and biographer Giorgio Vasari went out of his way to visit these most unusual women. Later, in his *Lives of the Most Eminent Architects, Painters, and Sculptors of Italy* (1568), Vasari would write: 'But Sofonisba of Cremona … has worked with deeper study and greater grace than any woman of our times at problems of design, for not only has she learned to draw, paint, and copy from nature, and reproduce most skillfully works by other artists, but she has on her own painted some most rare and beautiful paintings'.

Sofonisba's greatest early champion was her liberal father. When he recognised her budding creativity, he did something revolutionary: he provided her with three years of private instruction in the studios of two Cremonese artists, Bernardino

Campi (1522–1591) and later Bernardino Gatti (c. 1495–1576). Not only was it unheard of for a woman to become a painter, but it was considered highly distasteful for a member of nobility to assume such a low-class profession. Even Michelangelo's father, who was a gentleman, tried to discourage his son from becoming an artist. But the two strikes against her didn't stop Sofonisba from apprenticing under two great artists, and exposing herself to two divergent trends in sixteenth century art: the High Renaissance, with its controlled, ordered and graceful poses and balanced colours; and Mannerism, its antithesis.

Over the course of six years, from 1547 to 1553, Sofonisba painted a series of portraits—among them, one of her teacher Campi painting none other than Sofonisba herself; a few of her sister, Elena; and more than a handful of herself—and developed a quality in her work that was nowhere to be found in paintings by male artists, a true-to-life naturalism. While her male contemporaries were bent on portraying more operatic emotions—rapture, agony, devotion, adoration— Sofonisba was depicting the kinds of expressions that would be of no great use in grand historical or religious paintings: innocent pleasure, mischievousness, stifled giggles, playful fun. And she did this more keenly than anyone else had ever done.

With her masterpiece *The Chess Game* (1555), Sofonisba broke new artistic ground. In this group portrait of her sisters wrapped up in a minor episode in the life of an intellectual family, the twenty-three-year-old artist decided to throw solemnity and seriousness out the window and, instead, poke fun. The girls in her painting wear elaborate coiffures and are dressed in heavy brocades; the game is set in a garden, with a distant view of hills and chateaus, and with the chessboard placed on the type of oriental throw covering tables in plenty of paintings by Sofonisba's Dutch and Flemish

Following pages: 'The Chess Game': *Sofonisba's sister Minerva acknowledges defeat.*

contemporaries. But this is no conventionally formal, static, emotionless sixteenth century portrait. Sofonisba chose to depict the moment of victory in which one of her sisters, Minerva, signals her defeat to another, Lucia, who looks slyly pleased with herself, while Europa, the youngest of the group, shoots a reticent grin (but one that oozes with gleefulness) toward a chagrined Minerva, and a maidservant looks on sympathetically. In 1566, Vasari would see the painting during a visit to the Anguissola home in Cremona, and exclaim, 'It was done with such diligence and quickness that they all appear to be breathing and absolutely alive, and are wanting in nothing save speech'. Now, in the eyes of the influential art critic, Sofonisba was not merely a 'woman artist' but an artist in her own right, a representative of the School of Cremona.

Sofonisba's capacity for invention carried on in her correspondence with Michelangelo. In 1554, the aspiring painter had travelled to Rome to meet the aging seventy-nine-year-old titan. There, it is supposed, Sofonisba arrived elegantly attired, as was befitting a nobleman's daughter, sat and listened respectfully as Michelangelo pointed out the difficulties that she would face as an artist in a male domain. But she must have been persuasive, and Michelangelo eventually encouraging, for over the next two years he sent her sketches to copy, and tips for improving her canvases. It was Sofonisba's drawing of a girl barely stifling her laughter at an old woman she is trying to teach to read that really won over the master. Indeed, he challenged Sofonisba to make a drawing of someone crying, and in her characteristic cheeky way she did not depict what might be expected—a grief-stricken Virgin Mary or weeping apostles, for example—but, in Vasari's words, 'a little girl, who is laughing at a boy, because the latter, having plunged his hand into a basket of crabs, which she has held out to him, is caught by one of them, which is pinching his finger, and the boy is weeping and bemoaning his pain'.

With expert naturalism and imaginative composition Sofonisba met the mighty Michelangelo's challenge, and this feat did not go unnoticed by her contemporaries.

Vasari uttered the thoughts of many when he critiqued *Asdrubale Being Bitten by a Crab* in the words: 'One could not see a more graceful or realistic drawing than this one'. Years later, in 1562, a friend of Michelangelo's, Tommaso Cavalieri, would send Sofonisba's drawing as a gift, along with Michelangelo's *Cleopatra*, to the Duke Cosimo de' Medici; with them he sent a letter which said: 'I sent it [Sofonisba's drawing] to you with this one [Michelangelo's drawing], and I believe that it may stand comparison with many other drawings, for it is not simply beautiful, but also exhibits considerable invention'.

Between 1555 and 1559, Sofonisba's talent began to be recognised by those outside her immediate circle. She continued to paint her family and polish her self-portraits, and started to circulate her work among Italy's aristocratic families—including the Este, Medici, and Borghese clans—who didn't take long in becoming avid collectors. (In her lifetime, she would paint more self-portraits than any other artist between Dürer and Rembrandt.) Then word of Sofonisba reached the monasteries. Her status as a woman painter was still highly unusual, but her talent was too precious to overlook. In her *Portrait of a Dominican Astronomer* (c. 1555), the artist followed the sixteenth century tradition of painting a sitter with all the accoutrements of his profession, a way for the emerging bourgeoisie (and, in this case, the clergy) to be memorialised. Like Lorenzo Lotto's *The Astronomer* (1545), Sofonisba's painting shows the sitter behind a table spread with astronomical paraphernalia, and with a globe in his left hand. But where Lotto's painting is somber, Sofonisba portrays her bearded monk wearing a smile, capturing her subject looking up, lost in his calculations, an instant of pleasurable absorption clearly written all over his face. And, through this surprising work, she captured once again the attention of the world.

In taking commissions from those who led such spiritual and virtuous lives, and in signing her portraits 'Virgo' (an unmarried maiden), Sofonisba's motives

MARGARET BOURKE-WHITE

(1904–1971), an American photographer and journalist, was a woman of many firsts—the first female photojournalist for *Life* magazine; in 1930 the first Western photographer of either sex allowed into the Soviet Union; the first female war correspondent and the first woman allowed to work in combat zones in World War II. Beginning her career when photography and journalism were very much seen as male domains, Bourke-White paved the way for other women in these fields, and created some of the most enduring photographs of the twentieth century.

for painting could not be questioned. All this exposure eventually led to the great literary acclaim of writers and poets like Angelo Grillo, who had seen her work in these social settings and proclaimed her a '*miracolo di natura*' (miracle of nature). But the highest praise came in the form of an invitation from King Philip II of Spain, in 1559, for Sofonisba to attend his court.

At the Spanish court

Sofonisba's life, and her painting, changed when she joined the court of the most powerful ruler in Europe. Here she served as both court painter and lady-in-waiting to successive queens, Elisabeth of Valois and Anne of Austria, until 1578.

In the early 1550s, the Spanish court had been known for its somberness and tedious adherence to exacting ceremony. Inflexible, secretive and formal, the king himself only added to the oppressiveness. But with the arrival of Elisabeth, the sparkling fourteen-year-old daughter of Henry II and Catherine de' Medici of the opulent French court, the gloom began to lift. Philip called his new queen 'the light of my eyes.' The youthful Spanish queen, who had grown up around some of the century's most beautiful art, and the twenty-seven-year-old artist from Italy formed an immediate bond.

Sofonisba's court routine was a busy one: tutoring her royal pupil in painting and playing music with her, as well as tending to the regular court functions required of the queen's lady-in-waiting. There were sixteen ladies-in-waiting, and the pay was noteworthy. In addition to 100 ducats a year in ordinary salary, Sofonisba received money for two servants of her own, a lady's maid and a groom, a washerwoman, and even for candles and horse or mule feed. She also received a lifelong pension of 200 ducats. But she wasn't paid for her pictures.

It was customary for court painters to give their work as 'gifts' to the sovereign. At Philip's request, Spanish court portraiture in the 1560s was formal. Adhering to the king's wishes, in a severe and ceremonious environment, Sofonisba painted without the warmth and candid informality she expressed in her earlier family portraits. Just like everyone else, Sofonisba perceived royalty in almost godlike terms: living icons who, from their lofty perches, did not show emotions. And so, in her court portraits, she treated her noble benefactors formally, as would be expected by the state: the king wears around his noble neck the Order of the Golden Fleece;

Portrait from the Spanish court: Elisabeth of Valois, 1565.

Queen Elisabeth's face is framed by a small, lace ruff, with careful attention given to the smallest detail of the gold embroidery on the bodice of her gown and on her jewelled collar; in grand state portraits appear the king's two daughters dressed to kill. Nonetheless, the impudent artist couldn't help but add her signature touch—a hint of a smile, a sympathetic interpretation of a disturbed personality—in portraits of the monarchs in their royal splendour.

Although the king originally invited Sofonisba to his court as the queen's painter and companion, his initial scepticism at having a female court painter changed when he saw the caliber of her work. A portrait of his hunchbacked son Prince Don Carlos, which Sofonisba finished in 1567, so pleased the king that he ordered nineteen copies made. And the king—who was truly a shrewd judge of the arts—wasn't the only person pleased with her canvases. 'We have received the portrait of our dear daughter, the Queen of Spain', wrote the Pope, in October 1561, and 'we commend your marvellous talent which is the least among your numerous qualities'. By now, Sofonisba was good enough to assume a place beside Philip's preferred portraitists, Alonso Sanchez Coello and Anthonis Mor. Vasari tells us, 'Everyone considered the excellence and distinction of Sofonisba as something wonderful'.

In the autumn of 1568, Queen Elisabeth's health was deteriorating after a series of miscarriages and successful pregnancies. Sofonisba stayed with her, trying to lift her spirits. But Elisabeth, lucid although seriously unwell, was convinced she would not live long, and drew up her will. The final blow came when the twenty-three-year-old queen miscarried on 3 October, and died at noon. In her will she left her favourite lady-in-waiting 3000 ducats and a length of brocade, perhaps a hint that it was time she married.

Sofonisba's close relationship with Elisabeth had not gone unnoticed by the king, and he took a special interest in her future. While the queen's household slowly dispersed after her death, with the French ladies-in-waiting and staff returning to

FRIDA KAHLO

(1907–1954) was a Mexican artist who combined traditional Mexican Symbolism with Surrealism and Realism. Revered as a feminist icon, Kahlo endured a lifetime of acute physical suffering which revealed itself in her intensely personal artwork—her self-portraits deal with the subjects of truth, beauty, sexuality and pain. 'They thought I was a Surrealist', she said, 'but I wasn't. I never painted dreams. I painted my own reality'. In 2006, Frida Kahlo's painting *Roots* fetched US$5.6 million at auction, setting a record as the most expensive artwork ever painted by a woman.

Paris, Sofonisba stayed in Madrid, apparently at the king's request. She painted the official portraits of Philip and his new queen, Anne of Austria, his niece, whom he wed in Segovia on 12 November 1570. But she did not form the kind of friendship with the new, reclusive queen that she had shared with Elisabeth. French ambassador Pierre de Seguesson reported of Queen Anne: 'She never leaves her rooms, and her court is like a nunnery'. At thirty-eight, and technically a ward of the king, Sofonisba began to have her own thoughts about marriage. She shared her concerns with Philip—whose responsibility it was to choose her a husband—saying that if marriage were an option for her she would be 'inclined to marry an Italian'. The closest that Philip could come was the Sicilian Don Fabrizio de Moncada, from a family that was part of Spain's venerated nobility. Sofonisba received a sizable dowry from the king on her marriage in 1571, and stayed on at court with her husband for eight more years. Then she would receive the king's blessings, and go on her way. It was a tribute both to Sofonisba's artistic gifts and her personality that she had remained at the Spanish court for nearly two decades.

The return of an illustrious daughter

In 1579, when Sofonisba was forty-six, Don Fabrizio died, probably from the plague. They had lived in Palermo since their departure from Madrid, and Sofonisba had been painting and tutoring would-be artists. The thought of going back to the Spanish court, to dependence on royal whim, was out of the question. It was time to return home.

On the way back to Italy, she was swept off her feet by the ship's captain, the much younger Orazio Lomellino, and by the end of the voyage had agreed to marry him. In January 1580, Sofonisba and Orazio were married, and they settled in Genoa, the home of the Lomellino family, where Sofonisba became lady of her own palazzo. She lived another forty-five years, happily married, continuing to paint while her husband was at sea, and renowned as a *grande dame*. She divided her time between executing polished, courtly portraits for the nobility and paintings on religious themes, which she had not tackled since her days with her teacher Bernardino Campi. Her studio became a gathering place for the nobility and other artists.

In her twilight years, she found time to teach and was much sought out as an adviser to other women artists in northern Italy—Lavinia Fontana, Barbara Longhi and Artemisia Gentileschi, to name a few—who, like their famous role model, chose painting as a career, and whose own careers were on the rise. Sofonisba's work was by now well known all over Europe, and her sketches, as well as her life, were held up as ideals—but not only for other women. Caravaggio is said to have seen her sketch *Asdrubale Being Bitten by a Crab*, and adopted the motif for his *Boy Bitten by a Lizard*. The twenty-three-year-old Anthony Van Dyck met with Sofonisba in Palermo in 1624, when she was in her nineties, and commemorated the event with a drawing and a written account. He described the elder painter as growing feeble in eyesight but 'possessing considerable memory and a sharp mind' as she regaled him with stories of the Spanish court and advised him in his own work.

Eventually, Sofonisba was forced to get a document called a *fides vitae*, a certificate that proved she was still alive. She died in her ninety-third year. Sofonisba Anguissola—truly one of the wonders of her age.

—————⦁⦁⦁—————

Despite her success during her lifetime, Sofonisba's artistic fame slowly disappeared during the eighteenth century. But just a few decades ago, in the 1970s, she was back in the spotlight as an artist, recognised for her landmark achievement of resourcefully carving out a unique category for herself within the social constraints of her times. Indeed, it leaves one to wonder if she could accomplish all that she had within an established set of restrictions, what more she could have produced if those restrictions did not exist. Financially independent, renowned for her talent, and respected for her creativity and intelligence, Sofonisba Anguissola was a true Renaissance woman.

Right: Self-portrait of Artemisia Gentileschi.

ARTEMISIA GENTILESCHI

(1593–c. 1653)

*Italian early Baroque painter who
defied convention and torture*

The first female painter to become a member of the Accademia dell'Arte del Disegno in Florence, Artemisia Gentileschi suffered the blows of contemporary critics, a jealous father, rape and a sensational rape trial during her illustrious career. By the age of forty, she was considered practically a world wonder, and was celebrated by poets for her virtuosity. In the eyes of her peers, she stood as one of the greatest female painters of Roman and biblical history, perhaps the most brilliant of all.

Artemisia was born in Rome in 1593, the daughter of Orazio and Prudentia Monotone Gentileschi. Her mother died when she was twelve. Her father, a respected painter, took her under his wing and trained her as an artist. She had little schooling, and didn't learn to read and write until she was an adult, but she was a quick study when it came to painting. She is said to have been a follower, like her father, of the revolutionary Baroque painter Caravaggio, whose dramatic realism and chiaroscuro *style (use of light and dark to achieve a heightened illusion of depth) influenced her work. But in other ways she followed no one.*

Unlike any other female artist of her time, Artemisia tackled grand religious and historical themes, leaving landscape and portrait painting to others, even though these were considered more acceptable avenues for women artists. By the time she was seventeen, she had produced an accomplished work—the one for which she is now best known, but which was long attributed to her father—her stunning and highly original interpretation of Susanna and the Elders *(1610).*

Despite her evident talent, the professional academies denied Artemisia access because she was a woman. So her father enlisted one of his colleagues, the quadratura *(ceiling) painter Agostino Tassi, to continue her art training. Tassi proved to be a lousy tutor as well as a lecher and a lout. According to Artemisia, he repeatedly tried to get her alone with him, and raped her when he succeeded in cornering her in her own bedroom. Tassi asserted that on the day of the alleged rape he was patiently teaching her the rules of perspective, because her painting skills were so pitiful. It definitively came out that Tassi did try to placate the young artist by promising to marry her, but then reneged on his promise. Thus it was that in 1612, Orazio Gentileschi sued his closest* collaborator for breach of contract. The result: the century's first prominent rape trial, with the Gentileschi name enmeshed in scandal. During the seven-month court case, in which it surfaced that Tassi had tried to steal some of his employer's paintings, had had sexual relations with his sister-in-law, and had arranged for his wife's murder, Artemisia was tortured to make sure that she wasn't fabricating her allegations. By the end of the trial, Artemisia's reputation was restored, but the injustice of what she had to endure, compared to Tassi's mere one-year jail sentence, left its mark.

Artemisia's work began to exhibit an emotional power that set her paintings apart from those of her contemporaries. In her first version of a common religious account—Judith Slaying Holofernes (c. 1612)—Judith's expression is not one of horror, as usually depicted by other artists, but of grim determination, an innovative characterisation that in all probability reflects Artemisia's wish for psychological revenge.

Just one month after her trial, Artemisia was married off to a modest Florentine artist in a move by her father to restore his daughter's honour. They had several children, only one of whom, a daughter, lived. Eventually Artemisia separated from her husband and led a strikingly independent life for a woman of her time—even if there is no firm evidence for the reputation she suffered in the eighteenth century as a sexual libertine. Until 1620, Artemisia lived in Florence where, in 1616, she became an official member of the Academy of Design, a remarkable honour probably made possible by the support of her Florentine patron, the Grand Duke Cosimo II of the powerful Medici family. Artemisia's second, larger version of that tale of female triumph from the Apocrypha, Judith beheading the invading general Holofernes (overleaf), dates from this time and hangs in the Uffizi Gallery in Florence.

Over the next decade, Artemisia moved around—living and working in Rome, Genoa, and Venice, in search of more lucrative commissions—until in 1630 she settled in Naples. During this time, she was making a name for herself as a talented and coveted court painter. Her patrons included all the crowned heads of Europe, among them Philip IV of Spain and Charles I of England, and she moved in circles that included Galileo Galilei and Anthony Van Dyck.

In 1638, Artemisia travelled to England at the behest of Charles I, an avid art collector and patron eager to adorn his court with distinguished artists. She

'Judith Slaying Holofernes', *1620: Grand Duchess Maria Luisa de' Medici considered this painting so horrifying that she hid it from view.*

joined her father, already in the service of the king, in collaborating on a series of canvases for the ceiling of the Queen's House at Greenwich, London. Before the project was completed, Orazio died. It is speculated that Artemisia completed the work so that her father's fame and brilliance would go down in history.

Artemisia left England by 1642 and returned to Naples, where she lived until her death. She remained very active, continuing to paint graceful compositions with violent subject matter, among them yet another version of Judith slaying Holofernes and several portraits of Bathsheba.

The sympathetic and powerfully expressive way she evokes her biblical heroines courageously rising up against the tides of their predicaments may very well stem from the artist's personal history. However, some art historians suggest that she was playing on her notoriety from the rape trial to cater to male patrons looking for sexually charged, female-dominant art.

The only record of her death comes in two satiric epitaphs that figure her in exclusively sexual terms as a nymphomaniac and adulterer. No matter, Artemisia is admired today as a truly gifted painter and the earliest woman artist to show a feminist consciousness in her work.

LUCY STONE (1818–1893)

Yankee suffragist who spoke out for women

Lucy was suffering from another migraine. For almost ninety minutes, she had been listening to pairs of male classmates engage in heated debate, just as she did week after week at Oberlin College. She removed her bonnet and rubbed her temples for relief. As closing remarks were finally made, Lucy stood and turned to her friend, Antoinette, the only other female student in Professor Thome's rhetoric class. 'It's time', she said. The young women moved briskly down the steps of the lecture hall. Eyes flashing, they approached the lectern and Lucy made their plea: 'Professor, we want to have a turn at debate'.

Her words had a surprising effect. Professor James Thome was a man of liberal views—a Southerner who had freed his slaves—and he consented. 'Ladies, it would be against the policy of the college to let you take the speaking platform with men. However, you may debate each other'. Lucy considered her first argument already won, relishing the thought that finally she would get from Oberlin what she had come there for: training in how to stand and speak, put forth motions, debate and declaim … and maybe one day be as skilled an anti-slavery orator as famed abolitionist William Lloyd Garrison.

Then Thome cautioned her with hard reality: 'Just be prepared for an uproar'.

A daguerreotype of a young Lucy Stone reveals her determination.

Often facing hostile audiences, Lucy Stone lectured across the United States for most of her life, advocating for basic civil rights for all Americans at a time when women were discouraged and sometimes banned from speaking publicly. The first woman from Massachusetts to earn a college degree participated in anti-slavery conferences with Frederick Douglass, and led the call for the first National Woman's Rights Convention in 1850. Dubbed 'the orator' and 'the morning star of the woman's rights movement', Lucy stirred interest in 'the woman question' among obstinate male opinion leaders, and sparked other female leaders, like Susan B. Anthony, Elizabeth Cady Stanton and Julia Ward Howe, to take up the cause.

Early influences

Lucy Stone was born into a large family on a Massachusetts farm in 1818, apparently with a built-in radar for injustice. She was one of nine children of a hard-drinking, bad-tempered man, so tightfisted that his wife frequently had to filch money from him to buy household necessities. Lucy grew up particularly susceptible to disparities between the sexes, determined that when the time came to carve out a life for herself she would not be held down. At eighteen, the fight for equality was already in her. On landing a teaching position at a grade school in a nearby town and discovering she was earning less than half the salary of the male teacher she had replaced, Lucy mustered the courage to ask for equity, and her outspokenness got her a higher salary—but still less than her predecessor earned.

Unsurprisingly, when she decided three years later to continue her own studies, Lucy couldn't persuade her father to pay her tuition. Convinced that education was only for men, he would never come around to her way of thinking. It took Lucy another four years to save up enough money to attend Oberlin College at the age of twenty-five.

The Ohio school, a hotbed of abolitionism, was an easy choice; it was the first to admit African

---

OLYMPE DE GOUGES

(1748–1793) was a French playwright and political activist whose 1791 *Déclaration des Droits de la Femme et de la Citoyenne* (*Declaration of the Rights of Woman and the Female Citizen*) was the first manifesto to espouse equal rights for women. The document was a direct challenge to the *Declaration of the Rights of Man and of the Citizen*, a crucial document in the French Revolution and an important universal document on liberty and equality, which nevertheless ignored the rights of women. In 1793 Olympe de Gouges was sent to the guillotine.

American students, and at the time was the only college in the country that admitted women. Lucy had worked hard to prepare herself, studying at Mount Holyoke Female Seminary and two other private academies in Massachusetts while continuing to teach in order to pay for tuition and room and board at the academies, and put aside savings for college. She became an avid reader of the abolitionist journal *The Liberator*, and an admirer of abolitionist orators Abby Kelley and Sarah and Angelina Grimké, who publicly compared the second-class status of women with the plight of slaves, prompting Congregationalist church pastors to prohibit women from using the pulpit to deliver speeches.

By 1843, when she could finally afford tuition at Oberlin, Lucy held some firmly entrenched beliefs: she considered it wrong for one human to own another, and that slavery should be ended. She maintained that women should have the right to vote and hold political office. And she thought in no uncertain terms that women should have the opportunity to seek advanced education, in any institution and any field that was open to men.

Lucy was resolved to call no man master, and vowed that if ever she had anything of significance to say, she would make doubly sure to speak out in public, in spite of those who tried to muzzle women. Traveling by train, steamship and stagecoach to Oberlin College, Lucy was ready to study rhetoric and speak her mind in a public forum. Oberlin, however, was not ready for Lucy.

A collegian calls the shots

Lucy's alma mater may have pioneered coeducation, but like most of American society in the nineteenth century it strongly opposed women speaking in public on the grounds that doing so violated scripture as well as conventions of female propriety. Lucy didn't buy it. She had studied enough Hebrew and Greek to translate Bible passages for herself and, in her opinion, to correct popular mistranslations. Semester after semester, Lucy fumed as her male classmates received training in oratory and debate with weekly declamations and discussions, while the best she could hope for was to pick up a few techniques from the sidelines. She could sit quietly only for so long. Egging on her friend and classmate, abolitionist and suffragist Antoinette Brown, to join her, Lucy convinced their professor to let his only two students in petticoats take the podium and engage in debate.

The date arrived. The lecture hall was packed with curiosity seekers. The young women's anti-slavery debate turned out to be exceptionally brilliant. But the Ladies' Board (the faculty wives) grumbled about women making public statements on moral issues, and immediately got to work, invoking the Bible: 'Let a woman learn in silence with all submissiveness'. The college clamped down on any further experiment. This only served to fuel Lucy's aspirations. Before long, she organised an off-campus, all-girl debating society—the first of its kind among college women. With sentinels on the watch to warn of intruders, the first of many meetings was held secretly in the nearby woods. Topping the list of discussion topics was a woman's right to speak in public.

Confident in her oratorical skills after much surreptitious practice, Lucy made a bold move just before graduation. In the summer of 1847, she petitioned the Oberlin administration for permission to read aloud the commencement address she had been invited to write by a vote of her classmates. She was turned down, Oberlin offering to have a male professor deliver her speech. Lucy couldn't support a gesture that 'takes away from women their equal rights, and denies to them the privilege of being co-labourers with men in any sphere to which their ability makes them adequate', and in the end refused to write any speech at all. Lucy graduated with honours, nonetheless, and with college behind her, she set her sights on a life of public lecturing.

'I was a woman before I was an abolitionist'

The Stone family was proud to have Lucy back in Massachusetts—the first woman in the state to hold a college degree—but they thought her ambitions were outrageous. She was teaching again, performing her job well and finding herself popular with her students. Why, they wondered, couldn't she just stick with her comfortable profession? What they didn't realise was that Lucy was in the classroom merely to make the money she needed to pay back her student loans, and only until a public speaking position presented itself. That didn't take long. In 1848, she accepted an offer to become an organiser and lecturer of William Lloyd Garrison's American Anti-Slavery Society (AASS), in Boston. Lucy explained to her parents, 'I surely would not be a public speaker if I sought a life of ease ... I expect to plead not for the slave only, but for suffering humanity everywhere. Especially do I mean to labour for the elevation of my sex'.

Lucy's public speeches caused a hullabaloo from all corners, not in the least from the AASS. Most of America still wasn't welcoming public addresses by women to mixed male and female audiences, and Garrison and his abolitionist society did not appreciate Lucy mixing the women's cause with their own. The public tore down posters advertising her talks. Provocateurs drove out listeners gathered in lecture halls by scattering finely ground pepper. Some audience members flung rotten fruit, hurled hymnals, and threw icy water as Lucy took the stage. And to add insult to injury, the AASS's co-founder, Samuel Joseph May, eventually asked Lucy to cease and desist with any talk of women's rights. As righteous as ever, she decided to quit the society, declaring 'I was a woman before I was an abolitionist. I must speak for the women'. But Lucy's pulling power was too valuable to lose, much less ignore. The AASS persuaded her to stay and speak on abolition on weekends, on the condition that she limit her talks to women's rights to weekdays.

In May 1850, Lucy convinced Garrison to join forces with her and eight other women influencers, among them suffragists Harriot Kezia Hunt, Paulina Kellogg Wright Davis, and Abby Kelley Foster, to organise a national women's rights convention. Lucy was named secretary.

First National Woman's Rights Convention

As luck would have it, Lucy was kept from diving into event planning. Family obligations called her away to Illinois, so she had to hand the reins over to Paulina Davis. Lucy spent the summer of 1850 wishing for better days: her ailing brother, Luke, eventually succumbed to cholera, and after arranging his funeral she was stuck settling his family business. She then accompanied her widowed and very pregnant sister-in-law back to Massachusetts, only to witness the young woman prematurely deliver a stillborn son before they had left eastern Illinois; she had to arrange for another funeral, and care for the doubly grief-stricken widow in a hotel; Lucy herself nearly died after contracting typhoid fever and losing consciousness for eighteen days. By the time autumn arrived, Lucy was just barely able to travel again.

Held over two days, 23 October and 24, America's first National Woman's Rights Convention drew delegates from eleven states as well as hundreds of attendees; of the 900 attendees who showed up the first morning, most were men. Lucy, still weak and convalescent, sat absorbed, listening to the discussions without calling attention to herself for most of two days. At the last session, the organisers unexpectedly invited her to take the stage. She hadn't prepared a speech—at least not on paper—but she capitulated. Unrehearsed and without notes, Lucy spoke briefly in favour of women's property rights. Thrusting her arms out to the side, she emphasised her points: 'We want to be something more than the appendages of Society; we want that Woman should be the coequal and help-meet of Man in all the interest and perils and enjoyments of human life'. Finally, reaching a rapid crescendo, her chest heaving, Lucy addressed the crowd with a burst of righteous disgust: 'We want that she should attain to the development of her nature and womanhood; we want that when she dies, it may not be written on her gravestone that she was the "relict" of somebody'. The audience was at once moved and scared stiff.

The newspapers went wild. One journalist called the historic, two-day affair a 'hen convention', and wrote, 'When a hen crows like a cock, it is time to cut her head off'. The *New York Herald* referred to the delegates as a 'hybrid, mongrel, piebald, crackbrained, pitiful, disgusting, and ridiculous assemblage' and offered a benediction: 'May God have mercy on their miserable souls'. But Lucy's words and impassioned delivery absolutely floored newspaper publisher Horace Greeley, who ran possibly the only favourable account of the proceedings in his *New York Tribune*. Later, Susan B. Anthony would attribute to Greeley's flattering description of Lucy's speech the spurring on of her own involvement in the women's cause, and author Harriet Taylor would count the article as the catalyst for writing *The Enfranchisement of Women*.

From bloomers to Blackwell

Lucy threw herself with her customary drive into the nine National Woman's Rights Conventions over the ensuing decade. In between, she toured throughout the North and the South, earning up to $1000 a week for speaking engagements that were attracting audiences in the thousands, and using part of her earnings to print and circulate her speeches. Crowds grew ever bigger and ever more curious to hear, and see, the 'freak' in strange apparel speak.

By 1852, Lucy had taken to wearing the trousered dress first worn two years earlier by Amelia Bloomer, and later adopted by most of the women lecturing on women's rights, as a practical alternative to the long skirts of the day. Sporting 'bloomers' was for Lucy a trying experience—everywhere she went, she was accosted. 'I am annoyed to death by people who recognise me by my clothes', she wrote to Susan B. Anthony, 'and who will [sit] by me and bore me for a whole day with the stupidest stuff in the world'. As practical and comfortable as they were, Lucy eventually gave up her bloomers, realising that her style of dress was a distraction and a detriment to any cause she was supporting.

Temperance was one of those causes, because it attracted a wide range of men and women who were willing to push for change in society. For Lucy, the temperance movement was a stepping-stone offering a compelling reason for giving women further rights. But while she was making a name for herself as 'an agreeable orator', the press continued to attack the focal point of her speaking career as 'a disagreeable subject'. Of a lecture Lucy held on 'the wrongs and rights of women' in April 1853, the *New York Times* wrote, 'But one sentiment seemed to pervade it: what a delightful woman was spoiled when Miss Lucy Stone abandoned good sense, society and duty, and addicted herself to "Woman's Rights"'.

A young abolitionist named Henry Blackwell would beg to differ. Lucy's courage and clear, spellbinding voice had greatly impressed him when, in 1851, he heard her address the Massachusetts legislature in support of an amendment to the state constitution that proposed full civil rights to women. Within an hour of their first meeting, he proposed marriage. Lucy roundly turned him down. But Henry was not easily rebuffed, and became more involved in the women's rights issue and in scheduling speaking engagements for the object of his affection. Gradually, Lucy's resolve to never marry—not just Henry, but any man—began giving way under

---

KATE SHEPPARD

(1847–1934) was the leader of New Zealand's suffragette movement whose persistent lobbying led to a Women's Suffrage Bill being presented to the Parliament, and ultimately to New Zealand being claimant to the title of first country to give full voting rights to women, in 1893. Women in Australia would not gain suffrage until 1902, in the United Kingdom not until 1918 (although only for women over 30, younger women had to wait until 1928), and in the United States not until 1920.

Henry's assurances that their union would be one of equals. Finally, at the end of 1854, the woman who once wrote of marriage as death, as a 'suffocating sense of the want of that absolute freedom which I now possess', agreed to tie the knot with the man who had courted her for two years. Lucy and Henry set the wedding date for 1 May 1855, and wasted no time in crafting a piece of writing they would call the 'Marriage Protest' to distribute and read at their ceremony.

The marriage announcement elicited its share of adverse and antagonistic criticism. Many of Lucy's colleagues felt betrayed, thinking she was deserting the cause. Critics who considered her a nuisance felt relieved, asserting that now, bound to a husband, she would finally be silenced. But both camps were in for a surprise when they learned how Lucy's new husband had agreed to make 'a protest, distinct and emphatic, against the laws of marriage, [renouncing] all the privileges which the law confers on me [including] the custody of the wife's person [and] the exclusive control and guardianship of their children'. A year into her marriage, Lucy created more controversy when she wrote that, 'A wife should no more take her husband's name than he should hers', making it widely known, in no uncertain terms, that she was not to be called Mrs Blackwell, only Lucy Stone, and nothing else.

The campaigning continues

Marriage only temporarily slowed down Lucy's advocacy activities. For six years, between 1857 and 1863, she stayed home to raise her daughter, letting Susan B. Anthony take the helm of the suffragist movement. But by 1863, in the thick of the American Civil War, she was helping form the Woman's National Loyal League to abolish slavery through the passage of the Thirteenth Amendment to the US Constitution. By 1869, she was helping organise the American Woman Suffrage Association, dedicated to winning women the right to vote.

But now another struggle was rearing its ugly head: how to juggle home life and family responsibilities with an active career, or what she called her 'natural way'. With her commitment to women's rights unwavering, Lucy came up with a solution: she would start a women's rights newspaper, which would allow her to continue her campaigning from 'a snug home' and through the written word. Beginning in 1872, Lucy and her husband laid the groundwork for the launch of *Woman's Journal*, which she would write for and edit for the rest of her life.

Lucy gave her last public speeches at the World's Congress of Representative Women in May 1893 in Chicago. Almost 500 women from twenty-seven countries spoke at eighty-one meetings, and attendance topped 150,000 during the seven-day event. With her daughter Alice in the audience, Lucy spoke on 'The Progress of Fifty Years' and declared, 'I think, with never-ending gratitude, that the young women of today do not and can never know at what price their right to free speech and to speak at all in public has been earned'.

Forever pushing for the end of slavery, and for 'the right of woman to the control of her own person as a moral, intelligent, accountable being', Lucy Stone lived to see the emancipation of slavery, but not enfranchisement for women. The Nineteenth Amendment to the Constitution, giving women the right to vote, was not passed until 1920. She died on 18 October 1893, at the age of seventy-five. Her last words to her daughter were 'Make the world better'.

———❖———

Lucy Stone's refusal to take her husband's name as an assertion of her individual rights is largely what she is remembered for today. Fighting for both Black and woman suffrage her entire life, Lucy—or at least her place in history—has been surprisingly overshadowed by equally dedicated suffragists. Maybe it's because her leadership was the kind that was not grandstanding but more personal and mentoring. Inspired by a cause, this diminutive do-gooder shouldered its burdens without self-aggrandisement. She fought when she had to; when agitation served no purpose she retreated.

One of her greatest fans, William Lloyd Garrison, articulated what countless contemporaries concurred: Lucy had 'a soul as free as the air'. The mission she set for herself was to right the wrongs of society. 'If the right of one single human being is to be disregarded by us', she once said, 'we fail in our loyalty to the country'.

CHRISTABEL PANKHURST

(1880–1958)

*Militant suffragette went to
prison rather than pay a fine*

This fierce young Briton drew national attention to women suffragists at a Liberal Party meeting in Manchester in 1905, by taking a no-holds-barred approach that landed her behind bars. After heckling a government minister (culminating in the shout out: 'Will the Liberal government give votes to women?') and resisting expulsion from the meeting by kicking and spitting at a police officer, she became the first woman (along with Annie Kenney) to be arrested in the fight for women's rights. Her active opposition, and her decision to serve a short prison sentence rather than pay the five shilling fine for assault, marked the beginning of a more militant mode of suffrage campaigning.

Rejecting the deadening conventions of Victorian society, in 1901 Christabel, her sister Sylvia, and their mother Emmeline joined the National Union of Women's Suffrage Societies (NUWSS) to demand new freedoms and new rights. But when the organisation didn't make much headway, the three Pankhursts took matters into their own hands and, with three other women, formed the Women's Social and Political Union (WSPU) in Manchester, adopting a more aggressive stance and the slogan 'Deeds not Words'. With Christabel's calculated arrest in 1905, WSPU membership swelled and the 'lady campaigners' came to be called 'suffragettes'.

In 1906, Christabel relocated to the WSPU's London headquarters, where her strong personality and her mother's influence got her a director position. This move would allow England's most public suffragette to change the organisation's direction. But her next step, to start a campaign that would give the vote not to all women but exclusively to those with money and property, eventually lost her the support of a small group of prominent members of the WSPU who left to form the Women's Freedom League, and her sister, who also opposed partial enfranchisement but stayed on out of family loyalty. During this time, Christabel also advocated to replace a strategy of passive resistance with more militant action such as stone throwing and the destruction of property.

Left: Militancy was briefly set aside for this photographic portrait, c. 1912.

Earning the nickname 'Queen of the Mob', Christabel was arrested in 1908 for inciting riot and disorder when suffragettes attempted to rush the House of Commons. The demonstration was considered a humiliating failure; less-militant women's rights supporters charged Christabel with setting back the cause by a generation, one citizen called the campaigners 'infinitely greater social pests than the burglar or pickpocket'; and the Home Secretary warned that militant suffragettes, if sentenced again, would not be treated as 'first-class misdemeanants'. But the militants would not be discouraged. In 1912, with suffragettes indiscriminately smashing shop windows, doing jail time, and enduring extreme hunger strikes, London police began going after the Pankhursts. Christabel fled to France from where, without fear of imprisonment, she organised an ever-more militant campaign that saw suffragettes damaging public venues and attempting to burn down the homes of two members of government who were against women having the vote.

When England declared war on Germany, in August 1914, the WSPU agreed to end their militant activities to help the war effort. The British government announced it was releasing all suffragettes from prison, and Christabel returned to England. Her ferocious zeal for women's rights was now turned toward the fervent support of the National War policy. She toured the country to make recruiting speeches, and wrote scathing attacks in Britannia (the WSPU's newly named newspaper) against politicians and military leaders for not doing enough to win the war. In 1917, she and her mother formed the Women's Party, hyping a twelve-point program that included a fight to the finish with Germany, and 'equal pay for equal work, equal marriage and divorce laws, and equality of rights and opportunities in public service'.

In England's postwar general election of 1918—the first held after the WSPU had won partial enfranchisement for women—Christabel stood as a Women's Party candidate and polled more than 8000 votes. Though she was defeated—albeit narrowly—she received more votes than any of the other seventeen women candidates in that election.

In 1921, Christabel moved to the United States and turned her energy to the Adventist movement. In this later incarnation, she carved out a new career as a writer of best-selling evangelical books and as a high-profile speaker on the fundamentalist preaching circuit. In 1936, back in England for a period, she was appointed Dame Commander of the British Empire. She crossed the Atlantic once again, at the outbreak of World War II, and lived in the US until her death in Los Angeles, at the age of seventy-seven.

Christabel Pankhurst, her voice, her actions and her leadership changed how women were perceived in England at the turn of the century. Initially regarded with a tinge of amusement, the campaign for women's right to vote aroused serious public and political interest only after she began to lead the cause with her militant methods. Without her leadership, not even partial enfranchisement would have been granted in 1918. (Universal suffrage was not legislated until 1928.) What did she care if she were considered a nuisance? In the end, Christabel's rabble-rousing made a world of difference.

Christabel Pankhurst (standing centre) in London with a group of suffragettes in 1909.

ELIZABETH BLACKWELL (1821–1910)

American physician and rebel with a real cause

Elizabeth steadied her fragile, cancer-stricken friend, and helped her back into bed. The doctor came into the room, set down his black bag, and with a business-as-usual air began the unpleasant task of bleeding. Elizabeth noticed her friend's fear. She took her limp hand and said, 'Don't be afraid'. But unable to bear the sight herself, she had to turn her face away as the doctor made his incision. The blood was thick and came slowly. The doctor took one pint, then another. Finished, he patted his patient's hand, snapped his bag shut and, without a word, left her bedside.

Elizabeth's dying friend sighed and shut her eyes—more in resignation than weariness—and murmured: 'I know I would have been spared my worst sufferings, if only I had been treated by a lady doctor'. Then, opening her eyes and holding Elizabeth's gaze, she said firmly, 'You, my dear, are fond of study. You have health, leisure and a cultivated intelligence. Why don't you study medicine?'

Before she took her last breath, the Blackwells' family friend had managed to plant the most preposterous idea in Elizabeth's head.

Compassion for the unnecessary suffering of women led Elizabeth Blackwell to study medicine.

When she graduated from New York's Geneva Medical College in 1849, Elizabeth Blackwell became the first woman in the United States to earn the MD degree. While nineteenth century America considered an education in medicine a distasteful, even dangerous, pursuit for a woman, Elizabeth dared to be a doctor. Her entrance into medical school came after years of dogged persistence, although from the school's point of view her admittance was actually in jest. Still, Elizabeth had the last laugh. When the program was completed, Dr Elizabeth Blackwell graduated number one in the class.

At a time when Victorian-era prudery banned male physicians from properly examining their female patients, Dr Blackwell provided women with the skilled and sensitive care they so desperately needed, so that they would not have to 'die of humiliation' at the prospect of being examined by a strange man. Worse, many women actually did die because they outright refused to be examined by any male doctor. she not only improved the practice of medicine, but helped pave the way for women in the professions. A 'guiding star … to rebellious women everywhere', Elizabeth opened the first women's medical school in 1868, providing a venue for education and acceptance in the closed, males-only, mainstream medical arena, and establishing stricter standards for medical schools as a whole, everywhere.

Blackwell background

Elizabeth Blackwell was born in Bristol, England, in 1821, a port city which had become rich as one of the three points of the transatlantic slave triangle before the slave trade was officially banned in England in 1807. She was the third child and third daughter of the nine surviving children of a close-knit, highly religious and moral Quaker family. The most delicate of the three, she came to be called 'Little Shy' by her father, and never grew taller than five foot one. But Elizabeth proved to have a giant will. Even as a little girl, she would put herself up to difficult challenges. As a protest against slavery in other parts of the world, she refused to eat sugar, even though her father was in the sugar-refining business. Wanting to imitate the saints, she slept on the floor until her parents put a stop to it. At the age of six, she proclaimed, 'I don't know what I'm going to be when I grow up, but it's going to be hard'.

Elizabeth was eleven years old when the family migrated to America. Her father, wrestling with the fact that he morally opposed slavery while his sugar-refining business depended on it, had decided that he would be better able to support his large family in the New World, where he could also focus his energies on the American abolitionist movement. Vociferous abolitionist, dissenter of the Church of England, and strong supporter of educational reform and equal rights for women, Samuel Blackwell would see to it that his five daughters received in America an education comparable to that of their brothers—no small feat in a society that considered the proper education of girls to be one that left them, in the words of the 'Father of American Scholarship and Education' Noah Webster, merely 'correct in their manners, respectable in their families, and agreeable in society'.

The Blackwells landed in New York, and for six years Elizabeth soaked up the intellectual and cultural life of the city—taking advantage of Shakespearean plays, outdoor concerts, museum visits—while attending school, music lessons, and church socials with her sisters. But life wasn't all about education. While most girls her age stayed close to home improving their domestic skills, in her free time Elizabeth was exploring her environs and feeding her thirst for social justice. By the age of fifteen, yearning to be as socially active as Prudence Crandall—the controversial Quaker schoolteacher who became famous when she admitted a black girl into her Connecticut private school—Elizabeth was regularly attending anti-slavery fairs and the local meetings of no less than five abolitionist organisations.

In late 1836, disaster struck. As depression swept across America, Samuel Blackwell's refinery went up in flames, which destroyed his entire business investment. Elizabeth had no illusions about her family's situation. By spring 1837, she was writing about it in her diary: 'We have become so poor … We had no meat for dinner yesterday, today we had a stew composed of potatoes with a few bones which had been carefully preserved, and one penny leek'. A season passed, and another, with scarcely more hope or money to keep the household running. In early March 1838, she wrote, 'What [Papa's] plans for the future are we do not know.' She

---

AGNODICE

(c. 300s BC) was an Athenian who, while women were forbidden to study or practice medicine, managed to gain an education by disguising herself as a man and then distinguished herself as a doctor. When her true identity was discovered, she was permitted to continue practicing because of the reputation she had won for herself among the women of Athens, who insisted on her continued services. Despite many believing that Agnodice's story is nothing more than legend, she is credited with being the first woman gynecologist in history.

would soon find out. A few weeks later, Samuel Blackwell announced to his family that they would be packing up and moving west, to Ohio. An opportunity had come up to open a sugar refinery in Cincinnati—the first in the West. Elizabeth would have to say goodbye to the city in which she had outgrown her childhood. Worse yet, she would be leaving behind the two older sisters who had been helping her navigate her adolescent world, and who couldn't afford to give up their jobs in Vermont and Manhattan. So, at seventeen, Elizabeth was the oldest Blackwell child to embark on the daunting nine-day journey from New York. They travelled by steamboat, canal boat, horse-drawn carriage and rail car, crossing the Allegheny Mountains and carrying on down the wild and unpredictable Allegheny and Ohio rivers until they reached 'the prosperous little Western town' of Cincinnati.

Three months after their arrival in the Western frontier, Elizabeth's father unexpectedly died. He had just $20 in his accounts, leaving his family to depend entirely upon their own efforts to support themselves. The two boys next in age to Elizabeth, only fifteen and thirteen, weren't old enough to earn much, and there were four younger children who needed their mother's attention. With the older sisters still teaching back East, it was up to Elizabeth to bring in some money, fast, and the only way to do that in an era when ladies did not work was to teach. No sooner was her father laid to rest than she began giving private music and English lessons in the back parlour of the family home. Less than six weeks later, her sisters Anna and Marian arrived to pool their resources with those of the family. Together the three Blackwell sisters established a boarding school, the Cincinnati English and French Academy for Young Ladies.

Elizabeth threw herself into teaching. Still only seventeen, she was terrorised by the 'very wild Western' girls only a few years her junior whom she was expected to instruct twelve hours a day. 'I only controlled them by the steady quietness of demeanour which they took for sternness, but which really was fear', she wrote later.

FLORENCE NIGHTINGALE

(1820–1910), a pioneer of modern nursing and hospitals, a statistician and social reformer, fought against gender prejudices to serve in the Crimean War. There she was in charge of the Allied nursing unit and became known as the 'lady with the lamp' for her lengthy bedside vigils. Upon her return to Britain in 1860 she opened the first scientifically based nursing school, providing training for midwives and nurses, at the Nightingale Training School at St Thomas' Hospital in London. In 1907 she was the first woman to be awarded the Order of Merit.

The ability to look at least six feet tall, while all five foot one of her quaked in her shoes, would serve Elizabeth well in the years ahead.

Changing course

By 1842, the academy had closed. Times were tough for the entire nation and parents could no longer afford tuition fees for their daughters. It didn't help that the Blackwell women were friends and followers of outspoken abolitionist and transcendentalist William Henry Channing who, according to Elizabeth, was 'revolutionising American thought'—and who had been forced by conservatives to resign as pastor of the First Congregational Church in Cincinnati. What transcendentalism offered to Elizabeth was the idea of 'the power of me', the notion that she made her own circumstance.

Elizabeth was surprised to be approached to set up a girls' school in Henderson, Kentucky, a little tobacco-growing town, but the offer was too good to turn down—at least from an economic standpoint. She was just twenty-three when she headed down the Ohio River into the heart of 'the crude civilisation of a Western slave State'. The new teacher was a success, her white teeth particularly admired by the tobacco-using townsfolk. But Elizabeth found the community—though polite and hospitable—uncultured, stifling, and ultimately insufferable. Writing home, her growing disgust over slavery led her to say, 'To live in the midst of beings degraded to the utmost in body and mind ... utterly unable to help them, is to me dreadful'. She felt alone and alienated: 'I do long to get hold of someone to whom I can talk frankly: this constant smiling and bowing and wearing a mask provokes me intolerably'. At the end of her eighteen-month contract, her social conscience lacerated by her surroundings, Elizabeth felt that for the sake of her self-identity she had no choice but to resign.

Home again in Cincinnati, Elizabeth studied history, German, music and metaphysics. She attended meetings on abolitionism and women's rights. She joined a literary club and rubbed elbows with authors, astronomers, professors and lawyers. But she felt restless, unsatisfied. And it was then that the words of her dying friend would change the course of her life.

'Why not study medicine?' she was asked, the question initially leaving Elizabeth dumbstruck. Women simply did not pursue an education in medicine. And besides, metaphysics was one thing, medicine another altogether. The very sight of a medical book was a turn-off for Elizabeth, who noted that even 'the thought of dwelling on the physical structure of the body and its various ailments, filled me with disgust'. Still, the seed had been planted.

Tackling the impossible

Elizabeth was unable to put the extraordinary notion of becoming a doctor out of her mind. She broached the topic with several trusted friends, most of whom either tried to dissuade her or advised her to go the only route available to women: studying at one of the fringe sectarian medical schools, which trained women in homeopathy and hydropathy, but were not nearly as respected as a regular medical school. But these suggestions only served to infuriate her. Suddenly, overcoming her aversion to the physical aspects of a medical career took a back seat to the even greater challenge of enrolling in a mainstream medical school that taught the most esteemed, scientific medicine around—the kind that was closed to women for study.

At first Elizabeth had no idea of how to go about it, but with courage in one hand and pen in the other, she sent letters of inquiry to physicians all over the country. Some actually took the time to reply. Invariably, the message was the same: a worthy goal, but for a woman, 'impractical', 'eccentric', 'utopian', 'utterly impossible'. The negative attitude only fuelled Elizabeth's interest and cemented her determination. To shocked family members and friends, she declared, 'I will do it'.

To raise the money for tuition, in the unlikely event that she would eventually be accepted into a medical school, in 1845 Elizabeth took a teaching position in Asheville, North Carolina, at a school run by the Reverend John Dickson, a former doctor, who would guide her initial studies in medicine. Now her life took a definite direction. She knew she had found her true calling. 'My brain is as busy as can be', she penned to her mother, 'and consequently I am happy'. The next

MARY EDWARDS WALKER

(1832–1919) was an American feminist, abolitionist, prohibitionist, surgeon, alleged spy and prisoner of war during the American Civil War, and the only woman to be awarded the Congressional Medal of Honor, the nation's highest honour. Dr Walker's award was rescinded in 1917, possibly because she was a suffragette, although the stated reason was to 'increase the prestige of the grant'. She refused to return the medal itself and wore it until her death in 1919. Fifty-eight years later, the US Congress posthumously reinstated her award, which was officially restored by President Carter on 10 June 1977.

year, Reverend Dickson was forced to close his school, but by great good fortune his brother Samuel, an eminent physician and faculty member of the medical college in Charleston, South Carolina, invited Elizabeth to continue her studies with him. For the next sixteen months, Elizabeth toiled away, teaching by day, by night poring over Dr Dickson's medical books, and saving her pennies. By 1847, she was ready to do the unheard of: apply, as a woman, to the nation's leading medical schools.

Sixteen schools swiftly turned her down before the faculty of liberal Geneva College in upstate New York put her application to a student vote, never expecting that the all-male student body would agree to a woman joining their ranks. But the high-spirited students thought the whole thing was a hoax, and voted 'yes'. On 7 November 1847, sporting a plain bonnet and gray silk gown, Elizabeth Blackwell, a small, quiet Quaker with sheer determination in her eyes, reported to the dean's office at Geneva Medical College. The faculty was horrified.

First woman with a medical degree

Elizabeth considered the disturbance her presence caused: 'I had not the slightest idea of the commotion created by my appearance as a medical student in the little town. Very slowly I perceived that a doctor's wife at the table avoided any communication with me, and that as I walked backwards and forwards to college the ladies stopped to stare at me, as at a curious animal'.

Between semesters Elizabeth interned at Philadelphia's Blockley Almshouse, an infirmary for the poor, in the ward for female victims of venereal disease. The resident physicians and other interns made her long hours there difficult, openly snubbing her and refusing to complete patients' charts with critical information while she was in attendance. Even some of the patients resented her presence. One destitute woman told her: 'I may be poor and cast out by the Lord into a pauper's bed, but I'll have no woman to take care of me in my illness!' But every inch the gentlewoman, Elizabeth remained courteous, swallowed her resentment, and worked all the harder.

So seriously did Elizabeth take her coursework that she completed her studies at Geneva in practically half the time it took the other students. On 23 January 1849, Elizabeth Blackwell was granted a medical degree. It was an unprecedented occurrence, so odd that Britain's humour magazine, *Punch*, memorialised it in a set of rhyming verses ending in 'excellent Miss Blackwell!' Geneva's radical, if unintended, experiment had been a success: Miss Blackwell graduated first in her class. The struggle had been long and lonely but, at last, tenacious Little Shy was Elizabeth Blackwell, MD.

The story does not end with Dr Blackwell coasting on to fame and fortune. After several months in Pennsylvania, she understood that the doors to her chosen profession remained as tightly closed as before. Determined to become a surgeon, but unable to persuade any hospital in the United States or England to permit her practical experience, she eventually landed a position at La Maternité, a converted convent and midwifery school in Paris, France, in the summer of 1849. But La Maternité brought her no closer to her dream of practicing surgery—in fact, her work there destroyed the dream. Dr Blackwell lost an eye when she contracted a serious ophthalmic infection from a child patient suffering from gonorrhea. Still, the loss did nothing to dampen her desire for a medical career. She needed more clinical experience, and she got it during the winter of 1850–51, having gained unprecedented entry into St Bartholomew's Hospital in London.

Bolstered by this invaluable practical training, confident that she could now begin a medical practice in earnest, Elizabeth headed back to America mid-year, in 1851. But every effort to come into another physician's private practice as an associate, or land a hospital staff position in New York City, was met with scornful rebuff. If Dr Blackwell hoped to practice medicine in New York, she would have to do it alone. Even finding space to rent was a challenge; nobody could quite connect the dots. When a sympathiser finally allowed her to rent a boardinghouse room, all the other renters promptly moved out, scandalised at having to share quarters with a lady doctor. Eventually, Elizabeth bought a house, hung out her shingle, and waited for patients to appear. Later, she wrote: 'Patients came very slowly ... I had no medical companionship; the profession stood aloof, and society was distrustful of the innovation'.

In the spring of 1857, Elizabeth and her younger sister, Emily, who had become America's second female physician in 1854 (her path in no way smoothed by Elizabeth's pioneering efforts), together with German immigrant Dr Marie Zakrzewska (who had followed Emily's trail), took a house at 64 Bleecker Street, in the heart of the slums, and opened the New York Infirmary for Women and Children. It was a novel and exciting concept: a hospital for women, staffed entirely by women. The need for a clinic was enormous, and the beds were full within a month. At first the project and the intrepid trio who'd launched it attracted more than their fair share of scepticism, not least from a protesting mob convinced 'the lady doctors were killing their patients'. It mattered little to Elizabeth. Public doubt and disapproval had never discouraged her before—she wasn't about to be stopped now.

Rallying sufficient support to add a medical school to the infirmary, Elizabeth opened the doors of the Women's Medical College in November 1868. Medical education would never be the same again. Dr Blackwell's college was the first school devoted entirely to the medical education of women and to furthering that education. Not only that, its course of study was significantly more rigorous than in most other

An engraving from a US newspaper of 1870 showing the main dissecting room of the Women's Medical College.

medical schools of the day. The Women's Medical College later became one of the first medical schools in America to mandate four years of study, and awarded a medical degree to Rebecca Cole, the first African American woman to become a doctor. The Women's Medical College was to slowly turn doubters into believers.

In 1869, leaving the infirmary and the college in Emily's hands, Elizabeth set off for England. Certain that in America the early pioneer work of women in medicine was complete, she knew that in England there was still much work to be done. With her characteristic determination, Dr Blackwell once again would rally support for the acceptance of women in medicine. Princesses, dukes, bishops, and captains of industry helped champion the cause when she and Dr Elizabeth Garrett Anderson, the first woman to gain a medical qualification in Britain, led the campaign which resulted in the establishment of the London School of Medicine for Women in 1875. Dr Blackwell proudly accepted the Chair of Hygiene (gynecology) in the new medical school. She retired from medical practice a year later.

ELIZABETH GARRETT ANDERSON

(1836–1917) was the first woman to gain a medical degree in Britain and the first woman physician in Britain. She worked in London as a doctor and fought for the vote and equal educational opportunities for women. In 1872 she became the co-founder of the New Hospital for Women in London, run by women for women, where Elizabeth Blackwell, who had inspired her to become a doctor, was later appointed professor of gynecology. On Garrett Anderson's retirement in 1902 she moved to Aldeborough, where in 1908 she was elected England's first female mayor.

At her core, Elizabeth was a social reformer, and in her later years she worked tirelessly for a score of causes: women's suffrage, morality in government, better hygiene, inoculation, and the abolition of prostitution, white slavery, and circumcision, to name just a handful. She concentrated her efforts also on writing. Her most important work, *Counsel to Parents on the Moral Education of Children*, was written in 1876. At the age of fifty-eight, she moved permanently to the village of Hastings on the English Channel, where she eventually set to work writing her autobiography (published in 1895 under the title *Pioneer Work in Opening the Medical Profession to Women*).

By the time Dr Elizabeth Blackwell died at her home, Rock House, in Hastings on 31 May 1910, more than 7000 women were licenced physicians and surgeons in the United States. Her obituary in the London *Times* read: 'She was in the fullest sense of the word a pioneer'. Though she had won, for the most part, only grudging acceptance of women into medicine, Elizabeth believed the day would come when the rest of the world would see things through her eyes: 'The study and practice of medicine is … but one means to … the true ennoblement of woman, the full harmonious development of her unknown nature, and the consequent redemption of the whole human race'.

When Elizabeth Blackwell decided to pursue an education and career in medicine, she was as motivated by the opportunity for service as she was intent on feeding her powerful intellect and galvanised by the challenge of achieving the impossible. Fearing marriage would stifle her intellectual growth, she kept that institution at bay her entire life, and instead threw herself into the mission of leaving the world a better place. Given the handicaps and restrictions of her time, Elizabeth Blackwell's accomplishments inspire awe. Her clear vision, sheer courage and unassuming determination allowed her to ignore naysayers and the most infuriating disregard, and move on to achieve her lofty goals. Her pursuits went far beyond self-serving. One hundred years after her death, Elizabeth Blackwell's feats in educational and professional reform cannot go unnoticed. The hospital she founded, now vastly enlarged and renamed the New York Infirmary–Strang Clinic, still operates on East 15th Street.

DR JAMES MIRANDA BARRY

(c. 1789–1865)

*Cutting-edge surgeon whose gender
cuts a swath of suspicion*

One of the nineteenth century's most esteemed military doctors has also to be its most enigmatic. James Miranda Barry seemed to have appeared out of nowhere when, in 1809, he applied to the University of Edinburgh's prestigious medical school. Decades later, he would be a legend in medical and military circles, with a reputation as a genius surgeon, a distinguished officer in the British Army, and a progressive social and medical reformer with unflagging energy. After his death in London, rumours circulated that the doctor was, in fact, a woman. If this were true, then Dr Barry was the first female Briton to become a qualified medical doctor.

James Miranda Barry's early life remains obscure and subject to speculation. But original letters, legal documents and financial papers surrounding one James Barry, an artist living between 1741 and 1806, leaves no doubt that Dr James Barry began life as Margaret Ann Bulkley, niece of the artist whose name she would adopt. In Margaret Bulkley's time, British medical schools accepted male students only. Her entrance into the University of Edinburgh was the result of an ambitious plan concocted by her mother and a number of powerful protectors, including Venezuelan revolutionary General Francisco Miranda and notable Scottish eccentric David Stewart Erskine, 11th Earl of Buchan, who had studied at the university and was a proponent of equal education for women. With their encouragement, the soon-to-be-medical student dared to alter her appearance and arrive at the university in male guise, under a male pseudonym.

The plan was to keep up the ruse only until she finished her final examinations. Then, as a qualified medical doctor, Margaret would resume her female identity and relocate to Venezuela where, with General Miranda's assistance, she would practice medicine free of social constraints. But when the general was thrown into prison, the Venezuelan dream disappeared and Margaret had to choose between revealing her identity and ruining any chance of success as a physician in Britain, or continuing the masquerade. Dr Barry chose the

---

Left: The doctor's tendency to upset the establishment hampered recognition of his contributions to medicine.

latter, concealing her identity to her dying day. She carried it off without a hitch, joining the army, fighting duels, becoming the superhero of physicians in the Crimean War, and rising to the rank of Inspector General.

By the standards of the day, Dr Barry was considered a very handsome young man, even if of slight build, and had a winning smile when he wanted to put on the charm. He was known to have a quick temper and brusque demeanour, but he treated his patients with sensitivity and understanding. Strictly teetotal, and a vegetarian who drank only goat's milk, he was way ahead of his time when it came to preventive medicine and the promotion of health. His progressive ideas even extended to practicing such taboo subjects as psychosexual medicine.

Around 1815, he joined the British Army, the start of a career that spanned nearly fifty years, and was posted to Cape Colony (South Africa) where, in typically outspoken style, he informed the senior medical officer that he would serve as personal physician to the governor, Lord Charles Somerset, a close family friend and mentor from his youth. In this way, James avoided living in the barracks. He spent some thirteen years at the Cape, and during that time rumours circulated about his supposed sexual orientation and 'immoral relationship' with the governor. But he also developed a reputation as a highly skilled and conscientious physician, surgeon, and obstetrician. In July 1820, he performed an emergency caesarean section, delivering a baby boy and saving the mother's life; it was the first operation of its kind performed in the Colony where both mother and child survived. In 1822, he introduced smallpox vaccination to the Colony, twenty years before it was introduced in England.

Dr Barry moved from military posting to military posting—Mauritius, Saint Helena, Jamaica, Trinidad and Tobago, then Malta and Corfu. In each place, he continued the sweeping reforms he had begun in Cape Colony, setting standards for medical facilities and hospitals, and consistently monitoring the health and hygiene of the troops. From 1854 to 1856, with the Crimean War raging, wounded soldiers who were evacuated to the military hospitals under Dr Barry's command on the island of Corfu were the lucky ones; only seventeen troops died out of some 460 treated. In comparison, Florence Nightingale's base, the Barrack Hospital at Scutari, averaged twenty deaths a day.

Despite his lengthy career and many postings, Dr Barry received little recognition for his far-reaching contributions, due to his persistent knack for upsetting the establishment. In 1857, he was posted to Canada, a move orchestrated by Florence Nightingale, who found the doctor argumentative and had grown to really dislike him, and wanted him out of her sphere of influence. (That same year, Florence successfully promoted her Royal Commission on Army Health, which endorsed many of the cutting-edge reforms that Dr Barry had personally devised and initiated, and saw to it that the doctor was given scant credit.)

Retiring from the army in 1864, the doctor spent his last days in his house in London. He died from pneumonia in 1865. A military staff surgeon and long-time acquaintance named McKinnon, who had treated James through his sickness, never recorded any official examination of the body. However, a local nurse, Sophia Bishop, who undressed the body for the laying out, claimed that the famous physician was a woman. The idea took firm hold, and has long been believed. But renewed interest in this fascinating figure has brought another theory to light: the doctor may have been intersexed.

No one will ever know for sure what the doctor looked like under his clothes, or how he saw his own gender or sexual orientation. The speculation continues, but the things that cement Dr James Miranda Barry's place in history are his far-sighted belief in health care as much as sick care, and his choice to be a man in the eyes of the world in order to, above all, be a military doctor—and one who made such a difference.

MARY SURRATT (1823–1865)

Southern sympathiser was at the end of her rope over conspiracy

Mary was climbing the stairs to her bedroom when a battery of rapid-fire knocks at the front door stopped her in her tracks. It was 11 pm, and boarders at her H Street boardinghouse were preparing for bed. She grabbed hold of the handrail and, legs shaking, slowly inched her way down to the entrance, preparing herself for the worst.

Five military officers stood at the threshold. Major H.W. Smith informed Mary that they had come to take her and everyone else in the house down to the Provost Marshal's office for questioning on charges of conspiracy in the assassination of President Lincoln. Mary asked for a moment in her parlour to pray with her daughter and niece. The uniformed men waited in the entrance hall while the boarders gathered their things. Then there was another knock at the door, and the investigators were calling out for Mary.

A grimy man with a pickax, looking surprised, was explaining that he had been hired by Mrs Surratt to dig a ditch. Mary turned to Captain Wermerskirch and, raising her right hand theatrically, said, 'Before God, sir, I do not know this man, and have never seen him, and I did not hire him to dig a gutter for me'.

The fact that ex-Confederate soldier and Lincoln conspirator Lewis Paine had arrived at Mary's residence just as she was being arrested certainly did not help her situation.

Mary Surratt: not the epitome of the respectable boardinghouse keeper suggested by this photograph.

Mary Surratt was convicted of taking part in the conspiracy to assassinate Abraham Lincoln. The depth of her complicity has been debated since the day of her arrest on 17 April 1865, three days after John Wilkes Booth murdered America's Civil War president as he sat watching a play at Ford's Theater in Washington. Less than three months later, Mary would be sentenced to death by hanging, becoming the first woman ever to be executed by the US government, and the only woman in the history of the Republic to be hanged by officialdom. The military tribunal made a swift and unanimous decision in finding her guilty, but five of the nine commissioners petitioned President Andrew Johnson, Lincoln's successor, for clemency. President Johnson, unmoved, refused to stay her execution, convinced that Mary 'kept the nest that hatched the egg'.

Building the nest

Mary Elizabeth Jenkins, born in Waterloo, Maryland and schooled in an all-girl Catholic seminary, married twenty-eight-year-old John Surratt in 1839, when she was seventeen. By the time she was twenty-one, she had three children to care for: Isaac, Anna, and John Jr. In the spring of 1852, the Surratts bought 287 acres of land in Maryland's Prince George's County—about two hours' ride from Washington— where they farmed tobacco and built a two-story wood-frame and clapboard structure that, come September that year, would serve not only as family homestead but also as community tavern.

Mary had her hands full, tending to her family, helping manage the slave-run plantation, providing food and drink to hungry locals and offering lodging for weary travellers. Within two years, the Surratt House was an amalgamation of private residence, tavern, hostelry, polling house and post office to meet the needs of the growing community, with John Sr serving as postmaster for the community now known as Surrattsville. Meanwhile, Mary was serving to a host of farmers, carpenters, doctors, lawyers, merchants, and politicians her much-lauded Maryland beaten biscuits, something to drink at the bar, and a comfortable place to debate the issues that were dividing the country in the crucial decade before the dawn of the Civil War. By the time Union and Confederate forces were battling, the border state of Maryland—though officially Union—was a hotbed of Confederate underground activity, and the Surratt House a hub for Southern sympathisers.

Despite the amount of activity at Surratt House, the war meant money was scarce. Patrons weren't paying their tavern bills. Half of the family's slaves were missing—either having run away or been repossessed. To top it off, John Sr died suddenly in August 1862, leaving Mary under a mountain of debt. For two years, she tried desperately to hang on at Surrattsville, but it was an insurmountable task. Practically penniless, the widow leased the farm and the tavern to an ex-policeman named John Lloyd, and moved with twenty-two-year-old Anna to a small but comfortable townhouse she owned in Washington, converting its upper floor into a boardinghouse. There, she would eke out a modest living and, eventually, open her doors to 'a fiend with a heart as black as hell' named John Wilkes Booth.

Jubilation and bedlam

The boardinghouse at 541 H Street was dark and still against a backdrop of brilliant victory bonfires illuminating Washington, DC on 9 April 1865. The war was over. Earlier that day, General Robert E. Lee's Confederate forces had surrendered in northern Virginia. Evening came and brought jubilant revellers dancing, cheering and crowding the avenues of the Federal capital. Alone in her quiet living room, behind tightly closed drapes, Mary wrung her hands and wept. Her fervent hopes for a Southern victory had come to a sudden end.

Mary was also worried for her son, John Jr, who she knew was being pursued by the government for rebel activity ever since he had left for Canada, carrying Confederate orders from Richmond. Now, with the war over and no Confederacy in need of his services, she wondered where exactly John Jr was, and who he might be with. Her son's pal, the handsome, successful and smooth-talking stage actor John Wilkes Booth, came to mind. Booth had been coming around quite often to the H Street boardinghouse, even while John Jr was away, creating a fluster among the infatuated lady boarders, and holding forth with his Southern sympathising and denouncements of Lincoln. Mary didn't mind. His

SOPHIA PEROVSKAYA

(1853–1881) was a Russian revolutionary who helped plan the assassination of Tsar Alexander II. A member of the Zemlya i Volya (Land and Liberty) organisation, whose aim was to free political prisoners and lead the serfs to revolution, she held many secret meetings and plotted the tsar's murder in March 1881. One month later she was arrested and sentenced to death by hanging, becoming the first woman in Russia executed in connection with a political trial.

political beliefs were not out of step with her own—she was pro-South and devoted body and soul to the Confederate cause. She considered Booth fine company and welcomed his visits. But she hadn't seen him for about a week before the surrender.

It was close to midnight on 14 April when the streets of DC exploded again, this time in out-and-out pandemonium. President Lincoln had been shot while enjoying a show at Ford's Theatre, and bells were tolling the alarm, mounted patrols dashing every which way, nervous crowds rushing about, shouting out in horror and disbelief. Between two-thirty and three o'clock in the morning, as the president lay dying and his attacker was on the run, five detectives paid a visit to Mary's home.

> ### RUTH EISEMANN-SCHIER
>
> (c. 1941–) in 1968 became the first woman to be placed on the FBI's Ten Most Wanted Fugitives list, charged with kidnapping for a $500,000 ransom heiress Barbara Jane Mackle (a crime she carried out, disguised as a man, with Gary Krist, who was quickly captured). She was captured after seventy-nine days on the run, and spent four years in prison before being exiled to Honduras, her country of birth.

Long-time boarder Louis Weichmann called out, 'Who is there?'

Loudly, from behind the closed door, Detective James McDevitt from the Metropolitan Police announced, 'Detectives, come to search the house for John Wilkes Booth and John Surratt'.

As a search was underway in Weichmann's room, the agitated boarder demanded to know why they were looking for John Jr and Booth. Detective Clarvoe couldn't believe that Weichmann had not heard the news. 'I will tell you', he said. 'John Wilkes Booth has shot Abraham Lincoln and John Surratt has assassinated the secretary of state'. At the time the police were not aware that Secretary of State William Henry Seward had in fact survived the attack, and that his assailant was not John Surratt Jr but an ex-Confederate soldier named Lewis Paine.

Meanwhile, Mary, who had told another detective that she hadn't seen her son for two weeks, was scrambling to locate the item she claimed to have received just that day: a letter from John Jr, postmarked in Montreal on 12 April. She never managed to produce it, nor did she disclose that, earlier that day, Booth had been at the H Street house to give her a package and a message to take to Surrattsville for him.

By the time the detectives left, eventually satisfied that neither John Jr nor Booth nor any other suspicious characters were in the house, Mary's daughter was absolutely beside herself.

'Oh, Ma!' she cried out, 'That man [John Wilkes Booth] having been here in this house before the assassination! I am afraid it will bring suspicion upon us!'

'Anna, come what will', Mary coolly responded, 'I am resigned. I think John Wilkes Booth was only an instrument in the hands of the Almighty to punish this proud and licentious people'.

Less than five hours later, at 7.22 on the morning of Saturday, 15 April, the President of the United States was pronounced dead and Washington, DC was placed under martial law. Breakfast at the boardinghouse was tense and sombre. Weichmann—scared, restless, and by now thoroughly suspicious of Booth's

Mary Surratt's H Street residence still stands, most recently with the first floor converted to a Chinese restaurant.

many visits to the house, the comings and goings of strange men, and all the innocuous details that were now adding up—announced that he was going directly to police headquarters to tell them all he knew, though he was not yet clear about what exactly he did know. Anna told Weichmann to button his lip. As far as she was concerned, Lincoln was 'no better than the meanest nigger in the army'. Mary would not sleep well that night, nor the next. Late in the evening of 17 April, she was hoping she might get some real rest, but she never even made it to her bed. That fearsome knocking at her front door would be the harbinger of bad news: she and all the residents of the boardinghouse would soon be under arrest for conspiracy in the assassination of President Lincoln.

Face to face with Federal authorities, the mistress of the boardinghouse fell strangely calm. Mary showed Major H.W. Smith into the parlour, where Anna and her cousin sat terrified. The other officers rounded up the rest of the residents and carefully searched every room, collecting possible evidence. In Mary's room, they discovered a bullet mold and percussion caps (used to ignite gunpowder in the barrel of a gun), and a photograph of John Wilkes Booth secreted in the back of a framed picture.

Back downstairs, as she waited for the carriage that would take her and the others to Union commander General Augur's office for interrogation, Mary knelt to pray. And then came the fateful rap on the front door. Lewis Paine, cold, hungry, and desperate after hiding in a nearby cemetery ever since attempting to murder the Secretary of State at his family residence two days earlier, had foolishly come to Mary's home seeking shelter. That 'peculiar knock', the *Baltimore Clipper* reported later in the week, would start to unravel Booth's plot, and mark the beginning of the end for Mary.

Before the sun peeked over the horizon on the morning of 18 April, Mary found herself behind bars in Washington's Old Capitol Prison.

Incarceration and interrogation

By the time Lincoln's acknowledged assassin John Wilkes Booth was captured and killed by Federal troops on a farm in northern Virginia twelve days later, the police had rounded up most of his band of accomplices. Until the end of April, Mary would share with Anna a damp, filthy, roach-infested cell in the Old Capitol's Carroll Annex, where female criminals and Confederate spies were housed during the war. And here, Mary, Anna, and a number of other suspects would be subjected to extensive interrogation.

Mary had had three days from the time of Lincoln's murder to the day of her own arrest to craft a defence, or a confession, of her own. But she was not particularly forthcoming. Years of covert activity and clandestine relationships had presumably trained her well in cover-up tactics. She calmly and confidently received the questions her interrogators lobbed her way … for the first hour. But under extended questioning she grew more arrogant, evasive and, finally, outright defiant.

By the end of her three-hour interrogation, Mary had provided not a single lead about John Jr's whereabouts, not one piece of valid information about Booth's murderous plot. What the detectives did manage to glean, aside from repeated protestations of innocence, was a pretty good idea of the kind of woman Mary Surratt was: a fiercely proud and protective mother, especially when it came to her son.

But while Mary carried on with her protestations of innocence and uncooperative behaviour, the authorities were swiftly gathering important evidence pointing to her involvement in Booth's elaborate plans. It took only two short weeks to make sense of all the data and to decide that Mary's involvement in the assassination could not be ignored. There was no choice but to keep her in jail.

On 30 April, Mary was transferred to the Arsenal Prison on the banks of the Potomac and joined the seven male conspirators already charged to await their trial.

The trial

The trial proceedings began on 9 May 1865, and continued until the end of June. Because the US Attorney-General and President Andrew Johnson had decided that the actions of the conspirators amounted to a wartime act, the eight accused were tried not in a civil court but in front of a military tribunal of nine officers, who would sit as prosecution, judge, and jury. That didn't sit well with everyone. One former attorney-general griped: 'If the offenders are done to death by that tribunal, however truly guilty, they will pass for martyrs with half the world'. It would be a military trial, with a majority vote needed for conviction and no right of appeal but to the president for the most infamous crime of the Republic. Everyone had a pretty good idea what the outcome would be.

Mary had three attorneys—Reverdy Johnson, long-time Union man and friend of Lincoln's, took the lead, but rarely appeared in court, leaving Mary's defence to his two inexperienced associates. They prepared her as best they could, but ultimately the defence was hampered by Mary's refusal to give plausible explanations for her actions as the evidence mounted against her.

On 11 May, the first day of open court proceedings, Mary appeared in a long black veil that shielded her face from spectators and the press. She sat nearly motionless, separate from the rest of the defendants. The newspapers vilified her mercilessly, reporting on her steely resolve and describing her as fat and 'slovenly', 'very much broken down and humbled', with a 'cold, cruel gleam in her gray eyes'.

Louis Weichmann was among the first to testify, and he described Mary very differently. Hesitant to identify her as a co-conspirator, Weichmann called Mary sweet and caring, 'exemplary' in character and 'lady-like in every particular'. Nonetheless, his testimony over the next weeks would clearly incriminate his landlady. He described numerous private conversations at the boardinghouse between Mary and Booth. And he testified that Booth gave him ten dollars three days before the assassination and told him to use the money for a hired buggy to take Mary to Surratt House. On the day of the assassination, Weichmann reported, Mary asked him to hire a buggy and accompany her on the two-hour ride to her Maryland property. She carried with her 'a package, done up in paper, about six inches in diameter'.

> ## WAFA IDRIS
>
> (c. 1975–2002) was a Palestinian woman from the Amari refugee camp near Ramallah, who worked as a paramedic with the Red Crescent Society. She was also a member of the Fatah movement and in 2002 became the first female Palestinian suicide bomber, when a bomb she was carrying detonated in the heart of Jerusalem, killing an eighty-one-year-old man and wounding one hundred others. Whether or not the explosion was intentional is unknown, since Wafa carried the bomb in a backpack rather than strapped to her body, and left no suicide note. Israeli authorities concluded intent, however, and Fatah and other groups celebrated her as a martyr.

Mary stayed for two hours in Surratt House; Weichmann waited outside or spent time in the bar. The rest of Weichmann's account included telling observations: around six o'clock, shortly before they began their return trip to Washington, he saw Mary speaking privately in the parlour with John Wilkes Booth. At nine o'clock, Booth appeared at the H Street boardinghouse and spoke with Mary again. After this meeting, Mary's demeanor changed—she became 'very nervous, agitated and restless'.

But the most damning evidence against Mary came from her Surrattsville tenant and innkeeper, John M. Lloyd. Although Mary claimed to have made the 14 April journey with Weichmann to collect back rent owed by Lloyd, her tenant testified that she collected nothing—rather, she had given him a package containing field glasses and instructions to 'make ready the shooting irons', the two Spencer carbines that John Surratt Jr and two other conspirators—David Herold and George Atzerodt— had dropped off at the tavern five weeks earlier. According to Lloyd, the men had asked him to conceal the weapons, along with ammunition, about twenty feet of rope, and a monkey wrench, and John Jr had suggested a hiding place under joists in a second-floor room. After murdering President Lincoln, John Wilkes Booth did in fact first stop at the Surrattsville tavern with his accomplice David Herold. And, according to Lloyd's testimony, the innkeeper did as Mary had instructed him earlier that day: he handed over to Herold and Booth a pair of pistols, one of the two Spencer carbines, and the field glasses.

Another prosecution witness, George Cottingham, told the Tribunal that after learning of the president's assassination Lloyd had cried out, 'Oh, Mrs Surratt, that vile woman, she has ruined me! I am to be shot! I am to be shot!'

The deadly verdict

The case ended on 28 June. It would be a short deliberation, and the verdicts would be swift and deadly. The tribunal—relying heavily on the testimony of Lloyd—found Mary Surratt guilty of conspiracy and sentenced her to death. Three more of the eight co-conspirators (Lewis Paine, George Atzerodt, and David Herold) would also be executed; the other four would serve prison terms. Mary's death sentence bore a singular distinction: she would be the first woman ever to be executed by the US government.

Curiously, five members of the military commission recommended leniency for Mary, 'on the grounds of her sex and age'. (Southern womanhood had never before been so threatened by such harsh treatment, and at forty-two, and nearly twenty years older than the other conspirators, Mary was considered old.) Her lawyers tried in

Following pages: preparations for the execution of four of the Abraham Lincoln assassination conspirators at the Washington Arsenal on 7 July 1865.

vain to stay the execution. Her daughter, on the very day of the scheduled executions, visited the White House to plead mercy. But President Johnson was unmoved. The execution would proceed as planned.

Death by hanging

On 6 July, the verdicts were publicly announced, and almost immediately thousands of curiosity-seekers descended on Washington, hoping to catch a glimpse of the gruesome finale. But only one hundred spectators would be allowed in the Arsenal prison yard on the following, ill-fated day.

Up went a scaffold platform twenty feet high and thirty feet across, with two hinged drops. Captain Christian Rath prepared four nooses. One of them he tied with fewer knots, convinced that in just a matter of hours Mary's sentence would be commuted. Mary was not to be so fortunate. About ninety minutes to the impending hour on 7 July, Mary sat in her cell close to the yard, closing her ears to the loud clap of the gallows' heavy drops being tested over and over again.

At 1.12 pm the door to the yard creaked open. Mary was the first to emerge into the blazing sun, wearing a long black dress, black veil and bonnet. The sweltering humidity of the Washington summer only added to the oppressive atmosphere. Her legs could hardly support her. Two soldiers took hold of her and led her past four freshly dug graves, then up the fifteen steps to a chair on the gallows platform. Mary's noose hung before her. The male conspirators were dealt with first, their chains and shoes swiftly removed, their wrists and arms bound. But before Mary, the hangman hesitated, unsure of how to proceed. He had no choice but to do what he'd never done before, and prepare a woman for her execution. Awkwardly he wrapped the cotton ties around her billowing skirt. He bound her

PHOOLAN DEVI

(1963–2001) came from a poor Indian village where her early life was one of physical abuse at the hands of her husband. Abducted by a group of bandits, she first sought vengeance on her husband, then took to life as an outlaw, ransacking high-caste villages and taking rich landowners hostage. She became known as the Bandit Queen and was celebrated in India as something of a Robin Hood character, continually evading capture from the authorities. In 1983 she negotiated a surrender with elaborate conditions, and served eleven years in prison. Upon release, she was elected twice to Parliament, in 1996 and 1999. In 2001 Phoolan Devi was assassinated outside her house in revenge for an incident during her life as the Bandit Queen.

wrists, and Mary mumbled something about the pain. 'It won't hurt long', she was told. Finally, the hangman removed Mary's veil and bonnet, and slipped the noose around her neck. The crowd stirred and murmured uneasily. Then the white cotton hood descended over her head. In one last bid for sympathy, she said, 'I am innocent, but God's holy will be done'. Then she was told to move away from her chair.

As she stood on the brink of death, three claps sounded. Mary called out, 'Don't let me fall'. The support beams swung out from under four sets of bare feet, and the conspirators dropped to their death. At 1.22 pm on 7 July 1865, Mary E. Surratt met her death at the end of a rope.

⸺⸙⸺

During the weeks following the execution, the woman who had been assigned the role of wicked schemer during her trial was recast as the pitiable victim. In mid-nineteenth century America, it was still too difficult for anyone—male or female—to accept the idea that a mother and widow, much less a woman, period, could be so totally and unpardonably guilty. And for the next hundred-odd years, it would be through that sympathetic lens that Mary Surratt's historic part in the conspiracy would be most often described. Was she just another doting mother who had no idea what was going on at her inn? Was she sent to trial as bait for her fugitive son? Was the extraordinary use of military rather than civil justice unconstitutional? Would Mary's execution have taken place had she been tried in the civil courts? Indeed, a year later, the US Supreme Court forbade the use of military courts where civilian courts are open—which they were in Washington, DC in July of 1865. And it's interesting to note that, with virtually the same witnesses and for essentially the same crime, a civil court of the District of Columbia was unable to convict Mary's son when he was brought to trial in 1867.

More recent research leaves historians with little doubt that Mary Surratt knew exactly what was going on when the conspirators met at her boardinghouse. Should she have been executed for her collusion? The debate continues. The central truth remains that her unwavering loyalty to Booth, her son, and the other conspirators guaranteed punishment. Her treatment, at the hands of a vengeful, newly reunited nation and a terrified government, probably was all she could realistically expect.

PEARL HART
(c. 1870–1956)

❧

*Starry-eyed dreamer
turned desperado*

She was a girl who was easily seduced—first, by a gambler named Frederick Hart, then by images of the Wild West, and finally by a man who called himself Joe Boot. Born Pearl Taylor, her life started out with promise; she was raised in a respectable middle-class family in Ontario, Canada, and attended finishing school in her teens. But she would grow up to become the first known female stagecoach robber in the American West.

At the impressionable age of seventeen, Pearl fell for and eloped with the swaggering and seductive loser and abuser, Fred Hart. Five years later, they travelled to the Columbian Exposition in Chicago where Fred got a job as a sideshow barker. But he drank heavily, battered his wife, and lost his earnings at the gaming tables. Pearl escaped from harsh reality in the daily audiences of Buffalo Bill's Wild West Show, starring the amazing markswoman Annie Oakley, and grew ever more enchanted with the heroes and legends of America's frontier. Finally, having had enough of her good-for-nothing husband, Pearl packed her bags and took a train to Trinidad, Colorado, but an immediate gig as a saloon singer was cut short when she found out she was pregnant with Fred's child. Once again, she packed her bags, this time heading home to her family in Canada for support.

The next years of Pearl's life were all over the map, figuratively and quite literally. Having given birth to a son, Pearl left the baby with her mother to answer the insistent call of the American West. But in Phoenix, Arizona, Pearl discovered that the 'Wild West' of her romantic notions, with its unfettered women and laconic heroes, did not exist. Pearl had to wait tables and take in laundry to support herself, and eventually she took in her estranged husband as well, when he came chasing after her, begging forgiveness. The arrival of a second baby, a girl, brought fresh dissension, to the point where Fred knocked Pearl unconscious in a fit of drunken rage, and left her to fend for herself. Pearl had no choice but to take her daughter to live with her parents, who by now may have been residing in Ohio. But the American West still called, and Pearl didn't stay long. She returned to Arizona, and worked as a cook, moving from one mining camp to the next.

Left: Pearl Hart cut her hair and donned men's clothing to rob a stagecoach.

Just before her thirtieth birthday, Pearl took up with a miner who went by the name of Joe Boot. When she got word that her mother was ill and needed money for medical bills, Joe came up with a number of ideas for making some quick cash. One involved Pearl luring an unsuspecting man into their bedroom with the promise of romance so that Joe could sneak up behind him, knock him out, and pocket his wallet. This scheme worked more than once, but it wasn't lucrative enough. So Joe concocted a scheme to rob the Globe to Florence stagecoach.

On 29 May 1899, at Cane Spring in the Dripping Springs Mountains of Arizona, the two desperados stopped a stagecoach which had three passengers: a salesman who carried $380, a 'tenderfoot' with $36, and a Chinaman with $5. With guns drawn, Pearl and Joe ordered them to empty their pockets, and took all the money, a revolver, even the salesman's watch. Feeling somewhat badly about leaving her victims penniless, Pearl returned to each a dollar—'enough to eat on'. Then the two bandits disappeared on horseback. Only a few days later, however, on 4 June, Pearl and Joe found themselves surrounded by the sheriff and his posse just outside of Benson, Arizona.

Held in the Florence jail, Pearl milked her role as a lady bandit, posing for pictures and signing autographs for those who came to see the 'Bandit Queen'. Her trial for robbery took place in November, 1899. She admitted guilt, but the jury acquitted her. Trial magistrate, Judge Fletcher Doan, was furious, claiming that Pearl had 'flirted with the jury, bending them to her will'. Pearl was sent to trial a second time, on the charge of unlawfully carrying a gun. The new jury was not swayed by her charms, nor by her plea of temporary insanity at the time of the robbery, and she was convicted and sentenced to five years in the Yuma Territorial Prison.

While Pearl was serving time at Yuma, her notoriety grew. The tabloids constantly sent reporters to interview her about her life of crime and to snap pictures of the 'Bandit Queen' posing with a six-shooter or a Winchester. After just eighteen months, Pearl was paroled on 19 December 1902, and told to get out of town. The prison governor explained that Yuma Prison 'lacked accommodations for women prisoners'. But the truth of the matter was that she claimed to be pregnant, and the putative father would have had to have been a prison employee. To avoid a major scandal, the governor—at the behest of the warden—let her go. Pearl may have been playing a trick, though—there is no record of a third child being born.

Pearl moved to Kansas City to star in her sister's theatrical production about Pearl's adventures out West. The play ran only a short time, and Pearl's fame quickly faded. Many years later, in 1924, she visited the old courthouse in Florence where she was tried. Catching an attendant's eye, she smiled and said, 'Nothing has changed'. When the man asked who she was, she turned in the doorway and replied dramatically: 'Pearl Hart, the lady bandit'.

Later in life, Pearl purportedly married a rancher named Calvin Bywater and settled in Dripping Springs, Arizona. Legend has it that she became a hard-working, law-abiding citizen, a woman who chain-smoked cigars and cursed a blue streak, the likes of any male counterpart. Asked by a census worker where she was born, she is said to have replied, 'I wasn't born anywhere'.

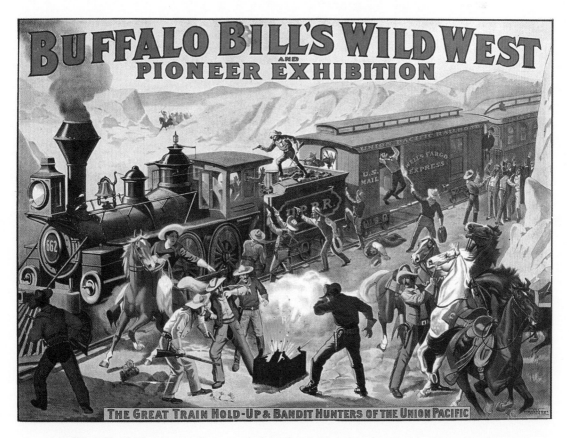

A Buffalo Bill's 1907 promotional poster included a 'female bandit', perhaps loosely based on Pearl Hart.

ISABELLA BIRD (1831–1904)

'Lady traveller' couldn't contain herself for long

Two days out from Auckland, the dilapidated steamer *Nevada* hit a hurricane. Isabella and the other seven passengers gathered in the deckhouse to watch the sea's fury battering the boat. The shrieking winds made it impossible for anyone to hear the captain's shouts. A wave crashed on deck and carried part of it away. Isabella knew that if the 'crazy engines failed at any moment to keep the ship's head to the sea, her destruction would not occupy half an hour'.

When the storm ended, the *Nevada*, her captain, her crew and all her passengers were still afloat—but the ship was sitting two feet deeper in the water. Isabella could not contain her excitement. She found a pen and wrote to her sister: 'The old Sea God has so stolen my heart and penetrated my soul … It is the perfect infatuation. It is to me like living in a new world, so pure, so fresh, so vital, so careless, so unfettered [with] no door bells, no "please ma'ams", no servants … Above all, no nervousness and no conventionalities. It seems to me a sort of brief resurrection of the girl of twenty-one. I cannot tell you how much I like my life!'

Isabella Bird circled the globe three times in her travels.

Traveller, writer and adventurer extraordinaire, Isabella Bird lived up to her name spectacularly—breezing around the world with her self-described 'up-to-anything and free-legged air', and in 1892 becoming the first woman Fellow of the prestigious Royal Geographical Society. But it was not until she was forty that Isabella—firmly rooted in the oh-so-conventional and stifling society of Victorian-era Britain—finally found her vocation, took off and soared. When she did—travelling to Canada, Australia, the Hawaiian Islands, the American West, Japan, China, Korea, Tibet, Morocco and the Middle East—she left all her cares and complaints behind, and never once had a dull experience, at least not by any of her vivid accounts.

Isabella's first journey was undertaken as a cure for her chronic ailments. It worked. But later, as she climbed volcanoes in Hawaii, rode horseback over hundreds of miles in Colorado in the dead of winter, and mingled with fascinating strangers, she became infected with something else entirely—the travel bug. Throughout her far-flung travels, Isabella Bird blazed with enthusiasm for the marvellous world around her. And with breathless, dramatic intensity, she wrote about everything she saw and experienced.

From pain to publication

For Isabella Bird, aches and ails were her almost constant companions throughout much of her otherwise comfortable youth. She was born on 15 October 1831, to a devout evangelical minister and his gentlewoman wife in Yorkshire, England. Her childhood days were filled with her mother's lessons in reading, writing, sewing, and religion, while several maids and a cook tended to the household tasks.

During summers at her grandparents' house in the country, she spent most of her time outdoors, rowing and acting the fearless horsewoman, mounting any horse however spirited. But back home in the quiet parish, Isabella more often than not complained of back pain, headaches and fatigue. At eighteen, she had a fibroid tumour close to her spine removed. When her doctor prescribed 'a change of air' to speed her recovery, Edward Bird took his family to the Scottish Highlands for six weeks. Amid the heather-covered hills, scrambling up steep trails for hours, Isabella forgot all about her pain. Ill-health followed by speedy recovery in new environs—usually those with fresh vistas and mountain air—was a pattern that would repeat itself over and over again in Isabella's story.

Her respectable, upper-class life in the mid-1800s, while easy, was bounded by the narrow routine of home and the acceptable limits of behaviour for ladies. Lively, curious, intelligent, and articulate, Isabella wanted something worth doing, not frittering her time away on pointless activities. Her only outlets were reading— she devoured her father's books on law, history, and religion—and writing, for which she had a natural gift. Her very first travel account was of her trip to the Scottish Highlands. She thought it made a good read, and submitted it to a popular family magazine. When the article was accepted, Isabella became emboldened; she declared herself a writer and started turning out human interest stories for *The Family Treasury*, *Good Words*, and *The Sunday Magazine*. But after a while, her niggling ailments started creeping back, signalling the return of an ongoing, nagging malaise. Her doctor again prescribed the nineteenth century cure-all of 'a change of air'. This time, it would come in the form of a long sea voyage.

On a warm June day in 1854, Isabella, now twenty-two, and the cousins who had been visiting from Canada boarded a boat in Liverpool for Halifax, Nova Scotia. Isabella carried a small bag of clothes, the £100 her father had given her, and a leather-bound notebook. Staying at her cousins' farm on Prince Edward Island, it was a matter of only a few weeks before she was struck with the urge to go to America. She packed her things again and, despite the dangers of travelling alone, boarded a boat to Portland, Maine. From Maine, she caught the train to Ohio. And from Ohio, it was on to Chicago, then Detroit, then across Lake Erie to Niagara Falls. By the time she returned to the port of Halifax, six months later, Isabella had covered more than 9600 kilometres—and she had never felt better.

On her lengthy trip, Isabella wrote with the liveliness of a young woman travelling abroad for the first time, filling the pages of her notebook with exuberant detail about the new sights and the 'prairie men' who 'could tell stories, whistle

---

ANNIE SMITH PECK

(1850–1935) was an American scholar and mountaineer, and the first woman to climb the Matterhorn in trousers rather than a skirt (and only the third woman to reach the summit). Her greatest triumph was the record-breaking ascent of the north peak of Peru's 6768-metre Mount Nevado Huarascán in 1908 (aged fifty-eight), never previously achieved by man or woman (twenty years later the peak was renamed Cumbre Aña Peck in her honour). A supporter of women's suffrage, she climbed Peru's Mount Coropuna in 1909 and planted a 'rights for women' pennant on its summit.

melodies', and were 'tall, handsome, broad-chested and athletic', not to mention 'chivalrous and as free as the wind'. Her notes formed the basis of her first published book, *The Englishwoman in America*, released in January, 1856. The *Times* of London and a whole slew of Canadian newspapers gave the book a thumbs-up. The royalty checks began to arrive. For the twenty-six-year-old Isabella, it was a heady and exciting experience—to discover that the two things she most loved to do—travel and write—could provide her with meaningful, and fairly lucrative, work.

But Isabella was unsettled by her success. Having been brought up to believe that a woman's role was to do good deeds, help others, and put her own interests aside, she found success difficult to accept. It was an era when members of the upper classes rarely worked to earn money, living on family inheritances and investments. Isabella decided to do as any well-bred lady would do, and used her book royalties to help those in need—specifically, buying new boats for impoverished Scottish fishermen. It was just one of many of her efforts in the years to come to be of service, to do what she believed was most fitting for the role of genteel lady. And, essentially, to keep the real Isabella Bird at bay.

> ## JUNKO TABEI
>
> (1939–) is a Japanese climber, who in 1975 became the first woman to reach the top of the world's highest mountain peak, Mount Everest. In 1992, she became the first woman in the world to reach the summit of the highest mountain on each of the seven continents. She now works as an environmental conservationist, specifically to preserve mountain habitats that increasing climber numbers now threaten, and is the director of Himalayan Adventure Trust of Japan.

When Edward Bird died, in May of 1858, Isabella felt the loss of her father all the more profoundly because she believed she had failed him. 'I feel as if my life were spent in the very ignoble occupation of taking care of myself', she wrote, and chided herself for not having a more natural 'self-denying spirit'. She vowed that from then on, she would stay put, do good service and dedicate her writings to religious topics.

For close to twelve years, Isabella held to her vow. Settled in Edinburgh, Scotland with her mother and her younger sister Henrietta (Hennie), she wrote for magazines to occupy her mind, and did good deeds to ease her conscience. In 1866, Mrs Bird died, leaving her two daughters, both single and now in their thirties, with a small inheritance that would allow them to live comfortably, sharing a house. Isabella continued to write to supplement their income. For a couple of years all went well, the sisters forming an unbreakable bond and depending on one another, almost exclusively, as friends and confidants. But by 1869, Isabella was starting to feel antsy. She wrote to her publisher, John Murray: 'I long for some more serious and engrossing literary occupation than writing papers for the *North British Review*, *Good Words*, etc'. Murray urged her to do what she did best: travel abroad and gather new and interesting material. She felt the tug of desire, but resisted. It would be too selfish.

True to form, however, Isabella's body told her what she needed to do. Nineteenth century doctors didn't know it, but Isabella's debilitating headaches, backaches and insomnia reflected mental and emotional anguish. Hennie couldn't bear to watch her sister deteriorate, and begged her to take an ocean trip. Eventually, in 1872, Isabella caved in. Her very real maladies had given her the excuse to satisfy her itchy feet.

A new lease on life

On the cusp of her forties, Isabella left the 'constant murk' of Scottish skies and set out, her destination the American West, via Australia and New Zealand. Her ultimate goal was to spend time in Colorado's Rocky Mountains town of Estes Park, where, she was told, she would find fresh, cool air and natural beauty that was unsurpassed. Perhaps with her sights set on the Rockies, Isabella found Melbourne too familiar and the heat of the city unbearable. She wrote miserably to Hennie: 'I don't know anything that could reconcile me to living in this country. The climate and the growths are so unlovely …' She moved on to New Zealand, but Auckland, where 'all nature was limp, dusty, groaning, gasping' and 'men on the verge of sunstroke plied their tasks mechanically', appealed to her even less. Frustrated and disappointed, she booked passage for San Francisco.

As luck would have it, the *Nevada*, having survived the wild storm a few days out of Auckland, made an unscheduled stop in the Sandwich Islands (Hawaii). 'Fair Paradise of the Pacific! Bright blossom of summer sea!' Isabella exulted, as the *Nevada* trundled through the clear turquoise waters of Honolulu Bay and was greeted by a crowd of brightly dressed 'rich brown men and women', who showered the passengers with flower wreaths of every colour of the rainbow. 'Everyone was smiling', she noted. And everything delighted her. So much so, that she remained for six months. Isabella ascended Mauna Loa (the world's largest volcano), watched transfixed the volcanic lake's molten fire hiss and crash in full eruption, and burned herself on the sulfurous steam. She adopted the 'gay, brass-bossed, high-peaked Mexican saddle' made for the jaunty bottoms of wild men of the open prairie, and rode horseback astride, sporting a lei of orange seeds around her neck, 'great rusty New Zealand boots', and a pair of 'jingling Mexican spurs'. She slept on mats in straw huts and swam in the rivers. As the days slipped by, far from censorious eyes, Isabella continued to shake off the grip of the prim and proper. Revelling in newfound good health, she confided to her sister: 'I saw myself looking so young in a glass that I did not know it was me … my cheeks have so much colour from sunburn and my eyes are so dark and shining that I look, I fear, younger than you'. When she felt herself succumbing to the temptation to stay in Hawaii forever, Isabella made a sudden decision to continue her interrupted journey to Colorado. On 7 August 1873, she bade farewell to her tropical dreamland, teary-eyed, but moving on as the independent and unusual lady traveller she had become.

Colorado

Ten hours a day in the saddle, crossing snow-covered peaks in subzero weather, was a far remove from sunny gallops through lush Hawaiian valleys. Nevertheless, after three months in the Rocky Mountains, Isabella wrote Hennie, 'Every day I admire it more, and the melancholy of its winter loneliness suits me. It is such a completely healthful life'. She described 'wild fantastic views opening up continually, a recurrence of surprise; the air keener and purer with every mile' and 'chasms of immense depth, dark with the indigo gloom of pines, and mountains with snow gleaming on their splintered cress, and still streams and shady pools'. She wrote, too, about the characters among whom she found herself—particularly one scruffy, gun-slinging desperado with a reputation for volatile binge drinking, fighting Indians, and tussling with a grizzly bear, an encounter which had cost him an eye. What Isabella failed to mention was that she had taken rather a fancy to Jim Nugent.

They made an incongruous pair—the English lady in her Hawaiian riding dress and the long-haired

ANN BANCROFT

(1955–) is the first woman in history to cross the ice cap to both Poles. In 1986, she travelled 1600 kilometres by dogsled from the Northwest Territories in Canada to the North Pole as the only female member of Will Steger's International Polar Expedition, becoming the first woman to cross the ice to the North Pole. In 1993, she led the American Women's Expedition to the South Pole, a sixty-seven-day trek of 1060 kilometres on skis.

mountain man from 'good Irish–Canadian stock'. 'I forgot both his reputation and his appearance, for his manner was that of a chivalrous gentleman, his accent refined …' He recited great reams of poetry for her. And, on 30 September 1873, she put her life in his hands. On that freezing day, Rocky Mountain Jim muscled Isabella up Longs Peak, 4480 metres of lofty inaccessibility that had been tantalising the intrepid English adventurer from afar. 'To me it was a time of extreme terror,' she later recounted. 'I was roped to Jim, but it was no use. My feet were paralysed and slipped on the bare rock.' Having no choice, Isabella let Jim toss her over his shoulder, then scrambled up a wall of pink granite 'as nearly perpendicular as anything could well be' and, 'gasping from the exhausting toil in the rarefied air', triumphantly reached the stalwart summit. Had Isabella known that only a few weeks earlier American writer Anna Dickinson had claimed the title of first white woman to climb Longs Peak, it would not have made the slightest difference. She wasn't out to break world records. But that doesn't mean she didn't want to impress on Jim that she was the bravest, toughest, most extraordinary English lady ever to come his way.

'There's a man I could have married', Isabella eventually told Hennie, but she was a little too old for such a preposterously reckless step, and her deep love for her sister pulled her homeward.

Falling into an old groove

From the moment she got off the steamer in Liverpool and hurried home to dear, predictable Hennie, Isabella was again the Christian do-gooder—one who had called on God to save the black soul of her hard-drinking Colorado companion during her American tour. Rocky Mountain Jim, now a repentant sinner, was stripped of all that 'certain dazzle about him'.

Over the next several years, Isabella would seesaw back and forth between hunkering down as the respectable Miss Bird in what she came to call 'criminal conventionality', and travelling abroad, clinging to the official reason for her travels: her health. The publication of *Six Months in the Sandwich Islands*, in February 1875, was an instant success and for the next year kept her engines humming on the new home front—a cottage she was sharing with Hennie in the village of Tobermory on Scotland's Isle of Mull. But then the old familiar syndrome reasserted itself: Isabella began to suffer from neuralgia and bouts of listless depression. This time she set her heart on the Far East—the beginning of a twenty-year passion for travel in Japan, China, and the Malay States.

Isabella wrote letter after letter to her sister from Japan in 1878, this time with a nagging undertone of peevishness as she journeyed 2250 kilometres off the beaten path, lived for a spell among the aboriginal Ainos (Ainu), and described in lurid detail their primitive living conditions. 'I write the truth as I see it … truly this is a new Japan to me, of which no books have given me any idea, and it is not fairyland.' By the summer of 1879, Isabella was back in Tobermory, putting together her new book on Japan, and waving off the overtures of an Edinburgh doctor named John Bishop who, in Isabella's mind, had fantastic notions of his own if he thought she would marry him.

Nevertheless, soon after Hennie died of typhoid in June of 1880, a heartbroken Isabella would agree to settle down with the doctor, who had become the rock she had leaned on through her sister's illness. Isabella was nearly fifty years old, and believed that the solid anchor of marriage, 'home and hearth' might be the only solution to her depression. Instead, her health took a turn for the worse, only improving after her husband's own 'long and weary illness' ended with his death in March of 1886. Assessing her situation calmly, Isabella noted, 'Henceforth I must live my own life'.

Back in the saddle

At the age of fifty-seven, Isabella was ready to begin again. Her best-selling book *A Lady's Life in the Rocky Mountains* (published in 1879) was into its umpteenth printing, and *Unbeaten Tracks in Japan* (published in 1880) was still selling strongly. Lengthy stories about her journeys in the Malay Peninsula and Sinai had run in the magazine *Leisure Hour* and doubled its circulation. By now, globetrotting and the name Isabella Bird were firmly associated in the public conscience. She had already travelled thousands of miles halfway around the world, and even greater adventures were on the horizon.

Deciding to travel as a missionary, Isabella undertook some basic medical studies before setting off for India, arriving in February of 1889. Within two months she had bought plots of land for the erection of two memorial hospitals, one in the name of her husband, the other of her sister. Over the next months, Isabella was again the lone woman traveller, commanding an assortment of servants, interpreters, guides and muleteers. From the lush valley of Kashmir she travelled on the back of a yak over the bare granite peaks of the Himalayas, reaching Tibet's ancient city of Leh,

> ## KAY COTTEE
>
> (1954–) is an Australian sailor who in
> 1988 became the first woman to sail
> solo, unassisted and non-stop, around
> the world, arriving back in Sydney on
> 5 June on her 11.2-metre yacht, the
> *First Lady*. Her adventure lasted 189
> days and included being capsized and
> washed overboard. In 1988 she was
> named Australian of the Year, and in
> 1989, received the Order of Australia.

crossing icy rivers and struggling up summits of up to 6000 metres.

More daring escapades, and another plug for good deeds, followed a year later. In January of 1890, in Simla, Isabella received 'the acme of good fortune as a traveller' when she got to go galloping away into the deserts with a dashing English officer of the Intelligence Department of the Indian Army. But it wasn't exactly a romantic adventure of the dime-store variety. The patently non-combative, middle-aged English lady would be the effective cover for Major Sawyer's military reconnaissance that would take them, and a handful of officers, on a 800 kilometre journey from Simla through Persia to Tehran. 'But *I* quite feel that it involves a certain abridgement of my liberty', Isabella points out. 'I should much prefer to travel alone.' Nevertheless, without disclosing any names in *Journeys in Persia and Kurdistan*, Isabella describes herself, with typical dramatic flair, in the company of the unit's commanding officer during his survey work in the region, armed with a revolver and a medicine chest. The English literary magazine the *Athenaeum* selected the book for review in its edition of 16 January 1892, concluding that: 'The reader will find much to instruct, interest and amuse'.

The indomitable Isabella is honoured

In November 1892, the Royal Geographical Society in London unexpectedly invited Isabella as a speaker, a great honour. The prestigious society had never before invited a woman to address their group—but also had never admitted women as members. So Isabella declined. At the same time she did agree to speak to the male and female members of the Royal Scottish Geographical Society. Out of sheer embarrassment, the president of the London society promptly proposed—and the council agreed— that they needed to bring women into their fold. Isabella L. Bishop would be the first woman Fellow of the Royal Geographical Society.

Five years would pass before 'the honourable Mrs Bishop' was again officially invited, in recognition of her status as exceptional explorer, to address the Royal

Isabella Bird photographed this cemetery of the Yu-Chom-Sa Buddhist Monastery in 1898.

Geographical Society; the request was specific: would she speak on her travels in Western China? Isabella's final great journey, as a sturdy widow of sixty-two, had been to Korea and the mountains of northwest China, essentially as a war correspondent and political interpreter. Much to her amusement, the writer who had once penned with breathless earnestness 'Oh the life on breezy hills, on countless horses! This is the life that's meant for me!', had been 'transplanted in to the ranks of political writers', and with the publication of her most recent books, *Korea and Her Neighbours* and *The Yangtze Valley and Beyond*, was considered an 'authority on the political situation in the Far East'.

Even in the last decade of her life, Isabella's spirit never faltered. The cycle continued: she travelled and came back invigorated. Then she wrote and published, lectured, and threw herself into one arduous round of 'missionary addresses' after another as a sort of amends for the days of unrestrained delight abroad. At the age of seventy she was at it again, making up her mind to 'quit civilisation for the wild' and undertaking a madcap fling in Morocco atop a black stallion mounted from a stepladder. Ironically, the woman who had risked danger so fearlessly in life met death peacefully. She died quietly in her own bed surrounded by friends, her bags packed for another adventure, two years later.

Isabella Bird said, 'I was born to travel'. If she were born today, it would take no guilt, and no time at all, to admit that. But globetrotting for Victorian women was not exactly respectable. And Isabella was diligent about preserving her image as a well-bred lady. She travelled as freely as Alexandra David-Néel, who roamed through Tibet in disguise, or Mary Kingsley, who explored Africa alone. But the last thing she wanted was to call attention to herself as pursuing her passion for travel simply for travel's sake. As it turned out, she was too good a writer to slip under the radar as adventur*ess* extraordinaire. Her gift was to journey far, have adventures better than anyone else, and tell her tales well. 'Miss Bird is the ideal traveller', announced the *Spectator*, but maybe the newspaper should have called her the 'ideal travel writer'. 'She can see and she can use the words that place what she sees before the reader … There never was anybody who had adventures so well as Miss Bird.' Perhaps the most telling thing Isabella herself ever wrote was this: 'Travellers are privileged to do the most improper things with perfect propriety'.

ALEXANDRA DAVID-NÉEL

(1868–1969)

Free-thinking explorer who
hobnobbed with high lamas

Even as a child, she ventured to expand her boundaries. The first European woman to enter the forbidden holy city of Lhasa, at a time when foreigners were banned from the mysterious land of Tibet, Alexandra David-Néel ran away from home for the first of many times at the age of two. Eventually, she went on to win world fame with accounts of her wanderings on foot in uncharted Asian territory, where she spent more than thirty years.

During her long life, she was a compulsive explorer of both her inner and outer worlds. She was born in Paris and grew up in a bourgeois household in Brussels— suffocation of the worst kind for this fiercely individualistic and spunky soul. When the adolescent Alexandra wasn't running off—much to her parents' chagrin—to England, Switzerland, Spain, or Italy—she was escaping into her studies of mysticism and Eastern religions and philosophy. In her twenties she joined the Theosophical Society in Paris, diving into Eastern studies and Sanskrit at the Sorbonne, and becoming a political radical. At twenty-three, disguised as a man, she joined a cult led by Sri Ananda Saraswati, who used hashish to obtain visions. When she received an inheritance from her godmother, she set sail for Ceylon (now Sri Lanka) on an eighteen-month journey that would take her through India, returning only when she ran out of money.

By the time she was in her thirties, she had established herself as a world traveller, independent-minded feminist, theosophist, and anarchist, who also happened to be a professional opera diva who played Marguerite and Carmen, among other leading roles. Not to mention she enjoyed her fair share of romances, becoming involved with a stagehand, having a live-in relationship with a fellow artist in France, and in Tunisia accepting an invitation to be seduced by the dashing railroad engineer who would eventually become her husband.

In 1904, thirty-six-year-old Alexandra agreed to marry Philippe Néel under his condition that she would give up acting. But she had conditions of her own: she got to travel, and at her husband's expense. Once the pact was made, Alexandra set out for what was supposed to be a twelve-month trek to India; she

---

Left: Alexandra David-Néel frequently wore Tibetan dress at her home in France.

was gone for fourteen years, during which time she slowly bankrupted her long-suffering husband as she milked him for the money to fund her expeditions.

Her journey to the East marked a new phase in Alexandra's life, renewing her studies in Buddhism and her spirit of adventure. Her entrance into Tibet counts as her most dramatic achievement. Tibet's location deep in the Himalayan Mountains made travel to the country extraordinarily difficult to begin with. Moreover, the political sensitivity of the area in the early twentieth century made entry for any European virtually impossible. These obstacles did not deter Alexandra, who was known to repeat the old saying: 'Who knows the flower best? The one who reads about it in a book, or the one who finds it wild on the mountainside?' Driven by a will of steel and the desire to find the Shangri-La that tantalised travellers and spiritual-seekers alike, Alexandra took fearsome chances.

In India, from 1911 to 1916, she took up with the Crown Prince of Sikkim (at the time a British protectorate near the Tibetan border) as either his spiritual companion or his lover; was granted the extraordinary privilege of being heard twice by the thirteenth Dalai Lama; lived for two years in a cave in the Himalayas, practicing meditation and studying spirituality under the tutelage of a hermit; and met a young Sikkimese monk named Aphur Yongden, with whom she trespassed into Tibetan territory in August of 1916. When the British authorities forced Alexandra and the boy monk to leave the country, they set out for Japan, and over the next several years slowly crossed China from east to west, always intending to make their way back to Tibet. On foot, and accompanied only by Yongden, whom she later adopted as her son, Alexandra surmounted the snow-covered peaks of the Himalayas. Finally, after numerous failed attempts to enter Tibet's capital, she disguised herself as a mendicant pilgrim with blackened face, and entered Lhasa in 1924, at the age of fifty-six becoming the first Westerner of her sex to crash the gates of the Forbidden City. Having achieved the impossible, the triumphant traveller remained in Lhasa for two months.

For this epic journey, Alexandra was awarded the gold medal of the Geographical Society of Paris, the French Legion of Honour, the Insignia of the Chinese Order of the Brilliant Star, and the silver medal of the Royal Belgian Geographical Society. In her later years, she settled in Digne, in the foothills of the French Alps, and wrote prolifically about the East. Her books run the gamut from anthropology to geographical discovery, history, politics, philosophy, and Western views of tantric sexual practices, and later influenced modern radical thinkers such as the Beats Generation's, Kerouac and Ginsberg. Her major works, published in both English and French, were My Journey to Lhasa, Magic and Mystery in Tibet *and* Initiations and Initiates in Tibet.

At the age of one hundred, Alexandra renewed her passport, thinking she would make her way to New York City. But her inability to walk, by this time, kept her homebound. She died at Digne, just shy of her one hundred and first birthday.

Expatriate British novelist and travel writer Lawrence Durrell anointed her 'the most astonishing French-woman of our time'. When the French government decided to cast a bronze medal in Alexandra's honour, she chose the motto to be engraved on it: 'Walk Straight on Following Your Heart's Desire'.

The Potala Palace in Lhasa, at the time when Alexandra David-Néel visited Tibet.

MARIE CURIE (1867–1934)

Two-time Nobel Prize laureate who lived, and died, for science

In a great pot over the fire, Marie stirred the boiling mass of pitchblende around and around and around with a heavy iron rod nearly as tall as she was. It was a crisp and sunny autumn morning in Paris, but inside the dimly lit work shed behind the School of Physics and Chemistry it was sweltering, and noxious fumes from the simmering chemicals made it difficult to breathe. Marie scooped out the heavy material that had sunk to the bottom of the pot, and began filling jars. Her arms ached with the strain of stirring, her shoulders stooped from the weight of the glass containers she repeatedly hefted from pot to shelves. And still the pitchblende kept its secret.

For four years, Marie had been toiling, trying to extract the tiny amount of radium contained in pitchblende, isolating it from the other metals in the brownish black ore. Time and time again she would collapse into bed at her workday's end, utterly spent and no closer to a finding. But this day was to be different.

Marie finished a crystallisation—one of more than a thousand such experiments—and suddenly the new element emerged from her tedious work. The unstoppable scientist had finally managed to isolate one mere decigram of almost pure radium chloride from the pitchblende. Finally, she had found what she was looking for. And now the rest of the scientific community would see that Marie had proven her theory was correct.

In 1903 Marie Curie was awarded her first Nobel Prize, for Physics.

On 25 June 1903, Marie Curie presented the findings of her work in her doctoral thesis titled 'Researches on Radioactive Substances'. The university's examination committee was astounded, declaring that her discovery of radioactivity represented the greatest scientific contribution ever made in a doctoral thesis.

Marie Curie's list of achievements is remarkably long. A true pioneer in two fields of science, she was the first woman ever to win a Nobel Prize. At the age of thirty-four, she became the first woman to earn her PhD in France; six years later, she would become the first woman professor at the Sorbonne in Paris. In the years between, she received her greatest honours: in 1903, she was awarded the Nobel Prize in Physics, along with her husband Pierre Curie and the French physicist Henri Becquerel, who opened the door to her research; in 1911, she won a second Nobel Prize, this time in Chemistry. She is the first and only woman among thirty-five women Nobel laureates to win the prize twice, and the only laureate (man or woman) to win the prize in two different fields.

A thirst for learning

Even among the brilliant members of her family, Marie Curie stood out as especially intelligent. She was born Marya Sklodowska in Warsaw, on 7 November 1867, when oppressive Russian rule was igniting a fierce sense of patriotism and loyalty in the hearts of Polish citizens. Her parents, Vladyslaw and Bronislawa, both dedicated teachers who believed that education was the key to liberating Poland from the Russians, instilled in their children not only a love of learning but a great love for their country. At home, the young Marya was as captivated by her father's collection of 'scientific apparatus' as she was by his passionate recitations of verses by the Polish poets. It has been said that, one time, at the tender age of four, she interrupted her older sister Bronislawa's reading lesson as she kept stumbling over the words, picking up the textbook and reading the passage aloud without a hitch. When Marya noticed the stunned looks on the family's faces she burst into tears, reportedly crying out, 'I didn't know I wasn't supposed to do that, but it was so easy!' It wouldn't be the last time Marya would find herself at the centre of attention for her brainy feats—and cringing in the spotlight at the same time.

Education in Poland under Russian control was a perplexing combination of subjects: those mandated by tsarist rule, and those—like Polish history and language—

that were banned but surreptitiously taught, anyway. Teachers and students were forbidden to speak Polish, but even the threat of arrest didn't stop them from doing so … unless Russian inspectors made a surprise visit to a school. When that happened, quick as lightning all Polish materials would be hidden away, and more often than not Marya—the prized student—would be selected to stand up and recite the day's lesson in her perfect Russian. This sort of display would be the only ugly memory she retained from her Polish schooldays. By the time she was sixteen, she had won her first notable award: a gold medal upon the completion of her secondary education at the Russian lycée in Warsaw. In another time or place, such a bright and devoted student would have continued her studies without much thought. But university was not an option for Marya, nor any other woman, in 1883 Poland. On the threshold of an unknown future with limited educational options, Marya was despondent. Throwing in the towel, however, was not her style.

LAURA BASSI

(1711–1778) was an Italian scientist, and the first woman to be appointed to a teaching position in a European university, becoming a Professor of Anatomy at the University of Bologna at the age of twenty. She was also the first woman professor of physics and one of the first women to be paid a salary in a university role. Remarkably, Bassi's career, which also included the publication of many scientific texts and treatises, was balanced by a busy family life—she was married to a colleague and possibly had as many as twelve children.

Vladyslaw had high hopes for all his children and wanted to send his daughters abroad to pursue an advanced education, specifically at the finest university in one of the most exciting and progressive cities in the world. But sending them to the Sorbonne, in Paris, was beyond his family's means. To solve the problem, Marya and Bronya came to an arrangement: Marya would go to work as a governess and contribute her earnings to her sister's savings, so that Bronya could enroll in the course in medicine. When Bronya had taken her degree she, in turn, would contribute to the cost of Marya's studies in mathematics and science.

So it was not until she was twenty-four, and with barely any savings, that Marya came to Paris to realise her dreams. She had been away from any kind of formal study for eight years. For a smart young woman, starved for both intellectual and cultural stimulation, what was there not to love about Paris in 1891? The Eiffel Tower, with its daring design, had recently taken shape on the city's skyline. The Impressionists Claude Monet and Mary Cassatt were defying conventions with their vibrant canvases.

The Lumière brothers were showing their new invention, moving pictures, to sold-out audiences. Everything about Paris enchanted Marya, most of all the way it filled her with a heady taste of freedom. She may have been a shy, penniless foreigner from a country under oppression. But for the first time since her secondary school days, she felt powerful and set on a vision. On 3 November 1891, Marya entered the gates of the Sorbonne and registered for classes in physics and mathematics in the Faculty of Sciences; they were not, by any means, popular class choices among women. With quiet deliberation, she signed the register 'Marie Sklodowska' and from then on was known as Marie.

The sacrifices Marie made as she worked toward her master's degree hardly fazed her. Living in a tiny, rented room near the Sorbonne, she studied far into the night by the light of a single oil lamp, and sometimes went without heat or a meal. Hers was a solitary life, but she wouldn't have it any other way. Time and again, throughout her life, Marie's love of learning would wreak havoc on her health as she ignored food, rest and troubling physical symptoms in her ardent pursuit of knowledge. But now her focus was wholly on her studies. 'It was like a new world opened to me, the world of science, which I was at last permitted to know in all liberty', she would come to write. Her professors were among the most distinguished scholars in France: physicist and mathematician Marcel Brillouin, mathematician Paul Painlevé, and future Nobel Prize-winner, the physicist and inventor Gabriel Lippmann. The master mathematician Paul Appell probably held the greatest sway over Marie. He fiddled with numbers and played with the stars, as keys to the natural laws. 'I take the sun and I throw it', the savant once offered his enraptured students, filling Marie with giddy delight. What could be more enthralling, she thought, than the exquisite, unchangeable laws that ruled the universe? She knew what her life's work had to be: to uncover the mysterious order in the universe's apparent disorder … that was, to be a scientist.

LISE MEITNER

(1878–1968) was an Austrian nuclear physicist, the first woman to be admitted to Max Planck's lectures, who became the first female full professor in Germany. She collaborated with the chemist Otto Hahn, working with him for over thirty years, combining her knowledge of physics with his of chemistry to research radiochemistry. In 1944 Hahn received the Nobel Prize for Physics for his research into fission, an award many believe should have been shared with Lise Meitner. In 1997 chemical element 109, meitnerium, was posthumously named in her honour.

By 1893, Marie was ready to take her final exams. The first woman ever to receive a physics degree at the Sorbonne placed first in her class. Thanks to a 600 ruble scholarship (equivalent to $5000 today), Marie was able to pursue a second degree, this time in mathematics. It took her just twelve months to complete her course, easily passing her exams and ranking second in her class. She was nearing her twenty-seventh birthday and her beloved homeland was calling her. Marie's next plan was to obtain a teacher's diploma and find a teaching position in Warsaw.

The discovery years

As fate would have it, Pierre Curie would change Marie's mind. He was a Frenchman internationally known for his work with crystals, electricity and magnetism, and whose published papers had earned him plenty of respect, even with a reputation in the French scientific community as somewhat of an eccentric. At the age of thirty-five, Pierre had also sworn off love. He did not have a very high opinion of women, and was convinced that no woman could possibly appreciate, much less understand, the dedication that a true scientist gave his work. This was, of course, before he met Marie.

In Marie, Pierre found a woman who spoke his language—not French, but the language of science. The man who declared he'd never get married proposed to Marie six months after they met. But in the early days of the summer of 1895, Marie's heart still belonged to Poland. And so she left for home, resolved that she would not be coming back. Pierre wrote to her. Again and again. 'It would be a beautiful thing which I dare not hope for if we could pass our lives close to each other, hypnotised by our dreams, your patriotic dream, our humanitarian dream and our scientific dream', he penned from Paris. Come autumn, Marie was packing her bags and heading back to France; she told herself it was for no other reason than to dive into another year at the Sorbonne. Ten more months would pass before Marie would turn her heart over to the man she had to admit she truly loved. On 26 July 1895, Marie Sklodowska and Pierre Curie married quietly in the Sceaux town hall, near Paris. They became partners in every sense of the word.

Motherhood came to Marie on 12 September 1897, with the birth of the couple's first child, Irène. Pierre arranged for his father to live with them and take on the baby's care, so that Marie could reach even higher in her professional life— working toward her PhD. She settled on a study of a little-understood phenomenon:

Marie Curie and husband Pierre processing radium in the first factory built for the purpose at Nogent-sur-Marne, Paris.

the emission of mysterious rays from the chemical element uranium. (Their colleague Henri Becquerel had recently made this discovery, but the door was open for further study.) Marie wanted to find out how these rays 'electrified' the air. 'What is the nature of radiation?' she asked herself. Her investigation would lead to the discovery of a lifetime.

In early1898 Marie made her first revolutionary conclusion: the ability to radiate did not depend on some outside energy force or the sun or even the arrangement of the atoms in a molecule, but it must be linked to the interior of the atom itself. This discovery is considered conceptually *the* most important contribution to the development of physics. Marie's next idea, seemingly simple but brilliant, was to systematically study samples of minerals to identify which ones contain uranium or thorium—the only two chemical elements known to emit the mysterious rays. In no time, using an invention of Pierre's called an electrometer, she identified that a brownish black ore called pitchblende not only gave off this strange radiation but was four times more active than was motivated by the amount of uranium in it. Thus, her second conclusion: an entirely new element that was far more active than uranium itself was present in pitchblende. Marie took her idea to her husband for his input, but she clearly established ownership of it. Later, in her biography of her husband, she twice recorded the fact that no one helped her formulate the idea, to ensure there was no chance of any ambiguity. There's a strong likelihood that, already, at this early stage of her career, Marie understood that scientists of the day would find it hard to believe that a woman could be capable of such groundbreaking work.

When Marie told her former Sorbonne professor Gabriel Lippmann about her findings, he wrote about them in a report to the Academy of Sciences. On 12 April 1898, the published report created a sensation in scientific circles all over Europe. A German professor commented: 'Nature is getting more disorderly every day'.

Here is where Marie's work became simply too extraordinary for Pierre to stand on the sidelines. Because of what Marie was uncovering, whole new vistas were opening up in the world of science. Pierre gave up his own research to join his wife in her project. By December of 1898, the Curie's had made it clear to the scientific community that they were positively certain of the existence of, not only one, but two new metals. They proposed naming them 'radium' and 'polonium', 'after the name of the country of origin of one of us'. Before long, scientists from all corners were popularising Marie's new term, 'radioactivity'.

Collaboration pans out

In order to prove radioactivity was a matter of two new elements, the Curies would have to produce them in demonstrable amounts, determine their atomic weight and preferably isolate them. At this stage, they needed more work space. It was far from ideal, but an unoccupied, poorly ventilated potato shed in the back of the school where Pierre taught would be the site where the very laborious work of separation and analysis would begin. Marie carried out the chemical separations, and Pierre undertook the measurements after each successive step. These would mark the happiest years of the couple's life. Later, Marie would write about the joy they felt when they came into the shed at night, seeing 'from all sides the feebly luminous silhouettes' of the products of their work. What Marie didn't realise was that the beautiful bluish glow was, among other things, the dangerous radioactive gas radon. Over time, with such prolonged exposure to radiation, both she and Pierre would suffer from a slew of symptoms, from severe headaches to scarred skin to chronic fatigue, and eventually, in Marie's case, leukemia.

On 12 January 1902, after thousands of crystallisations, Marie finally isolated —from a whopping tonne of pitchblende—one mere decigram of almost pure radium chloride, and determined radium's atomic weight as 225.97. Radium was, in fact, 5 million times more radioactive than its equal weight in uranium! Seventeen months later, on 25 June 1903, to a thunderstruck Board of Examiners at the Sorbonne, Marie presented the findings of her research in her doctoral thesis, 'Researches on Radioactive Substances'. Her dissertation resulted in the first doctorate awarded to a woman in France, and the first doctorate in science awarded to a woman in all of Europe.

The price of fame

The 1903 Nobel Prize for Physics was awarded jointly to Pierre and Marie Curie and to Henri Becquerel, arousing at once more than a little curiosity from both the press and the general public. Marie Curie—the first woman ever to be honoured with a Nobel Prize—caught the attention of the entire world. Science didn't seem so dull anymore. The magical, new element that could disintegrate and give off heat from what was apparently an inexhaustible source was the stuff of a sci-fi novel. And the story's central characters—Marie and Pierre—were besieged by journalists and photographers. The couple could not handle all the fanfare. Marie wrote, 'The shattering of our voluntary isolation was a cause of real suffering for us and had all the effects of disaster'. 'From the intellectual point of view', wrote Pierre, 'it is a question of life or death'. Ironically, Pierre's demise, in the very literal sense, would come sooner than anyone could have expected.

On 19 April 1906, Pierre Curie was run over by a horse-drawn wagon near the Pont Neuf in Paris and killed. Marie's almost mythic collaboration with her husband was over. She mourned her terrible loss by escaping to the lab. Eventually, free of any self-pity, Marie prepared herself to singly face the demands of two young daughters (Eve was born in December, 1904) and her responsibilities as both a professor and a researcher. When she was offered a national pension, she refused it: I am thirty-eight and able to support myself, was her answer. She did, however, accept the Sorbonne's offer to succeed Pierre as head of the laboratory. Two years later, in 1908, she was elected a full professor, becoming the first woman to hold a chair at the Sorbonne.

The next several years for Marie would mark another period of relentless hard work and refusal to accept defeat, ever the fundamental aspect of her character. The difference, this time around, was that by now her life was fully in the public eye. While she was attending high-profile conferences and accepting honours in her own right from around the world, there were some who still had a hard time with a woman of high rank in the sphere of science. Marie's greatest honour, in 1911, was a second Nobel Prize, this time in Chemistry. Another important honour would be an invitation to the first Solvay Conference with the world's leading physicists, including Einstein, Poincaré and Planck. But 1911 was also one of the darkest years in Marie's life, thanks to two smear campaigns driven by a French press caught up in the dark currents of prejudice against women, anti-Semitism and xenophobia.

IRÈNE JOLIOT-CURIE

(1897–1956) was a French scientist and daughter of acclaimed scientists Marie and Pierre Curie. In 1935 she and her husband Frédéric Joliot-Curie received the Nobel Prize for Chemistry, making her the second woman after her mother to receive a Nobel Prize for Science, and her family the most awarded by the Nobel Prize committee—with three awards shared between Irène and her parents. In 1936 Irène, and two others, became the first women to serve in the French Parliament, Irène becoming Undersecretary of State for Scientific Research (although women in France did not get the vote until 1944).

The year would begin with Marie being denied election to the French Academy of Sciences. Her brilliant scientific merits took a back seat to unfounded rumours that Pierre's research had given her a free ride and that she might be Jewish, among other discrediting accusations. Deeply wounded, Marie prohibited the Academy from publishing any of her work for ten years.

GERTY CORI

(1896–1957) was an American biochemist, raised in Czechoslovakia, who was awarded her medical degree in Prague in 1920. She worked with her husband, mainly studying the workings of metabolism. In 1947 she became the first woman to win the Nobel Prize in Physiology or Medicine, and the first American woman to win a Nobel Prize in the sciences.

In November, it would be her private life to figure front and centre and as fair game for the press, when the anti-Semitic *Petit Journal* ran, on 5 November, a front-page story under the headline 'A Romance in a Laboratory' publicising a love affair between Marie Curie and fellow physicist Paul Langevin. Day after day Marie had to run the gauntlet in the newspapers: a Polish, Jewish (purportedly but untrue) researcher supported by French scientists was a home wrecker who had torn a father of four from his family with 'the fires of radium'. The details of the affair, if overblown, were essentially accurate. While Langevin and a journalist who was especially antagonistic toward Marie held a duel (which would turn out to be an emotional but bloodless 'affair of honour'), Marie issued a statement in the less hostile *Le Temps*, declaring 'all intrusions of the press and of the public into my private life as abominable'. That same day, Marie received word from Stockholm that she had been awarded the Nobel Prize in Chemistry, 'in recognition of … the advancement of chemistry by the discovery of the elements radium and polonium, [and] by the isolation of radium'. In scientific circles, Marie's discovery was considered the greatest event in chemistry since the discovery of oxygen. However, the news was completely overshadowed by the love scandal that shook France. It took enormous effort for Marie to give her Nobel speech on 11 December. Afterward, she collapsed and sank into deep depression. A whole year passed before she could begin work anew.

Valuable efforts continue

When a reinvigorated Marie went back to her lab at the Sorbonne, in late 1912, she decided to step up a push for more funding for her research. She managed to get something better: a state-of-the-art facility devoted exclusively to the study of radioactivity. The Radium Institute was completed in 1914, just before the outbreak of World War I. Marie's work with the Institute would have to be put on hold, but that didn't mean she was about to sit back and wait, doing nothing. Promptly putting her prize winnings into war bonds, she would direct her energy to France's war effort.

Seeing the potential for X-rays as a tool for doctors in diagnosing and treating injuries, Marie went about setting up 200 radiology units in hospitals throughout

Marie Curie and Albert Einstein (third and fifth from left in front row) attended the fifth Solvay Conference on Electrons and Photons in 1927.

France and Belgium, and fitting ambulances with portable X-ray equipment (the vehicles would come to be known as *petites Curies*). With her characteristic single-mindedness, she trained young women in X-ray technology and sometimes drove the cars to the front lines herself. By the time the Peace Treaty was signed in 1918, Marie's simple idea had saved the lives of countless soldiers by utterly transforming medical practice at the time.

Uncorrupted by fame, but died from exposure

Now, in view of the potential for the use of radium in medicine, factories for its large-scale production were shooting up in the United States. The Radium Institute became internationally celebrated. Countries around the world owned significant quantities of Marie's precious radium. In comparison, France owned almost no radium, and did little to support Marie's work. This didn't sit well with a prominent American women's magazine editor, Marie 'Missy' Maloney, who interviewed Marie in 1920 and came up with a bold plan. Like Marie, Missy had enormous reserves of strength and stamina under a frail exterior.

After organising one of the largest and most successful research-funding campaigns the world has ever seen, Missy raised $100,000 for the purchase of one gram of pure radium for Marie's research. Marie took her first trip to the United States in May 1921, where she accepted the gram of radium from President Warren G. Harding, in Washington, DC, in front of an excited throng of onlookers. Her second American tour, in 1929, would succeed in equipping the Warsaw Radium Institute, founded in 1925 with her sister Bronislawa as director.

By the end of the 1920s, Marie's health was seriously declining. More than twenty years working with radioactivity had taken its toll on her. She still carried scars from burns on her fingers from handling radium. Cataracts contributed to her failing vision. She was becoming frailer. Nonetheless, before retiring completely, she continued to attend conferences and even wrote a biography of Pierre. In May of 1934, her health finally got the best of her. Accompanied by her daughter Eve, she retired to Sancellemoz, a sanatorium in the mountains of Savoy. At dawn on 4 July 1934, Marie Curie died from aplastic pernicious anemia, due to 'a long accumulation of radiations'.

Marie Curie has been lauded for her 'immortal achievements' and called the 'Copernicus of the world of the small'. Suffering from severe health problems that would have incapacitated the average person, she carried on with her epoch-changing work. Ironically, while radiation was her claim to fame, it was also the very thing that caused her to quietly slip away. Had she known about the dangers of radiation, surely she would have taken precautions. Still, it is hard to imagine Madame Curie *not* choosing uranium's glow, even if it would have meant avoiding dangerous rays and—perhaps even more important to the self-effacing scientist—no more time in the limelight. Albert Einstein is supposed to have remarked that she may have been the only person untouched by fame so deservedly won.

Some sixty years after her death, the remains of the celebrated scientist and her husband were re-interred in the Panthéon in Paris, making Marie Curie the first woman at the memorial dedicated to the 'great men' of France. It would mark the final 'first' for Marie Curie—once again, an honour bestowed for her own outstanding merits.

BERTHA VON SUTTNER

(1843–1914)

All her paths were peace

She wanted to be an opera singer, but used her voice in an even more powerful way. 'Lay down your arms! Tell this to many, many people!' declared Baroness Bertha von Suttner, the first woman Nobel Peace Prize winner, and the first woman to be awarded a Nobel Prize in any category in her own right. They were to be among the last words uttered by someone who had spent her last forty years urging peace.

Tireless Austrian writer turned vigorous activist, Bertha von Suttner became a leading figure in peace activism at the turn of the twentieth century with the publication of her anti-war novel, Die Waffen nieder! (Lay Down Your Arms!) *in 1889. Bertha continued her efforts as a public speaker and played a key role in the formation of the first Hague Peace Conference and the Nobel Peace Prize. For her efforts in the peace movement, she received the Nobel Peace Prize in 1905.*

In her youth, however, Bertha, born Countess Kinsky, was not focused on fighting war. She came from a family with a long military tradition, and was born shortly after her father died in combat, but had a more personal kind of battle to reconcile: all her training in singing versus not a hint of the talent required to perform professionally. Her mother had gambled away the family's resources, and Bertha needed to find work. So, at the age of twenty-nine, the impoverished Countess Kinsky left the Austro–Hungarian city of Prague for a job as governess to the four daughters of the von Suttner family, in Vienna. But when Baroness von Suttner realised that her youngest son, Arthur, had taken a romantic liking to the new governess (seven years older than he was), Bertha lost her job.

Now thirty-two, Countess Kinsky went to Paris in answer to an advertisement that would change the course of her life: 'A very wealthy, cultured elderly gentleman, living in Paris seeks a lady, also of mature years, well-versed in languages, as secretary'. The elderly gentleman—fourty-two-year-old Alfred Nobel, Swedish millionaire and world-famous maker of explosives—was instantly drawn to this aristocratic (and quadrilingual) applicant. Every afternoon, for eight days, they sat in Nobel's apartment and discussed poetry, art, music, life, love, and how to make war impossible. Theirs was a deep connection that would, alas, not lead to

---

Left: Aristocrat who vigorously opposed the militaristic traditions of her upbringing and class.

marriage (a hope that perhaps Nobel had entertained), for Bertha would go back to Vienna to elope with her young baron, but one that would be sustained by an exchange of many letters up until Nobel's death in 1896.

Bertha spent close to a decade with her husband in exile in the Caucasus, in Russia, together studying, writing, and hatching ideas about combating war. 'War is not necessary to achieve glory', she would write. 'In technology, art, science, charity, everywhere, more beautiful goals than those on the battlefield beckon to ambition.' Delighted to see one of her published articles, Alfred Nobel wrote her a letter: 'I see that your eloquent pleading against the horror of horrors, war, has found its way into the French press'.

When, reconciled with the von Suttner family, Bertha and her husband returned to Europe and met the co-founder of a peace organisation, the impassioned writer was galvanised to tackle a book that she was sure would be controversial at a time when nationalism was high, and war threatened. It would be a book with a clear anti-war message, and that would include, in her words, 'not what I thought, but what I felt, felt passionately'. She wanted it told in the voice of a heroine; it would be a novel. Lay Down Your Arms! ran to more than thirty-five editions and was translated into almost every European language.

The book's spectacular success brought Bertha to the forefront of the peace movement. Russian novelist Leo Tolstoy recognised the potential of Lay Down Your Arms! and compared its influence on the peace movement to the impact of American author Harriet Beecher Stowe's Uncle Tom's Cabin on the anti-slavery movement. Bertha continued to propagate her views in print, writing more novels, articles, letters, and petitions, and starting a peace newsletter. She set up branches of the international peace movement in Austria and Germany. She made public speeches (the first at the 1891 International Peace Congress in Rome) and went on lecture tours, including a six-month trip to America when she was nearly seventy. Though she was only allowed as an observer (and the only woman admitted to the opening ceremony), she took the unofficial spotlight at the First Hague Peace Conference in 1899. She cultivated her aristocratic connections, met President Roosevelt, enlisted the aid of luminaries such as Andrew Carnegie, Theodor Herzl and Alfred Nobel, and raised funds. And it was through her passion and eloquence that Arthur Nobel was persuaded, in 1892, to add a Peace award to his other awards. Thirteen years later, after

Arthur Nobel had already passed away, Bertha von Suttner would become the first woman Peace laureate, and the first woman to receive any Nobel Prize unshared with a man.

Bertha was described as a powerful lady, who could 'move not only mountains but also emperors and kings'. Sadly, just a week after her death, the assassination of the heir to the Austrian empire launched the Great War, and a world where peace was the next sensible step in humankind's progress to higher good was over. In spite of it all, she showed the way to a world that 'could be', and can be.

When naysayers would denounce the peace movement as unrealistic, Bertha von Suttner would always rise to her feet. Her efforts were made, and she made her mark, through a strong practical intelligence and a personal charisma of which she was fully aware. Indeed, it may truly be said of this great woman that 'all her paths were peace'. And if she could speak to us today, her message would surely be the same: lay down your arms!

Die Waffen nieder!, *published in 1889, was translated into numerous languages.*

DOROTHY LEVITT (1882–UNKNOWN)

By land and by sea, the fastest woman around

The Napier sliced through the water, sending up an enormous rooster tail that continually drenched Dorothy and her co-pilot and engineman Selwyn Edge. People on both sides of the river cheered and waved as they whizzed by. The 50 hp engine shook every bone in her body as it furiously cranked out the 800 rpm that drove the propeller. Dorothy struggled to keep the sleek 12.2-metre, steel-hulled launch in the centre of the narrow river as she manoeuvred to dodge flotsam and jetsam. As her soggy Biggles-style hat drooped off her head she began to laugh.

The Napier was more than two lengths ahead of any competitor and she could see the spectators crammed along the promenade of the Royal Cork Yacht Club for a glimpse of Dorothy Levitt. Just a week earlier, on 4 July 1903, she had shocked British society by racing at the Southport Speed Trials. Today she was racing in the first powerboat competition in history. This was only her second race and the start of a skyrocketing, gender-bending career that would earn her the title of 'the fastest girl on Earth'.

Sheer delight: A 1903 London newspaper presented
Dorothy Levitt at the controls of a 12 hp Gladiator.

Wholly deserving of the term 'pioneer', Dorothy Levitt paved the way for many more famous women racers on the land, sea and in the air. A giant of early motor racing from the day she first burst onto the scene at the Southport Speed Trials, she set new records and shattered existing ones year after year.

In 1904, she raced the Hereford 1000-mile (1600 kilometres) race and, in the following year, established the longest drive achieved by a lady driver—330 kilometres. And in 1906, her crowning glory, Dorothy broke the woman's world speed record at a then unbelievable 154 kilometres per hour.

She became a leading exponent of a 'women's right to motor'. In 1909 she wrote and published *The Woman and the Car: A Chatty Little Handbook for Women Who Motor or Want to Motor*. She wrote articles and lectured to encourage women to take up driving. In this regard her accomplishments went far beyond sports. She was the epitome of a new kind of twentieth century woman, breaking the bonds of body and mind that had kept Victorian ladies in the parlour. Racing gave her the feeling of freedom without limitations. Her presence on the water, road and racetrack sent a powerful message to all women—'anything is possible now'.

From tea to tires

Born in 1882, Dorothy Levitt's earliest years are largely undocumented, but it is believed that she was the daughter of Jacob Levi, a tea merchant in London. Records indicate that her given name was Elizabeth.

At the turn of the century, Britain was in the midst of a colossal economic and social shift and Dorothy embodied this transformational energy. A new merchant class was emerging and the shopkeeper was the cornerstone. One can imagine this young woman working in her family's shop on a bustling street in Covent Gardens or other fashionable centre of London. However, her family also enjoyed a more bucolic home in the West Country. Here Dorothy became an accomplished rider to hounds as well as a good shot with rifle and gun.

Dorothy's father had anglicised his name to John Levit by the 1901 British census and it appears Dorothy added a 't' when she set out to make her own way in the world. A journalist tells the story of a family friend with a motorcar who visited the Levitts' country home in 1902. Within a few days Dorothy had become acquainted with the intricacies of the motor and the art of driving as well. She and the family friend attended a country competition nearby. She drove with such instinctive prowess that it caught the attention of Selwyn Edge, who offered her a job at Napier & Sons motor works in London. Selwyn F. Edge was already emerging as a force in the motor-racing world and Dorothy caught his eye and his imagination. It seems Mr Edge was looking for a way to promote his revolutionary petrol engines and saw the charming Miss Levitt as the way to do this. Their collaboration began with a city driving lesson.

Dorothy connected with her destiny the moment her hands touched the steering wheel. After only one lesson at Hampton Court she took to the streets of London, dashing down some of the most congested thoroughfares in the world. This fiery 'chauffeuse', as female drivers were termed, challenged the horse-and-buggy traffic that dominated London at the time. They were the 'competition', and if she were anything, Dorothy was a competitor. However, it soon became apparent that this young woman belonged on motor-racing courses, not city streets.

On 6 November 6 1903 she found herself appearing before the magistrate at the Marlborough Street Assizes in Hyde Park. The court reported that Miss Levitt 'had driven at a terrific pace' and, when stopped, apparently said she 'would like to drive over every policeman and wished [she] had run over the sergeant and killed him'. It appears that her intentions had not changed much since the incident, because she had been advised not to appear in person. The Honourable Mr Denman fined her £5, with 2 shillings costs. Other court appearances, nonetheless, worked in her favour. Indeed, it might be said that she was a harbinger of the automobile insurance industry.

In 1903 Dorothy and her friend, Hena Frankton, claimed and received damages of £35 from the owner of a horse-drawn vehicle that collided with her motorcar. Dorothy's victories, however, were not to be in courtrooms, but on motor-racing courses throughout Great Britain and Europe.

AUGUSTA AND ADELINE VAN BUREN

(1884–unknown and 1889–unknown) were a duo of pioneering motorcyclists, who rode across the United States in 1916, from New York to Los Angeles, becoming the first motorcyclists to scale the 4300 metre Pikes Peak in the Colorado Rockies in the process. Descended from President Martin Van Buren and with a reputation as New York society girls, the Van Buren sisters set out on their epic journey to protest against women's limited opportunities in war efforts—America was on the verge of entering World War I—and by extension in the American political process.

Smashing records and barriers at 154 kph

By the time Dorothy Levitt made her debut at the Southport Speed Trials on 4 July 1903, she knew that she was addicted to speed. The crowd that had gathered around the starting line near the city centre drew a collective breath when she drove into the line-up in her 12 hp Gladiator. She wore a loose coverall coat that reached to her ankles and a matching veil and hat that sat upon crimped hair. She did not look like a racer. She was medium height, slim with what was described as 'fine and diminutive features'. Her green-grey eyes twinkled with a subtle mischief.

Trials were intended to test automotive engines and designs, but on this day, the Southport Speed Trials tested the norms and mores about a woman's place in the world. Dorothy won her class and opened the door to countless other victories over the next six years that would put women in the driver's seat.

Eight days later she, along with Selwyn Edge, would pilot the Napier launch in the inaugural British International Harmsworth Trophy race, which continues to this day. The publisher of the influential *Daily Mail*, Sir Alfred Harmsworth, created the event as 'a way of bringing marine motors and design of launch hulls to a state of perfection'. Many boats were far from perfect, and several would not even start. However, it was a perfect Sunday afternoon. Curious spectators gathered at Cork Harbour, Ireland and all along the 14-kilometer river route to witness not only the first powerboat race in history, but the first woman to drive a powerboat.

The Napier, which was formed from 20-gauge rolled steel, sported a 50 hp engine and a novel three-blade propeller that allowed it to easily win the contest. As Dorothy headed toward the Royal Yacht that marked the finish line, she twisted the wheel sharply, sending up a spray that rained down over the crowd. The Napier ran twice around the Royal Yacht as King Edward VII and Queen Alexandra bowed their acknowledgment to the craft and its bold and daring female pilot.

ALICE HUYLER RAMSEY

(1887–1983) was the first woman, in the summer of 1909, to cross the United States by automobile. Twenty-one years old and president of the Women's Motoring Club of New Jersey, she set off from New York in a 30 hp Maxwell and arrived in San Francisco fifty-nine days later. Over the next sixty-six years, Ramsey drove across the country more than thirty times. On 17 October 2000, she became the first woman inducted into the US Automotive Hall of Fame.

Early the following year, in 1904, Dorothy Levitt entered the Hereford 1000 Mile Trial. Only mechanical problems, which she repaired herself, prevented her from winning. This plucky motoring maven set another record for the longest drive achieved by a lady driver on 29 March 1905. She drove a De Dion-Bouton motorcar from its showroom on Marlborough Street in London to the Adelphi Hotel in Liverpool. She completed the 330 kilometres in eleven hours, averaging 32 kilometres per hour. She travelled without the aid of a mechanic, but was accompanied by an official observer. She was on her way to becoming an icon, and she frequently dressed the part. She often wore colourful dresses that she tied to her ankles to prevent the hem from flaring as she breezed by. She also carried with her a loaded Colt revolver and her pet Pomeranian, Dodo. This 330-kilometre drive required more than driving prowess, endurance, and mechanical know-how. Long-distance drivers had to be resourceful, navigating the byways of England before there were road maps or petrol stations. Petrol was obtained from hardware stores and chemists. Directions came from local villagers along the way.

Month after month, Dorothy entered every trial or race she could. In 1905, she drove an 80 hp Napier at the annual speed trials in Brighton, winning her class and the coveted Autocar Challenge Trophy. Once again, those who thought she would not have the strength to control the car at high speeds were proved wrong.

In 1906, Dorothy Levitt went into the history books for all time. When her 6-cylinder Napier motorcar finished two passes along a road outside Blackpool, the official stop watch revealed that she had broken the record for the fastest speed achieved by a wheeled vehicle on land. She broke the women's world speed record driving an astonishing 154 kph. The *Daily Mail* dubbed her 'the fastest girl on Earth'. Her record would stand for another seven years.

KITTY O'NEIL

(1946–) is a stunt car driver from Texas who in 1977 clocked the fastest quarter mile in automotive history, 3.22 seconds at 396 miles per hour, driving a hydrogen peroxide-powered rocket dragster. The record, however, does not officially stand as the drive did not occur under official conditions. O'Neil, deaf since she was four months old, has also succeeded as a Hollywood stuntwoman and high-speed water-skiing champion along the way.

Following pages: Dorothy Levitt in a 26 hp Napier at Brooklands in 1908; she was not allowed to race there.

Dorothy was now a celebrity. Her success began to attract other women into the world of motor sports, and garnered her invitations from society's notables. She travelled thousands of miles a year for competitions and recreation. She lived what has been described as a 'gay whirlwind life'—a weekend at Ascot, a hunt in Goodwood, boating in the azure waters off the sunny Riviera coast. One day London, the next day Paris.

In late 1906, she won the 'ladies record' at the Shelsley Walsh Speed Hill Climb, making the run in 92.4 seconds. Interestingly enough, this was also faster than any male competitor.

Then in 1907, Dorothy Levitt hit the remnants of a formerly huge barrier that had been thrown up against women in British culture. Hugh Locke King, a racing fanatic, built the first professionally designed circular racetrack in Britain on his Surrey Estate. The Brooklands, as it was called, was a 4.9-kilometre track with curved banks that swept 9 metres into the air. It had a concrete amphitheatre and seating for hundreds of spectators. The precursor to today's huge NASCAR tracks, the Brooklands quickly became the coliseum of motor sports in Britain. Dorothy was first in line to race at the Brooklands, knowing that the improved track would allow her to set and break even more records. However she, and all women, were banned.

Not to be stopped, Dorothy set her sights across the Channel and beyond. In October 1907 she won her class in the Gaillon Hill Climb in France. The following year was even bigger for this singular woman.

In 1908, she walked away with the Prinz Heinrich Trophy at the Herkomer Trophy Trials in Germany, the best in class prize at the Aston Clinton Hill Climb, and competed in the prestigious Côte du Calvaire Hill Climb in Trouville, France. Her string of victories across the Continent solidified her reputation as a top competitor—period. Her on-the-track successes, together with her articles and lectures, allowed her to break through the final barrier at the Brooklands. She returned triumphantly to that celebrated racetrack and in her wake marched Gwenda Hawkes, Mildred Bruce and Kay Petre, among others.

Toast of London, first lady of motoring

Dorothy's fame prompted offers from throughout Britain and across Europe and North America as well. She travelled continuously, judging and attending races, although not all of them were motor related. In 1906 the Aero Club sponsored an event in the nature of a fox and hounds contest. In this case the contestants were hot-air balloons, with one playing the role of the fox, and the other hotter-than-air craft chasing after.

In just three short years she had risen from relative obscurity to being the toast of London. She had hosts of friends, including those in the upper circles of society as well as more bohemian members of the art and literary community. She became an inveterate first-nighter, appearing in lush, ravishing gowns.

She resided in a modest West End flat, its distinctive interior belying its exterior. Her treasure was a Louis XIV drawing room. Her travels and experiences allowed her to develop an eclectic taste and her Flemish dining room created a casual ambience for the luncheon parties for which she became famous.

Over time, cheering racing fans gave way to applauding audiences. Her accomplishments and notoriety gave her access to the public ear, and she had plenty to say. She had her own column in the *Daily Graphic* newspaper, and wrote countless articles on motoring. A frequent theme was the 'accursed' pedestrian. 'Recent cases declare that it lies with drivers to keep clear of pedestrians who have the right to walk on highways at their own pace, whether paralytics or cripples. Dogs, chickens and other domestic animals at large on the highway are not pedestrians however, and if one is driving at a regulation speed, one is not responsible for their untimely end.'

In 1909 Dorothy Levitt published *The Woman and the Car: A Chatty Little Handbook for All Women Who Motor or Who Want to Motor*. This well-illustrated volume provided comprehensive advice on everything from what kind of car to purchase, to motoring manners, and the twelve commonest breakdowns and repairs. She is credited with inventing the rear-view mirror in one of her driving tips: 'If you have a closed-in car, see to it that there is a mirror attached to the dash-board so that the chauffeur can see what is behind him'.

While her book, lectures, columns and articles always focused on the pragmatic side of motoring, by her very presence she became the world's strongest advocate for

---

DANICA PATRICK

(1982–), in 2008, at the age of twenty-six, became the first woman ever to win an IndyCar race, the Indy Japan 300, demolishing the male stranglehold on modern-day professional motor sports. In 2005 she was named rookie of the year on the IndyCar circuit, and in 2009 she placed third in the Indy 500, the highest place for a woman in IndyCar history.

putting women behind the wheel. Without a doubt her single-handed effort created a movement wherein the fairer sex was able to exercise what might be seen, in her time, as one of the largest freedoms.

Unfortunately, little was recorded about Dorothy Levitt after 1909. It is known that she began taking an interest in flying and attempted to qualify as a pilot at the Hubert Latham School of Aviation near Reims in France. There is probably little doubt, given her tenacity and her propensity for the mechanical, that she eventually took to the air somewhere. And it would seem fitting that she should conquer all of the earthly domains—land, sea and air.

————◦———

If Dorothy Levitt had a motto, it would have to have been 'speed is my forte'. Although comfortable in polite society, she was in her element when she was speeding down a country road with her long brown hair waving in the breeze. When she was presented to King Edward VII after her 1903 boating victory at Cork Harbour, he complemented her skilful driving. She replied, 'I prefer steering a really fast motorcar to anything else in the world'.

Dorothy Levitt came into the world at a time when women were obliged to live within a paternalistic ideal that barred them from most professions and minimised their political and cultural influence. But at the age of twenty-one she burst onto the scene in the driver's seat of a motorcar appropriately named a Gladiator. The barriers she shattered went far beyond those of distance, time or speed. Her accomplishments tore through the fabric of society and transformed archaic notions of who a woman was and what she was capable of accomplishing.

Most pictures of Dorothy Levitt show her in, or standing next to, an automobile. This seems more than appropriate, for the motorcar reflected her dynamic personality and values.

Today's teenagers long for the day when they get their driver's licence because they know that a car is their portal to personal freedom. And it is that same knowledge that beckoned Dorothy Levitt a century earlier—freedom without boundaries.

Right: Bertha's demure exterior concealed a practical and intrepid soul.

BERTHA BENZ
(1849–1944)

*Inventor's feisty wife finagles
world's first road trip*

Bertha proved that her husband's invention was both useful and reliable.

If it weren't for her gumption, who knows how long it would have taken for the automobile to replace horse and carriage as the favoured mode of transportation for long-distance journeys? Thanks to Bertha Benz in the driver's seat—literally—of the world's first engined car, and her historic 105 kilometre drive, we can all breathe easier cruising our favorite highways and byways.

Wife and business partner of brilliant German inventor Karl Benz, Bertha was the kind of woman who acted on instinct. In 1888, while her husband tinkered away on his new invention—a three-wheeled wooden vehicle boasting a 2.5 horsepower engine—Bertha was itching to show the world the benefits of this new 'horseless carriage'. So, on the morning of 5 August, Bertha quietly slipped out of bed, so as not to disturb her husband, and crept out of the house with her two teenage sons. They stealthily entered Karl's workshop out the back, and rolled the fruit of his hard labour right out the door.

Karl Benz's Patent Motorwagen automobile—roofless, hoodless, horseless, with two back wheels and one in the front, a long handle for steering instead of a wheel, and powered by a single-cylinder petrol-fuelled engine—had come a long way since the inventor had registered it two years before. Still, Mr Benz believed there were more improvements to be made, and he hadn't yet considered introducing it to the general public. Bertha, on the other hand, was sure the time had come for her husband's invention to make its debut. Her plan was to get into that powered tricycle and take a long-distance drive, demonstrating just how useful and reliable it could be for daily use.

Mother and sons set off from the workshop in Mannheim, in southwestern Germany. The journey over the hills of the Black Forest to the town of Bertha's birth, Pforzheim, was not without its complications, but the adventurous automobilists were dedicated to their cause. Short on spare parts (and with mechanic shops and petrol stations non-existent), Bertha fortunately had plenty of ingenuity. When the engine needed to be cooled, Bertha and her boys gathered water from village wells and puddles along the roads. When the brake lining wore down, they visited a shoemaker to have pieces of leather nailed to the brake blocks. When the chains broke, they found a blacksmith who was able to fix them. Bertha even cleaned a clogged fuel pipe with a hairpin, and mended a frayed ignition cable with a piece of her garter belt. In Wiesloch, several kilometres south of Heidelberg, the car ran out of petrol and Bertha sent one of her sons into the local pharmacy to buy Ligroin, a petroleum ether used as a stain remover at the time; the boy walked out with the entire stock, enough to fill the vehicle with 2 litres of fuel.

On the last leg of the trip, with the sun setting behind rolling hills, our determined driver came up against one final challenge: a slope that was just too steep for the car to climb. It took the exertions of the boys and additional help from a farmer pushing from behind to get the vehicle to the top of the hill. Bertha and her boys arrived in Pforzheim, utterly spent, grimy, but grinning from ear to ear knowing they had prevailed. Their novel journey—the longest distance ever driven in an automobile at the time—gave the motorcar the breakthrough it needed. The rest is history.

Bertha lived to be ninety-five. Her historic journey is celebrated as a public holiday in Germany. In 2008, the Bertha Benz Memorial Route was officially signposted, from Mannheim to Pforzheim and back, passing through the cities of Ladenburg, Schriesheim, Heidelberg, Wiesloch—with its now famous pharmacy, aka the world's first filling/petrol station—Bruchsal, Karlsruhe, Bretten, Hockenheim and Schwetzingen. The same year, in May, a Bertha Benz monument was unveiled in Pforzheim to commemorate 120 years since this famous traveller made her mark not only on the German landscape but on the world at large.

Right: Outside the Harley-Davidson dealership in Salt Lake City, Utah in 1905.

AVIS AND EFFIE HOTCHKISS

(UNKNOWN AND 1894–1966)

❧

Mother—daughter duo who
made motorcycle history

At the age of twenty, Effie Hotchkiss wanted nothing more than to break out of her Wall Street job as a bank clerk and see America. The year was 1915 and Ford Motor Company had just reached a major milestone rolling its one-millionth automobile off the Michigan assembly line. But Effie wasn't interested in travelling by Model T. She was going to take to the open road on a motorcycle—something she had been dreaming about since she was sixteen.

By now, the petrol engine had revolutionised travel. America's vastness, at the turn of the century, seemed to shrink a little with each passing year. Still, much of the nation was regarded as frontier, and to traverse long stretches of unpaved territory was a bold and risky undertaking, especially for a woman alone. So, when Effie purchased a 1915 three-speed V-Twin Harley-Davidson with a small family inheritance, and set her sights on the West Coast, her mother, Avis, had strong reservations about letting her go. Effie persisted, and rather than dig in her heels with a final 'no', Avis gave in—on one condition: she got to go along.

Effie and Avis Hotchkiss crossed America on motorbike from coast to coast in 1915.

Rigging a sidecar to the bike, mother and daughter would ride the Harley—Effie at the controls, Avis in the sidecar—from Brooklyn, New York to California to attend the Panama–Pacific International Exposition, and then return home. It was a rigorous trip, kicking off on 2 May 1915. They had to navigate less than desirable roads and trailblaze through dangerous land. They had to be on guard for preying bandits, cowboys, and Indians. They had to endure torrential rain, floods, mud, rattlesnake-infested byways, and extreme cold and heat—such as when they crossed the San Marcos Pass, in California, where temperatures rose to 49° Centigrade. Effie also had to use some ingenuity and prove her worth as a mechanic many times along the way. On one occasion, in New Mexico, they ran out of inner tubes. The women cut down a blanket, rolled it into a doughnut shape and stuffed it into the tire until they could replenish their stock of inner tubes. According to a 1915 Harley-Davidson dealer magazine, the women managed it all 'with a shrug of their shoulders'.

In August, the intrepid Effie and Avis dipped their wheels, and toes, into the Pacific Ocean at San Francisco, and made a splash on the front pages of newspapers across the country. They were the first women to cross the United States on a motorcycle. Taking barely any time to rest, they began the return leg. But before heading back east, Effie made another impact: on a street in San Francisco, she met her future husband when she ran him over as he stepped unsuspectingly in front of her moving bike. Avis and Effie Hotchkiss returned to their home in Brooklyn in October 1915, having crossed the deserts of Nevada and Utah, and having cruised through the cities of Reno, Salt Lake City, Omaha, Davenport, Chicago, and Milwaukee. Their round trip logged more than 4400 kilometres.

Effie declared that she never intended to make news, but just 'wanted to see America and considered that the three-speed Harley-Davidson for myself and sidecar for mother and the luggage was best suited for the job'. With their historic road trip, Effie and Avis had ridden their way not only into the record books, but into the hearts and minds of plenty of Americans.

AMELIA EARHART (1897–1937)

American aviatrix mesmerised the world

The weekend crowd was jammed into the airfield. Amelia and Muriel found a spot away from the throng, off to one side in an isolated clearing, and turned their expectant faces up toward a cloudless, blue sky. The stunt pilot was wowing the crowd with another feat of aerial daredevilry, turning his Jenny biplane upside down into a loop. Cheers erupted. Then suddenly, the pilot put the Jenny into a dive, aiming straight at Amelia and her sister. Muriel dashed for safety. The small red plane buzzed precariously closer, but Amelia stood her ground, swept by fear and exhilaration. Common sense told her that if something went wrong with the mechanism, or if the pilot lost control, he, the airplane, and she would all be rolled up in a ball together. Still she didn't budge. The plane swooped by and something inside Amelia awakened. 'Some day', she thought, 'I will ride one of these devil machines'.

Advised to hide her 'gap-toothed' smile, Amelia kept her lips together in formal photographs.

On 28 December 1920, Amelia Earhart paid a professional pilot by the name of Frank Hawks (who would one day become famous as a record-breaking aviator) one dollar for a ten-minute ride over Hollywood, California that would forever change her life. 'By the time I had got two or three hundred feet [61 or 91 metres] off the ground', she said, 'I knew I had to fly'.

Nothing ever stirred Amelia as totally as soaring into the sky. At the age of thirty-one, she became the first woman to be flown across the Atlantic Ocean, when she accompanied pilot Wilmer Stutz in the Fokker F7 *Friendship* on a twenty-hour-plus flight from Newfoundland to Wales. After the *Friendship* flight, Amelia was often compared to Charles Lindbergh (the first solo pilot and the first American to cross the Atlantic non-stop in a fixed-wing aircraft, and winner of the much-publicised Orteig prize for flying first from New York to Paris). The parallel distressed her; she considered his role heroic and her own no more important than 'a sack of potatoes'. Four years later, she was determined to make the flight, again. But this time, she would pilot her own plane.

In 1932, she was the first woman to fly solo non-stop across the Atlantic, travelling from Newfoundland to Ireland faster than anyone on record, a feat for which she received the Distinguished Flying Cross from the US Congress, the Cross of Knight of the Legion of Honour from the French government, and the Gold Medal of the National Geographic Society from President Herbert Hoover.

Over the course of her life, Amelia set such an impressive number of records, and broke so many stereotypes about women, that her place in history was assured even before her plane disappeared over the Pacific.

'Aviation caught me'

Amelia Earhart was not raised to be 'a nice little girl'. Born in Atchison, Kansas at the turn of the century, she often shocked neighbours with her unconventional antics. Her progressive mother encouraged both Amelia and her younger sister, Muriel, to wear knickerbockers—baggy knee-length trousers that were essentially second-generation 'bloomers', the controversial 'reform costume' first worn by women activists a few decades earlier—even though other girls in the neighbourhood were still sporting dresses. Amelia climbed trees, 'belly-slammed' her sled to start it downhill and hunted rats with a .22 rifle. By all accounts, she was a regular tomboy. She was also fascinated by mechanical things, and she once designed a trap to catch stray chickens. When she was ten years old, she cobbled together a ramp fashioned after a roller-coaster she had seen on a trip to St Louis and secured it to the roof of the family tool-shed. Amelia's well-documented first flight ended dramatically. She emerged from the broken wooden box that had served as a sled with a bruised lip, torn clothes and a 'sensation of exhilaration'. She exclaimed, 'Oh, it's just like flying!' But not long afterward, when Amelia caught sight of her first aircraft at the Iowa State Fair, a rickety old 'flivver' that she described as 'a thing of rusty wire and wood and not at all interesting', she turned down her father's offer to take a flight, and hightailed it back to the ferris wheel—in that way satisfying her love of heights.

> ## SOPHIE BLANCHARD
>
> (1778–1819) was a French aeronautical pioneer who became the first woman to pilot her own balloon. On her third-ever ascent she flew solo from Toulouse, and became the first woman to work as a professional balloonist, gaining fame across Europe. She was also the first woman to be killed in an aviation accident. A favourite with Emperor Napoleon (on the birth of his son she flew a balloon over Paris and scattered leaflets announcing the birth), she also experimented with parachutes, parachuting small dogs, and on other occasions baskets of pyrotechnics, from her balloon.

It wasn't until she was in her twenties, working as a volunteer nurse's aide at the University of Toronto's Spadina Military Hospital, and spending weekends with her sister, that Amelia would discover her fascination with flight. Barnstorming was fast becoming one of the most popular forms of entertainment, with stunt pilots performing daring loop-the-loop and barrel-roll manoeuvres with old warplanes. At one of these crowd-pleasing flying exhibitions in Toronto, Amelia stood transfixed as a World War I veteran pilot 'looped and rolled and spun and finished his little bag of tricks' and, probably bored, 'felt there was nothing left to do but watch the people on the ground running as he swooped close to them'. Amelia held her ground, but she was undeniably moved. 'I did not understand it at the time', she later recalled, 'but I believe that little red airplane said something to me as it swished by'.

Amelia took her first flying lesson on 3 January 1921. Her instructor was Neta 'Snooky' Snook, a 'top-notch flier' and one of the first women to get a pilot's licence in Canada. Amelia noted, 'She dresses and talks like a man and can do everything around a plane that a man can do'. To finance her lessons, she got her first paying job, sorting mail for the telephone company in Los Angeles, where she was living with her parents.

From then on, the family scarcely saw her. She spent every non-working hour at the airfield on the outskirts of town, learning the name and function of every mechanical part and crawling under the Curtiss Canuck training plane to make repairs, emerging covered in grease and grinning from ear to ear. At last the time came for her solo. Amelia took to the sky in a Model K Kinner Airster biplane, rose 1525 metres and, as she put it, 'played around a little and came back'. Her landing was less than perfect, but the young aviatrix was thrilled. 'It's so breathtakingly beautiful up there', she said. 'I want to fly whenever I can.'

Flying, which had begun as a casual interest, was rapidly developing into an obsession for Amelia. Even two crash landings—the first one leaving her suspended upside down by her safety belt, and the second flinging her from the cockpit—were not enough to deter her. In 1922, she gave up her plans to return to college and got her pilot's licence from the Fédération Aéronautique Internationale (the only agency that issued licences at the time). Fortunately, Amy Earhart was an enthusiastic supporter of her daughter's novel pastime, declaring that when Amelia did things, 'she always did them very carefully ... She thought it out and her mind was quick'. For Amelia's twenty-fifth birthday, Amy and Muriel pooled some of their money with Amelia's savings, and put the lot into the purchase of Amelia's first plane. The second-hand Kinner Airster was a two-seater biplane painted bright yellow. Amelia named her plane the *Canary*, and used it to set her first women's record by rising to an altitude of 4260 metres.

> ## PRINCESS EUGENIE M. SHAKHOVSKAYA
>
> (1889–unknown) was Russia's second female pilot, and possibly the world's first female military pilot after she applied directly to the Tsar to fly in war missions. It is likely that she flew artillery and reconnaissance missions on the northwestern front during World War I, and after the revolution joined the Red air force.

In the summer of 1924, when her parents ended their twenty-three-year marriage and the three Earhart women decided to move to Massachusetts, Amelia revved herself up for a cross-country flight, intending to take her mother along. But Amy Earhart would have none of it. And so the *Canary* was traded in for the *Yellow Peril*, regrettably not another winged vehicle but a bright yellow Kissel sportscar. Far from the airfields of California, Amelia threw herself into social work at a Boston community center, teaching English as a second language. But her love of flying never waned. In September 1927 she wrote to fellow aviatrix Ruth Nichols proposing they establish an association of women aviators. Amelia noted, 'Personally I am a social worker who flies for sport. I cannot claim to be a feminist, but do rather enjoy seeing women tackling all kinds of new problems—new for them, that is'. It would be the launch of a great friendship, but business plans would have to wait.

One afternoon in April 1928, Amelia received a phone call that would change her life forever. Hilton Railey, a public relations man who represented aviation notables, including Ruth Nichols, asked her, 'Miss Earhart, would you be interested in doing something important for the cause of aviation?' Sceptically, she asked what. His answer: 'Fly across the Atlantic'. The flight aboard the trimotor Fokker F7 *Friendship* would be a goodwill gesture between the United States and Great Britain. Two expert male pilots had been hired to make the flight, but they wanted 'an American girl of the right image' to go along, too. It was an adventure impossible for Amelia to refuse.

All preparations were kept secret, to avoid a transatlantic race against any potential competitors. Amelia didn't say a word about it to anyone—although she did make sure to leave farewell letters for her family, just in case she didn't return. To Muriel she wrote, 'If I don't succeed, I shall be happy to pop off in the midst of such an adventure'. On 17 June 1928, Amelia joined pilot Wilmer 'Bill' Stultz and co-pilot/mechanic Louis E. 'Slim' Gordon at Trepassey, Newfoundland. The *Friendship* didn't take off on the first try. Amelia noted, 'I was crowded in the cabin with a stop watch in my hand … and with my eyes glued on the air speed indicator as it slowly climbed … Fifty, fifty-five, sixty. We were off at last'. Nearly twenty hours and forty minutes later, the team spotted 'out of the mists … a blue shadow … It was land!' Amelia recalled, 'I think Slim yelled … Bill permitted himself a smile'. The *Friendship*, specially fitted with pontoons for a water landing, touched down safely in the harbour at Burry Port, Wales. Since Lindbergh's famed flight, fifty-five people in eighteen planes—hailing from both sides of the Atlantic—had attempted to make the crossing; only three flights had made it. Now, with the success of the *Friendship* flight, three names could be added to the short list of people who had crossed the Atlantic by air. And for the first time one of those names belonged to a woman.

Railey, who had flown from England, greeted Amelia ashore. 'How does it feel to be the first woman to have flown the Atlantic?' Smiling, and shrugging her shoulders, she said, 'Like a sack of potatoes. Bill did all the flying. I was just baggage'.

Following pages: 1932—Broadway salutes 'Lady Lindy', the first woman to fly across the Atlantic Ocean solo.

JACQUELINE COCHRAN

(1906–1980) was an American aviator who had a distinguished career during World War II and was a key instigator in the establishment of the Women's Auxiliary Army Corps and the Women Airforce Service Pilots. Among Cochran's many flying firsts, in 1960 she broke the sound barrier by flying an F-86 over Rogers Dry Lake, California, at the speed of 1049.8 kilometres per hour. Eleven years later, she flew at a speed of 2300 kilometres per hour, more than twice the speed of sound.

Regardless, Amelia Earhart was an instant celebrity. Her name made banner headlines around the world, and she quickly became known as 'Lady Lindy', the female counterpart to Charles Lindbergh, one of the world's best-known celebrities since he made the first solo flight across the Atlantic just over a year earlier, in May 1927. Stultz and Gordon were virtually ignored, while the world reacted with stunned amazement to the fact that a woman had managed to make the treacherous crossing in one piece and utterly unshaken. It just seemed too incredible to believe. When the *Friendship* crew returned to the United States they were greeted with a ticker-tape parade in New York and a reception held by President Calvin Coolidge at the White House.

But Amelia would not let herself be swept up in all the fanfare. In fact, she was more than a bit embarrassed. She didn't think her role as passenger warranted a reputation as heroine. In the weeks that followed, Amelia persisted in setting the record straight about her part in the venture, giving all the credit to her fellow crewmates. Later, Hilton Railey would recall, 'She remained herself, serious, forthright, no bunk in her makeup. Even in those days, I sensed she would write drama in the skies. Her simplicity would capture people everywhere … in calm pursuit of an end not personal she would achieve greatness'. The legend was born; Amelia Earhart, 'First Lady of the Sky', had become America's flying sweetheart.

America's flying sweetheart

Amelia's life, now, was all about flying—if not necessarily going aloft, then at least talking and writing about it. Publisher George Putnam, who had played a role in preparations for the *Friendship* flight, was now figuring front and centre in Amelia's world. He planned her lecture tours, scheduled her interviews, and offered her a contract to write a book, which was to become *20 Hours, 40 Min: Our Flight in the Friendship*. She wrote for *Cosmopolitan* magazine, demystifying the new world of aviation and encouraging young women to try explore it. Through Putnam's efforts, photographs of Lady Lindy appeared in newspapers and magazines across the country. Amelia's cropped hair became a style copied by thousands of American women. The warm smile, the tousled hair, the well-tailored attire, the cool independent stance had all come to symbolise the independent spirit of modern womanhood.

Still feeling something was fraudulent about her fame, and determined to prove herself worthy of all the attention, in 1929 she got herself to California and entered the first cross-country competition for women, the Santa Monica to Cleveland Women's Air Derby, which would be dubbed the 'Powder Puff Derby' by amused male onlookers. But to the twenty entrants, it was no joke. The winner was to receive $2500. But the real prize, for many of them, was the chance to prove that women had a rightful place in the future of American aviation. Amelia placed third (after losing her turn to take off at the beginning of the final leg when she rescued another participant from a crash), and three months later became the first president of an all-female aviation society, the Ninety-Nines (still in operation today), formed by some of the participants. Topping the agenda was an endeavour that the members believed would erase any public doubt about women in aviation: a solo flight across the Atlantic.

Solo flight across the Atlantic

In February 1931, Putnam started promoting Amelia's career with renewed vigour. The publisher and the aviatrix were newly married. He had proposed to her five times and each time she had responded with a resounding 'no'. 'I'm still unsold on marriage', she wrote to a friend. The sixth time, she handed him an unusual contract, 'brutal in its frankness but beautiful in its honesty', Putnam would note. With characteristic gutsiness, she laid out who she was, how things would be between them and damn the consequences, declaring: 'In our life together, I shall not hold you to any medieval code of faithfulness to me, nor shall I consider myself bound to you similarly'. On 7 February they exchanged vows, but not before Putnam had taken all the words of her contract to heart, including: 'Please let us not interfere with each other's work or play'.

And so, together they worked secretly on plans for Amelia to make a solo flight across the Atlantic. In her twelve years an aviatrix, Amelia had chalked up more than 1000 hours in the air. Just after her *Friendship* flight, she flew from New York City to

Amelia Earhart beside the new Lockheed Vega 5B which she would use to cross the Atlantic.

Los Angeles and back, the first woman to make a solo round trip across the United States. The apex of Amelia's career would be a 3220-kilometre Atlantic crossing. On 20 May 1932, exactly five years after Lindbergh had made his celebrated transatlantic crossing, a slim, thirty-four-year-old woman pilot stepped calmly onto the airfield at Harbour Grace, Newfoundland, with her maps, toothbrush, a thermos of soup and a can of tomato juice under her arm. A red and gold single-engine Lockheed Vega 5B stood near the hangar. At 7.12 pm Amelia was airborne, heading for the British Isles. Hardly anyone in the United States knew she was setting out on this daring adventure, and not a soul in Europe expected her. Strong northerly winds, icy conditions and mechanical problems plagued the flight and forced her to land in a meadow near Londonderry in northern Ireland, 'frightening all the cows in the country' in the process. She asked a lone farmer, 'Where am I?' The man replied, 'In Gallegher's pasture … have you come far?' 'From America', she answered. In fifteen hours and eighteen minutes she had made the crossing—the first woman to accomplish the feat alone, faster than anyone on record, and the only person to fly it twice.

As word of her flight spread, Amelia was lauded by dignitaries and the press and showered with international honours. From London, Lady Nancy Astor, the first woman elected to the British Parliament, wired: 'Come to us and I'll lend you a nightgown'. The US Congress awarded her the Distinguished Flying Cross—the first ever given to a woman. President Herbert Hoover invited her to the White House, where he presented her with the National Geographic Society's coveted Special Gold Medal for distinction in aviation. At the ceremony, he praised her for her 'splendid courage and skill' and placed her 'in spirit with the great pioneering women to whom every generation of Americans has looked up'. Amelia accepted the honour with typical self-effacement, saying, 'I hope the flight has meant something to women in aviation', she said. 'If it has I shall feel justified. I can't claim anything else'.

Passions prevail

By the mid-1930s, Amelia was a one-woman industry. She was writing for women's magazines. She was designing wearable women's clothing. She encouraged flying competitions among women pilots. She put herself on a gruelling lecture circuit—speaking to packed audiences 136 times in 1935 alone, earning $250 a lecture, at a time when the average full-time stenographer was paid $20 a week. She even started two airlines. Responding to Eleanor Roosevelt's interest in flying, she arranged to get the American First Lady a student pilot licence and offered to privately instruct her. (President Franklin D. Roosevelt quickly put the kybosh on that idea.)

Amelia also served as aeronautical adviser and women's career counsellor at the progressive Purdue University, which had a growing aviation department and female student body. In April 1936, Purdue announced that it had raised $50,000 to purchase a 'flying laboratory' for Amelia Earhart. She was anxious to put the Lockheed Electra 10E to work.

As she neared her fortieth birthday, Amelia was ready to take on one last, monumental challenge. She wanted to fly around the world. 'I have a feeling that there is just about one more good flight left in my system, and I hope this trip is it', she said. To organise a trip of such magnitude would require the help of her dear friend and purported lover Eugene Vidal, who held the post of director of the Bureau of Air Commerce (the Federal agency charged with regulating civil aviation), thanks in no small part to Amelia's efforts lobbying President Roosevelt. In fact, not only had Amelia been instrumental in getting Vidal appointed in 1933, but she had helped him keep the job, when FDR—under pressure from certain senators—decided just before the 1936 election that he would replace the director. When Amelia heard about it, she sent a bold and blistering telegram to the First Lady threatening to back out of campaigning for the President if the replacement went through. Within forty-eight hours FDR changed his mind, understanding the repercussions of losing the public support of America's celebrated sweetheart, and Amelia was sending another telegram to her friend Mrs Roosevelt that read, 'Thanks very much. Appreciate your help'.

In February 1937, at a buzzing New York City press conference, Amelia announced her plans for a 46,670 kilometre, round-the-world equatorial flight.

Around the world at the waistline

The first attempt, on 17 March, starting from Oakland, California, on a westerly course to Honolulu, resulted in a disastrous mishap, a crash in Honolulu that required extensive repairs. On 21 May, Amelia tried again; this time she left California going east, to Miami, Florida, making several stops and testing out the plane. With her was her navigator, renowned celestial navigator and ex-Pan American Airways chief inspector Fred Noonan, who had been fired for drinking on the job. Alcoholics were nothing new to Amelia. She had dealt with one in her father, and in Bill Stultz, who had piloted her across the Atlantic in 1928. She was confident Noonan would stay sober during the flight. On 1 June, in Miami, pilot and navigator 'sat for a last breathing spell on the concrete apron beside the hangar watching the rising sun brush back the silver gray of dawn … I closed and fastened the hatch. The gathering crowd safely distant from the propeller blades, ground attendants signalled "All clear".' When the Electra was 160 kilometres out to sea, a Miami radio station broadcast a bulletin announcing the start of Lady Lindy's historic flight.

Over the next thirty-two days, Amelia's reports on her progress made headline news. After refuelling at Natal, Brazil, Amelia and Noonan flew northeast, crossing the Equator for the second time. Their route took them over the Atlantic, on to the African continent, then over the Red Sea to Arabia, Karachi in Pakistan and beyond.

Everywhere she landed, Amelia noted the surprised reaction of locals to a woman piloting a plane. 'I'm stared at in the streets', she wrote, 'I feel they think, "Oh well, she's American and they're all crazy".' On 29 June, Amelia and Noonan arrived in Lae, New Guinea, having covered the remarkable distance of 35,400 kilometres. They had 11,265 kilometres more to go. And the most dangerous part of the trip still lay ahead.

The next hop would be 4110 kilometres to Howland Island, a tiny US territory, virtually a pinprick in the middle of the immense Pacific Ocean. Howland Island government officials were standing by at the new runway. The US Coast Guard cutter *Itasca*, their radio contact, was stationed just offshore. Three other US ships, ordered to burn every light on board, were positioned along the flight route as markers.

After takeoff from Luke Airfield near Pearl Harbor in 1937, Amelia was forced to make an emergency crash-landing on the runway.

KENDRA WILLIAMS

(c. 1973–), a US Navy lieutenant, became the first American female pilot to fly in combat when, in 1998, she flew her Boeing F/A-18 over Iraq as part of the attack force that launched from the aircraft carrier USS *Enterprise* in the Arabian Gulf. Although female pilots have been flying American military helicopters since 1973, and U.S. Navy F/A-18s since the mid-1990s, their activities had been limited to flying patrol missions (like those over Iraq). That is, until Lieutenant Williams' bombing mission during Operation Desert Fox.

'Howland is such a small spot in the Pacific that every aid to locating it must be available', Amelia said.

On the morning of 2 July, Amelia removed every non-essential item from the plane to make room for additional fuel—4360 litres of petrol. Noonan, unfortunately, had refuelled himself the night before at a bar, and had a massive hangover. Amelia had to help him into the cockpit. At ten o'clock in the morning, the Electra took off. They were expected to reach Howland Island in eighteen hours. Seven hours and twenty minutes into the flight, Amelia called the Lae radio station and announced that she was dead on course. The operator told her that her signal was clear. It would be the last two-way conversation the Electra would have with anyone.

From then on, radio transmissions from Amelia would be irregular and faint or interrupted with static. At 7.42 am the *Itasca* picked up Amelia's voice, crisp and clear, 'We must be on you, but we cannot see you. Fuel is running low. Been unable to reach you by radio. We are flying at 1000 feet [305 metres]'. During the next hour, Amelia's voice was heard twice, but she was still apparently unable to pick up signals from the ship. At 8.45 am, almost two hours past due, Amelia came through again, her voice almost panicked, 'We are running north and south'. After that, only silence.

A massive sea and air search followed, and would become the most extensive search of its kind in naval history. On 19 July, after spending $4 million and scouring 650,000 square kilometres of the Pacific, the US government reluctantly called off the operation. The only memory of Amelia on Howland Island would be a small lighthouse named in her honour, constructed in 1938.

Amelia Earhart's disappearance and death remain a mystery. The story of her life, however, is a testament to courage and its rewards. She was catapulted to fame because she was the first woman to fly across the Atlantic when almost everybody who had

AMELIA EARHART'S RECORDS AND ACHIEVEMENTS

- Woman's world altitude record: 14,000 ft/ 4270 m (1922)
- First woman to fly the Atlantic (1928)
- Speed records for 100 km (and with 500 lb (230 kg) cargo) (1931)
- First woman to fly an autogyro (1931)
- Altitude record for autogyros: 15,000 ft/ 4570 m (1931)
- First person to cross the US in an autogyro (1932)
- First woman to fly the Atlantic solo (1932)
- First person to fly the Atlantic twice (1932)
- First woman to receive the Distinguished Flying Cross (1932)

- Received the Cross of Knight of the Legion of Honour from the French government in June 1932
- First woman to fly non-stop, coast-to-coast across the US (1933)
- Women's speed transcontinental record (1933)
- First person to fly solo between Honolulu, Hawaii and Oakland, California (1935)
- First person to fly solo from Los Angeles, California to Mexico City, Mexico (1935)
- First person to fly solo non-stop from Mexico City, Mexico to Newark, New Jersey (1935)
- Speed record for east-to-west flight from Oakland, California to Honolulu, Hawaii (1937)

attempted the feat before her had dropped into the ocean. And then she remained in the public eye, not only as a very fine flyer, but as a speaker and writer forever exhorting women to chuck the ridiculous notion of inferiority, and encouraging them to be the best they could be.

In a letter to her husband, written in case her dangerous around-the-world flight proved to be her last, Amelia Earhart's inimitably brave spirit shined forth. 'Please know I am quite aware of the hazards', she said. 'I want to do it because I want to do it. Women must try to do things as men have tried. When they fail, their failure must be but a challenge to others.'

RAYMONDE DE LAROCHE

(1886–1919)

*Barnstorming belle
who tempted fate*

The most remarkable thing about the story of 'Baroness' Raymonde de Laroche is that she was still alive ten years after she first flew an airplane. At the turn of the twentieth century, flying was not for the faint of heart. The first woman in the world to obtain a fixed-wing pilot's licence miraculously survived three serious crashes before the fourth claimed her life at the age of thirty-three.

She was born Elise Raymonde Deroche, into a working-class family in France. Flamboyant and headstrong to the hilt, she fancied up her name—adopting her middle name as her first, and changing her surname to 'de Laroche'—when she took up acting, in her early twenties. Years later, Flight magazine added the title 'Baroness' in reporting her air show before Tsar Nicholas in St Petersburg, and it stuck. But, before she ever flew an airplane, she was taking to the skies in hot-air balloons, and claiming to be a race-car driver.

At the age of twenty-two, Raymonde was dining with early aviator and airplane designer Charles Voisin when one or the other of them, or both, had a brainstorm: Raymonde should learn how to fly. It was 1909; five years earlier, the Wright brothers had made aviation history, birthing fearless pioneers in the sky who would hold spectators spellbound with their loop-the-loops, spiralling nosedives, and other barnstorming stunts. The daredevil male pilots of the time, and most of the watching world, were convinced that flying was not fit for a woman. Apparently, both Raymonde and a smitten Charles, who was utterly captivated by his companion's charms, thought otherwise.

On 29 October 1909, just after her twenty-third birthday, Raymonde met Charles at the Chalons airfield where he and his brother, Gabriel, built and flew their own planes, and where Raymonde had been taking lessons under Charles' supervision. The time had come for her initial voyage into the air. Raymonde made herself comfortable in the open cockpit of the one-seater classic 1907 Voisin pusher-engined biplane—one of the most significant and popular aircraft of the pre-World War I era—and waited for instruction shouted from the ground. When she got the verbal signal, she revved up the 50 hp motor and taxied across the field. She raced down the airstrip. Suddenly, her wheels left the ground. She

Left: A French postcard featuring the first woman to hold a fixed-wing pilot's licence.

rose about 4.5 metres and continued in the air for 275 metres before settling gently on terra firma and taxiing back. Loud cheers erupted from the ground crew, and Charles and Raymonde's instructor, the Voisin company engineer M. Chateau, nodded approvingly to the fledgling flyer.

Some years later Raymonde would be quoted as saying, 'Flying is the best possible thing for women'—this despite the fact that these novel machines were seriously unpredictable and dangerous, and she did not get by unscathed. Just ten months after she first lifted off the ground, she suffered a serious crash when the tail of her airplane brushed a tree during a landing. After she mended a concussion and a broken collarbone, she hopped right back into the cockpit, performing in air shows across Europe and keeping her passion for flying alive.

On 8 March 1910, Raymonde became the first woman in the world to receive a fixed-wing pilot's licence, issued by the Aero Club of France. Four months later, competing with a group of male pilots in an air show at Reims, France, she flew into the wake of another airplane, was knocked into a dive and crashed, breaking several bones and suffering from multiple internal injuries. As soon as she was fit to fly, two years later, she was at it again. Then, in September of 1912, she had a third near-fatal accident, this time on the ground: she and Charles Voisin crashed the car they were driving, killing Charles. But Raymonde was unstoppable and, in 1913, she went on to win the Aero Club of France's Femina Cup for a long-distance, non-stop flight of four hours. She would not be prevented from flying until the onset of World War I, when all women flyers were grounded and she took up service as a military driver for the French army, chauffeuring officers through artillery fire to the front lines.

Raymonde was back in the air in 1919. Just one month after she set an altitude record at 4785 metres, she answered a call to help test-pilot an experimental aircraft. On 18 July, she showed up at the airfield at Le Crotoy to join her co-pilot. Had she successfully executed the test, she would have become the first professional woman test pilot. But as the aircraft approached landing (whether she was at the controls or the co-pilot was flying the plane is not known), it suddenly went into a dive and crashed, killing both Raymonde and her companion. At a time when flying friendly skies is safer than driving a car to the corner store, a statue of Raymonde de Laroche stands at Le Bourget Airport, in France, reminding us of the terrible toll in human life that early air travel exacted.

Raymonde de Laroche posing for a photograph in her biplane.

BESSIE COLEMAN

(1892–1926)

*The sky was the limit for
this American legend*

From the moment young Bessie Coleman looked up from the cotton fields where she toiled in Waxahachie, Texas, and caught sight of a plane soaring overhead, she knew she wanted to fly.

The first African American to earn an aviation pilot's licence (and the first American of any race or either gender to hold an international pilot's licence) grew up in a world of poverty and the cruel double difficulties of gender and racial discrimination in early twentieth century America. Before she turned ten—living in a household with a single, hardworking mother and three young sisters who needed looking after—Bessie was serving as a surrogate mother and housekeeper, picking cotton during harvest and, when time allowed, attending an all-black school in a one-room wooden shack, a 6.4-kilometre walk from her home. It was a time when segregation was a way of life in Texas, when African Americans attended separate schools and rode in separate rail cars and could even find themselves lynched for scant evidence of wrongdoing.

But Bessie was not the kind of girl to resign herself to her conditions. After completing all eight grades of her simple school, she yearned for more. In 1910, she used most of her savings to enroll in the Colored Agricultural and Normal University in Langston, Oklahoma. Sadly, her academic plans were thwarted after only one term, when she ran out of money and was forced to return to Waxahachie and make a living there for the next five years as a laundress. At the age of twenty-three, she was even more determined to find a way to 'amount to something'. So, she set out for Chicago to look for a new way of life, grateful to be taken under the roof of one of her elder brothers.

The Windy City, as it turned out, offered little more to an African American woman than did Texas. During the summer of her twenty-seventh year, Bessie was still looking for a way to make something of herself. She was working as a manicurist at the White Sox Barber Shop, when World War I came to an end and returning American soldiers started livening up the shop with exciting tales of feats of flying, sparking Bessie's interest in aviation. Spurred on by her brother, who would tease her about the superiority of French women who made careers as airplane pilots, Bessie decided what she wanted to do. Now she had a dream.

Left: 'Queen Bess' thrilled audiences as a barnstormer, but she had a more serious side as well.

For a black woman in America, in 1918, it was impossible to get admitted into flight school. Training in France was the only option. So on 20 November 1920, with savings she had accumulated, as well as additional financial support from Robert Abbott, African American millionaire publisher and founder of the Chicago Defender *newspaper, Bessie set sail from New York City for Paris. In seven short months, it was evident that she took her fearlessness to the skies. The only non-Caucasian student in her class, she learned to fly in a 8.2-metre Nieuport Type 82 biplane, known to fail frequently, sometimes in the air. In June 1921, the Fédération Aéronautique Internationale awarded Bessie Coleman an international pilot's licence (two years before Amelia Earhart). She was the first African American to hold a pilot's licence, and the only international pilot licenced American in the world.*

This 'full-fledged aviatrix, the first of her race'—as noted by The Air Service News—*became a media sensation when she returned to the United States, in September 1921. 'Queen Bess', as she soon came to be known, was a highly popular drawcard for the next five years. She not only thrilled audiences as a barnstormer (stunt aviator) with her daredevil airborne manoeuvres—figure eights, loop-the-loops, and near-ground dips—but she also served as a role model for both women and African Americans, bucking prevailing stereotypes by her very presence in the clouds.*

Adopting a no-holds-barred attitude in the sky, this daring pilot similarly stopped at nothing to use her celebrity whenever she could to effect change, such as refusing to perform unless African American spectators were allowed to enter an airfield through the same gate as white spectators, and walking off a movie set as a statement of principle when she learned that she was required to appear in the first scene in tattered clothes, with a walking stick and a pack on her back.

Bessie would not live long enough to realise a long-held dream—establishing a flight school for young black aviators. She took to the skies for the last time on 30 April 1926, in Jacksonville, Florida, in her very own plane—a $400 Jenny. At 1065 metres, with her mechanic at the controls during a routine test flight, the aircraft unexpectedly plunged toward earth. The 'très chic aviatrix' who often told others, 'You can be somebody, too', fell from the open cockpit to her death.

Only after her death did Bessie receive the kind of recognition she had always desired. In 1929, African American aviator and aeronautical engineer William J. Powell established the Bessie Coleman Aero Club in Los Angeles, California. Her legacy has continued until this day, in the form of aviation clubs and tributes. Each year (since 1931), pilots fly over Brave Bessie's grave in Lincoln Cemetery in Chicago on the anniversary of her death. In 1977, a group of African American women pilots founded the Bessie Coleman Aviators Club. In 1995, she was inducted into the Women in Aviation Hall of Fame, and a US postal stamp was issued in her honour.

Bessie Coleman's pioneering achievements defied convention and discrimination, and to this day continue to inspire others with the underlying message: dare to dream.

Bessie Coleman receiving a bouquet in 1922 from fellow African American aviator Edison C. McVey, aeronautical instructor for United Air Lines.

VALENTINA TERESHKOVA (1937–)

Russian cosmonaut is the first woman in space

Valentina was taking the longest walk of her life, moving awkwardly in her bulky, bright orange flight suit. Ahead of her the Soviet spaceship *Vostok VI* rose up from its launching pad. At the launcher, she paused, shook a round of hands, clanked helmets with her backup in a traditional farewell, then rode the elevator 32 metres up to the platform. Before climbing aboard her spacecraft, she took a deep breath, turned around and, looking at the crowd of spectators below, clasped her hands above her head like a champion boxer, for one final farewell.

Now on board, Valentina closed her helmet and put on her gloves. Ground control read their meters. The suit was pressurised and holding steady at 5.7 pounds per square inch (psi); the cabin temperature was 20° Centigrade; cabin pressure: 14.5 psi. 'T minus 5 minutes', came a voice through her headphones. The countdown continued. Then Valentina felt the rocket's engines fire.

At 12.30 pm, 16 June 1963, Valentina heard, over the deafening roar of the rocket engines: 'Lift off! We have lift off!'

The call sign for the first woman in space was Chaika (Seagull).

Valentina Tereshkova was the first woman in space, orbiting the earth forty-eight times during a solo flight that lasted 70.8 hours, and travelling a total of 1.2 million miles. There were plenty of female candidates for cosmonaut training who were more qualified than Valentina. Some were highly educated scientists. Others were skilled pilots. Valentina was neither when she joined the space program—but that was one reason why she was chosen.

Soviet Premier Nikita Khrushchev wanted the first woman in space to be an ordinary worker. Valentina was just the type of person he wanted. She had two other things in her favour: she was a highly trained parachutist, and she was a keen member of the Young Communist League.

Soon after touching down, Valentina began the work she had really been intended for. She moved into the office of the president of the Committee of Soviet Women on Pushkin Square in Moscow, and toured the world as a goodwill ambassador. Though another woman would not enter space for almost another two decades (Soviet cosmonaut Svetlana Savitskaya, who was launched aboard a Soyuz flight in 1982, was the next), Valentina proudly presented herself as a symbol of liberated woman in Soviet Socialist society, and the world at large.

Valentina takes to the air

Born on 6 March 1937, Valentina Vladimirovna Tereshkova knew the value of hard work, having grown up on a collective farm in the tiny hamlet of Maslennikovo, in Russia. When 'Valya' was just four years old, her father was killed fighting for the Soviet army in World War II, leaving her mother to single-handedly support three young children (Valya, her older sister, and a baby brother). If her mother didn't work, the family didn't eat. So, Valya stayed home with her sister to help care for the baby, missing out on school until she was ten years old.

Valya pitched in with household chores, milked cows and worked in the fields, but she still found time for fun and games. Among even the bigger boys, she usually stood out as the daring one, climbing to the top of a tree and plummeting into the pond below. Or hurling herself off a tall bridge into the Kotorosl River, arms out to the sides, plunging toward churning water amid cheers and a shout that she looked just like a seagull. Or, playing 'paratroopers', a game she invented out of, perhaps, a prophetic vision of things to come.

At twenty-two, Valentina was a recent graduate from the Light Industry Technical School, employed as a loom operator at a cotton mill near Yaroslavl, and was a member of the mill's Komsomol (Young Communists League). Life was humming along when, one day, something caught her eye that she could not get out of her mind: her friend Galina, dressed in a blue flight suit, tumbling out from the open door of a Yak-12 airplane 1525 metres up, parachute blooming above her against a cloudless sky. In no time, the tomboy who had been the first girl to jump from the bridge over the Kotorosl joined her friend as a member of the amateur parachuting group, the Yaroslavl Air Sports Club.

Her first jump almost got her thrown out of the club, when she leaped from the plane before her instructor gave the command. But she would have 125 successful jumps after that. Her ninth one got a grade of 'excellent' and a photo opportunity with the local newspaper, when she leaped from 805 metres and landed with precision in a bull's-eye on the ground. Within a few months, she received the rating of parachutist third class. Two years later, she was awarded her first-class rating.

While Valentina was stacking up her jumps, her country was making history in space exploration. On 4 October 1957, the Soviet Union sent the first ever man-made object into orbit around the Earth, when it launched *Sputnik I*, the world's first artificial satellite.

> ## JERRIE COBB
>
> (1931–), American aviator, first woman to fly in the world's largest air exposition, the Salon Aéronautique Internacional in Paris, and chosen pilot of the year by the National Pilots Association in 1959, was the first woman to undergo astronaut testing and be cleared for space travel, in the Mercury 13 Space program in 1959. Although she successfully completed her training, women were dropped from the program in 1960, and thus Cobb never became a candidate for the Mercury space flights, despite her petitions to Congress. In 1963 the women's program was cancelled altogether, and it was not until 1983 that an American woman was sent into space.

That single event caught the world's attention and changed the face of things to come, marking the start of the space age and the heated USSR–US space race. Then the Soviets struck again; on 3 November, *Sputnik II* was launched, carrying a much heavier payload, including a dog named Laika. The United States shot back with its own satellite launch (*Explorer I*), on 31 January 1958. And one year later, the launch of the Soviet *Luna I* marked man's first probe to the moon. It was during this period that Vasily Romanyuk made his record-breaking three thousandth parachute jump. In an interview with a reporter from *Pravda*, Romanyuk said, 'And who knows, perhaps the time will come when the world's first cosmonauts will also return to our planet under the canopy of a parachute'. The words of one of Valentina's greatest idols were not in the least lost on the young parachutist.

A woman's turn

When Valentina heard the news on 12 April 1961 that a man was actually in space, and that the cosmonaut was fellow countryman Yuri Gagarin, she was electrified. Her patriotism swelled, and so did the idea that a woman could also accomplish that feat. After reading Gagarin's book, *The Road to the Stars*, with a section devoted to the importance of parachuting as a part of the cosmonaut's training, Valentina's notion of a woman in space became personal. She was galvanised into action. Writing a letter to the Supreme Soviet in Moscow, asking that she be considered for cosmonaut training, was purely spontaneous, a move driven by the heartfelt conviction that gender didn't have to make a difference when it came to space exploration. Little did she know that her timing couldn't have been any better.

Cosmonaut Gagarin's historic flight had been all that Premier Khrushchev could have hoped for: it had reasserted Soviet space supremacy and had given the world a stunning demonstration of his nation's technological virtuosity. To remain frontrunner, and beat the United States to another space 'first', Khrushchev was convinced he needed to do something really spectacular, something like launching into space none other than a woman.

Khrushchev set the standards for the USSR woman-in-space project: the world's first female cosmonaut must be a run-of-the-mill Russian girl, a factory or farm worker, whose flight would demonstrate that under socialism anybody at all could go into space. The selection process, under the direction of veteran cosmonaut Yuri Gagarin, began in the summer of 1961. It consisted of poring through the thousands of letters from wanna-be spacefarers who, like Valentina, had written with a dream just after a Russian man came closest to reaching the stars. Valentina, with her simple origins, her prominent role as chapter secretary in the Young Communist League at her factory, and her by now extensive experience as a parachutist, fit the bill. In 1962, she and three other women made the final selection for cosmonauts-in-training. Valentina was twenty-four years old when the call to Moscow came.

A secret and arduous mission

Valentina's own mother had to wait until her historic flight was announced over Radio Moscow to learn not only that Valentina was the cosmonaut in orbit, but that she was a cosmonaut at all. For eighteen months until that momentous date, Valentina trained in secrecy, using the cover story that her move to a training camp was with a women's precision skydiving team slated to enter international competition.

The Soviet Union's team of cosmonauts came together for a group portrait in 1964.

'Let me tell you, when I entered the Star City of cosmonauts, my heart was about to stop', Valentina later recalled. 'How will they meet me there? I didn't do anything great in my life; and these were real pilots'. Just like their male counterparts, the young female candidates had to meet strict medical and psychological standards before taking up their training. But this novice group of trainees lacked a key element that had earned the male cosmonauts their ticket into space: piloting skills. Some of the men were sceptical of the women's abilities. 'Space flight is no picnic', one told a journalist. 'It will be hard on them.'

The training was certainly arduous. There were long days in the classroom studying spaceship designs and equipment. There were tests to determine the effects of solitary confinement for long periods, tests under extreme gravity conditions to simulate lift off, and tests to duplicate zero gravity weightlessness in space. Parachute jumps were regular occurrences. The training also included at least two long simulations on the ground, of six days and twelve days duration. And the four women, who were all made second lieutenants in the Soviet air force, had to go through an extensive jet aerobatic program in two-seater Mig trainers. Their training was made all the more rigorous with the added component of competition. For, while each and every trainee in the men's program would eventually fly in space, only one of the female trainees would be selected to make the space program's one-time-only woman-in-space flight. The pressure to perform exceptionally must have been intense. Admiring fellow cosmonaut, Gagarin, was quoted as saying about Valentina, 'It was hard for her to master rocket techniques, but she tackled the job stubbornly and devoted much of her own time to study, poring over books and notes in the evening'. Which of the four women would be the one to go would not be decided until the very end of training.

As the launch date approached, the time came to pick the primary pilot and her backup. Valentina's tough-as-nails temperament, no less than her commitment to her cause, would eventually pay off.

SVETLANA SAVITSKAYA

(1948–) is a former Soviet cosmonaut, who became the first woman to perform a space walk, during the Soyuz T-12 mission in July 1984. Cosmonaut Savitskaya was also the second woman in space, achieving this distinction on the Soyuz T-7 mission in 1982, and the first woman to fly twice in space. She has twice been honoured with the Hero of the Soviet Union award and serves as a member of the Russian Parliament.

First woman into space

At 12.30 pm on 16 June 1963, Junior Lieutenant Tereshkova was launched into space aboard *Vostok VI*, and soon thereafter became the world's first woman to be hurled into orbit. Using her radio call sign Chaika (Seagull), she reported, 'I see the horizon. A light blue, a beautiful band. This is the Earth. How beautiful it is! All goes well'.

Vostok VI made forty-eight orbits (1.9 million kilometres) in seventy hours, fifty minutes, coming within 5 kilometres of the previously launched *Vostok V*, piloted by cosmonaut Valery Bykovsky. Rumours—not taken too seriously—circulated in Moscow that the two cosmonauts might attempt a his-and-hers rendezvous in space, although Valentina was neither a trained pilot nor skilled enough to carry out her part in a complicated manually controlled link-up manoeuvre. When Valentina reported she was feeling fine, she promptly stole the show from Bykovsky in *Vostok V*. Apparently aware that she was being watched by television viewers all over the Soviet Union and satellite nations via the Soviet bloc television network, she smiled and waved greetings at the camera, pencil and logbook floating weightlessly before her face.

Premier Khrushchev said: 'A happy journey to you. We will be extremely glad to meet you on our Soviet soil'.

Valentina sent back: 'I am deeply moved by your kindness. Many, many thanks for your hearty words, for your fatherly concern. I feel fine. I wholeheartedly thank the Soviet people for the good wishes. I assure you, dear Nikita Sergeyevich, that the honourable assignment of the homeland will be carried out'.

To return to Earth, Valentina allowed the autopilot to line up the spacecraft and fire the braking rocket engine. After riding *Vostok VI* through its blazing high-G re-entry for sixteen minutes, and once the capsule had stabilised under a small parachute, Valentina was ejected through the side hatch. She felt the familiar jerk as the canopy of her personal backpack parachute filled with air. And Seagull made her silent final descent to the ground below, feeling ecstatic beyond words.

EILEEN COLLINS

(1956–) is an American astronaut and US Air Force colonel who has clocked up thirty-eight days in space. In 1995 she became the first female pilot of a Space Shuttle, aboard the *Discovery* as it carried out a rendezvous with the Russia space station *Mir*. In 1999 she became the first female commander of a Space Shuttle, aboard *Columbia* on its mission to set up the Chandra X-Ray Observatory. In 2005, aboard *Discovery* again, Collins became the first astronaut to fly the Space Shuttle through a complete 360-degree pitch manoeuvre (rollover).

Valentina Tereshkova prepares for her departure into space.

After landing, Premier Khrushchev boasted, 'It is our girl, a girl from the land of the Soviet, who is first in space'.

According to an Associated Press report, the successful flight was 'expected to provide the Soviet Union with its propaganda keynote for several weeks to come'.

Rocketing from glory to glory

On 22 June, cosmonauts Tereshkova and Bykovsky were hailed in Moscow's Red Square. Striding down the red-carpeted 'one hundred steps to glory', Valentina reached out and took Valery's hand. Thus, another first for the Soviet space program: for the first time, two cosmonauts walked hand in hand to report to the premier of the Soviet Union that they had completed their space mission. At the Kremlin, Valentina was named Hero of the Soviet Union (the USSR's highest award), and Presidium Chairman Leonid Brezhnev decorated her with the Order of Lenin and the Gold Star Medal.

Two days later, Valentina addressed a Soviet-sponsored World Women's Congress in Moscow, with delegates leaving their seats to crowd around and reach for the world's space heroine. After pointing out that Valentina had lost her father in World War II, Khrushchev beat the drum for Communism. 'She stood firmly on her feet and now has risen to such heights as no person in the capitalist world brought up by wealthy daddies and mommies can rise', he boasted.

The first-woman-in-space mission was the propaganda triumph Khrushchev had planned. Valentina assumed dozens of ceremonial posts and moved into the office of the president of the Committee of Soviet Women on Pushkin Square in Moscow. And as she embarked on a world tour that would take her through India, Pakistan, Mexico, the United States, Cuba, and the Eastern Bloc, Valentina made sure to parrot the official Moscow line while embellishing the women's angle: 'Since 1917 Soviet women have had the same prerogatives and rights as men. They share the same tasks. They are workers, navigators, chemists, aviators, engineers. And now the nation has selected me for the honour of being a cosmonaut. As you can see, on earth, at sea and in the sky, Soviet women are the equal of men'.

Nonetheless, Soviet chauvinism was hard to shake. For twenty years following Valentina's launch into orbit, there would be no other spacewoman (hailing from either the Soviet Union or, for that matter, the United States). Russian cosmonaut

Alexei Leonov summed things up succinctly, in an interview in 1975: 'When we analysed the results of [Tereshkova's] flight afterward, we discovered that for women, flying in space is a hard job and that they can do other things down here [laughs] … After training, she will be twenty-eight or twenty-nine, and if she is a good woman she will have a family by then. Now, you don't subject a mother to such severe physical loads that go with the training, aside from physical tensions'. The next year, Valentina's husband of thirteen years, cosmonaut Andrian Nikolyev, elaborated: there never were any more spacewomen 'because this kind of work is tough. The mission program makes big demands on her, especially if she is married. So nowadays we keep our women here on Earth. We love our women very much; we spare them as much as possible. However, in the future, they will surely work on board space stations, but as specialists—as doctors, as geologists, as astronomers and, of course, as stewardesses'. And cosmonaut chief Vladimir Shatalov told the Russian press in 1980 that space flight was too demanding for women: 'In such conditions we just had no moral right to subject the "better half" of mankind to such loads'.

KATHRYN SULLIVAN

(1951–) is an American geologist and former NASA astronaut. With a background in oceanography and Earth science, Sullivan was a mission specialist on three Space shuttle missions, studying the Earth's atmosphere. On her first flight, in 1984, she became the first American woman to make a space walk. Logging 532 hours in space, in 2002 she was inducted into the Astronaut Hall of Fame.

After her famed flight, Valentina continued as an aerospace engineer in the space program, earning a doctorate in engineering in 1977. She later became a prominent member of the Soviet government and a well-known representative abroad. She was made a member of the World Peace Council in 1966, a member of the Yaroslavl Soviet in 1967, a member of the Supreme Soviet of the Soviet Union in 1966–1970 and 1970–1974, and was elected to the Presidium of the Supreme Soviet in 1974. She was also the Soviet representative to the UN Conference for the International Women's Year in Mexico City in 1975. She attained the rank of deputy to the Supreme Soviet, membership of the Communist Party of the Soviet Union Central Committee, Vice President of the International Women's Democratic Federation and President of the Soviet–Algerian Friendship Society. Valentina headed the USSR's International Cultural and Friendship Union from 1987 to 1991, and later chaired the Russian Association of International Cooperation.

After the collapse of the Soviet Union, Valentina lost her political posts but none of her prestige. To this day, she is revered—not just as a Russian hero, but as a woman's hero. Whatever their national or political leanings, women everywhere around the world in 1963 reacted with pride and exuberance when Seagull broke into the male preserve of 'manned' space flight. Once considered a simple everyday Russian girl, Valentina Tereshkova today represents the magnificent power of the everywoman.

In October 2000, at the age of sixty-three, the first woman in space was awarded the Greatest Woman Achiever of the Century award, in London, by the International Women of the Year Association. According to the Russian news agency Itar-Tass, 'her unsurpassed successes in the cause of equality, exploration of the outer space for the benefit of peace, and protection of the planet's ecology', made her the association's unanimous choice. In her memoirs, she wrote, 'Those who have already been in space yearn with all their heart and soul to hasten there again and again'. For the celebration of her seventieth birthday, Valentina was invited to President Vladimir Putin's residence in Novo-Ogaryovo; while there she said that she would like to fly to Mars, even if it meant a one-way trip.

SALLY K. RIDE

(1951–)

*First American woman to take
the ride of a lifetime*

'There is no amusement park ride even close to the experience of flying into space', Sally Ride has said. She would know. In 1983, this southern California native became the first American woman and youngest American to be sent into space, as a crew member on the Space Shuttle Challenger. She took another flight on board the Challenger in 1984, and has accumulated more than 343 hours orbiting Earth.

Excelling in both athletics and academics, Sally seriously considered a career as a professional tennis player—until it hit her that she would never make a fortune with her forehand. So she enrolled at Stanford University, where she would play on the university tennis team and focus on physics for her bachelor's and master's degrees. She was just months away from getting her PhD in astrophysics when she saw an ad in the school newspaper that the National Aeronautics and Space Administration (NASA) was accepting applications for astronauts for the new Space Shuttle program. Instantly, Sally knew that's what she wanted to do. Though she wasn't a test pilot and had never flown an aircraft, Sally had the solid science background NASA was looking for in candidates. It was the first time in ten years that NASA was taking astronauts, and the first time ever that the administration was looking to bring women into the corps. Still, the odds of being selected for the program were very slim. Out of 8000 applicants, NASA would pick just thirty-five to make up the first Space Shuttle astronaut class. Sally—the kind of student who trembled at the thought of being called on in class—made the final selection, along with five other women.

Sally joined NASA in 1978. The training to become a cosmonaut was as mentally rigorous as it was physically taxing. For five years, she learned everything there was to know about the Space Shuttle and how to handle emergency situations, training in radio communications, navigation, parachute jumping and water survival, and performing gravity and weightlessness exercises until they became as automatic as starting a car and driving away. During this time, Sally was the Capsule Communicator for the second and third Space Shuttle flights, relaying radio messages from mission control to the shuttle crews, and was a member of the team that developed the Space Shuttle's remote mechanical arm.

Left: Sally read that NASA was looking for female applicants …

On 18 June 1983, Space Shuttle Challenger *lifted off from Florida's Kennedy Space Center and roared into the skies, launching astronaut Sally Ride into history. On this second* Challenger *mission, the five-member crew deployed satellites for Canada and Indonesia, and Sally became the first woman ever to operate the shuttle's robot arm in space. Her second space flight was in 1984, also on board* Challenger, *for an eight-day mission that saw Kathryn Sullivan become the first American woman to make a spacewalk. Sally had completed eight months of training and was preparing for her third mission when* Challenger *broke apart just over a minute into its flight in January 1986, killing all seven crew members and resulting in a thirty-two-month hiatus in the shuttle program. Sally was chosen to serve on the Presidential Commission investigating the accident. Following the investigation, she was assigned to NASA headquarters to lead the effort in long-range and strategic planning, serving as the first Director of Office of Exploration, and authoring a report entitled 'Leadership and America's Future in Space'.*

Surprisingly, America's first female cosmonaut did not appreciate just how much of a trailblazer and role model she was for women until after she completed her first mission in space and was propelled into the public eye. It didn't take long for her to become a big ticket item on the speaking circuit, and a featured subject for interviews. She travelled widely, addressed the United Nations, and talked to women's groups and science clubs, collegians and schoolchildren, educators and engineers about her experiences in space, the job of an astronaut, and her opinions on the importance of studying Earth from space. In 2001, she directed her attention to what she sees as a brewing crisis in the United States: a severe shortage of female students pursuing science and engineering careers. Set on keeping girls interested in mathematics and science as they move into middle school, Sally established Sally Ride Science, an organisation that provides hands-on science programs and camps, national invention contests, and educational materials aimed at making science interesting, fun, and accessible for female 'tweens'.

Sally continues to advocate for space exploration and for combating climate change and global warming. She has written and co-authored a number of children's books addressing these issues, including To Space and Back, Voyager: An Adventure to the Edge of the Solar System, The Third Planet: Exploring the Earth from Space, Mission: Planet Earth: Our World and

Its Climate—And How Humans Are Changing Them *and* Mission: Save the Planet: Things You can Do to Help Fight Global Warming!

No matter what Sally Ride sets her sights on, she does it in the spirit of challenge. Her smarts, her focus and her heartfelt advocacy have earned her numerous awards, including the Jefferson Award for Public Service, the Women's Research and Education Institute's American Woman Award, and, twice, the National Spaceflight Medal. She was inducted into the Astronaut Hall of Fame at Kennedy Space Center on 21 June 2003.

Sally Ride was the only woman in the crew of the second Challenger *mission.*

PEGGY WHITSON

(1960–)

*ISS's first female commander has
accumulated over a year in space*

She was inspired, at the age of nine, by the men who walked on the Moon. 'What a cool job!' she thought. But it wasn't until she graduated from high school and six women were chosen as astronaut candidates by NASA that Peggy Whitson actually believed the job of flying in space could one day be hers. Not only did this girl from America's heartland grow up to be an astronaut, but in 2007, at the age of forty-seven, she became the first woman ever to command the International Space Station.

Peggy has said that what kept her pursuing her goal was a double dose of dedication and stubbornness that she acquired from her hardworking parents. She was born on a farm in rural Iowa, and took an early curiosity in animals and plants and how things grow, fueling a love for biology. Throughout her education, she pursued those avenues that would get her closer to her dream of one day being a part of NASA, double-majoring in biology and chemistry at Iowa Wesleyan College and later graduating with a PhD in biochemistry from Rice University in Houston. Fresh out of school in 1989, she began working for NASA as a research biochemist. Seven years down the road, Peggy would be selected as an astronaut.

On 5 June 2002, Expedition 5 launched forty-two-year-old Peggy Whitson into space for her first time. Peggy's first stint on the International Space Station (ISS) was a six-month tour of duty as a flight engineer installing equipment and conducting investigations in human life sciences and microgravity sciences. The fledgling cosmonaut found many things were different when she left Earth, including a new fondness for peanut butter and a sudden aversion to shrimp cocktail. She returned to Earth on 7 December.

Peggy would go up into space, again, five years later, this time as commander on Expedition 16 to the ISS. It was a mission not only with greater responsibilities, but with a much livelier pace than that of her first, with three shuttle flights and crews delivering new hardware coming from four different space agencies, and more than a dozen spacewalks. Moreover, Expedition 16 would mark the first time a female was to command the station, with a number of women in other leadership roles, including lead flight director Holly Ridings,

Left: Peggy farewells the crowds before takeoff from Baikonur cosmodrome in Kazakhstan.

Peggy Whitson participating in an Expedition 16 spacewalk from the ISS, a sparkling blue and white Earth in the background.

Pam Melroy commanding the first shuttle mission, and Dana Weigel and Sally Davis serving as lead flight directors for two different shuttle missions.

Peggy and her crew kick-started Expedition 16 without delay, hosting visiting NASA colleague Pam Melroy and her crew on the orbital outpost just two weeks after their 8 October 2007 launch (this marked the first time two female mission commanders were simultaneously in space). By the end of November, shuttle and ISS astronauts had accomplished quite a bit: they had relocated a massive solar-power tower, manoeuvred a tricky robotic crane to attach a new module to the space station, and performed seven spacewalks. Two more shuttle flights arrived in February and March, delivering Europe's $2 billion Columbus laboratory and a storage room for Japan's giant Kibo science laboratory (itself launched on 31 May aboard the shuttle Discovery and attached to the ISS on 3 June). The commander and her crew also squeezed in a few unscheduled spacewalks to inspect one solar wing joint and repair another. On 18 December, during Expedition 16's fourth spacewalk, Peggy received some exciting news from the ground team in Mission Control: the commander had become the woman with the most cumulative EVA (extra-vehicular activity) time in NASA history. Three hours and 37 minutes into the spacewalk, Peggy exceeded NASA astronaut Sunita Williams' total time of 29 hours and 18 minutes.

Commander Peggy Whitson and two crewmates arrived safely back to Earth on 19 April 2008. When the Russian Soyuz TMA-11 spacecraft touched down in Kazakhstan, Peggy had spent 192 days in space on the Expedition 16 flight, 190 of them on the ISS. With the completion of her second mission to ISS, Peggy set a new spaceflight record for the most cumulative time spent in space by any other US spacefarer, giving her a career total of 377 days, and breaking the previous mark of 374 days set by Mike Foale on his six flights.

Today, Peggy hopes that her feats will encourage other women to take the risks necessary to go one step further, no matter the endeavour. 'I think that history has demonstrated for us that exploration is worth doing', she says. For Peggy Whitson, 'it's the risk that makes exploration so exciting'.

DAWN FRASER (1937–)

Australian Olympic champion has had 'one hell of a life'

It was a sweltering summer day when five-year-old Dawn and her older brother Don crept up to the fence at the Elkington Park Baths in Sydney, Australia. The pool was alive with the splashes and shouts of kids who blanketed the surface of the water. With a wink and nod Don hoisted his sister over the fence and climbed up after her. They paced the deck from side to side looking for a place to jump in. They could have walked from one head to another without getting wet. Finally they spied their spot. Don held his little sister's hand and lowered her into the warm water.

Don watched over his sister as she gleefully flapped her arms in the air and bobbed up and under the waves, swallowing mouthfuls of water. The swimming pool became a magical place for Dawn. She felt a kinship with the water that she had never known before.

This was not just an inaugural swim, but a baptism. Little Dawn Fraser was born again in that moment.

*Dawn Fraser won her first
Olympic gold in 1956.*

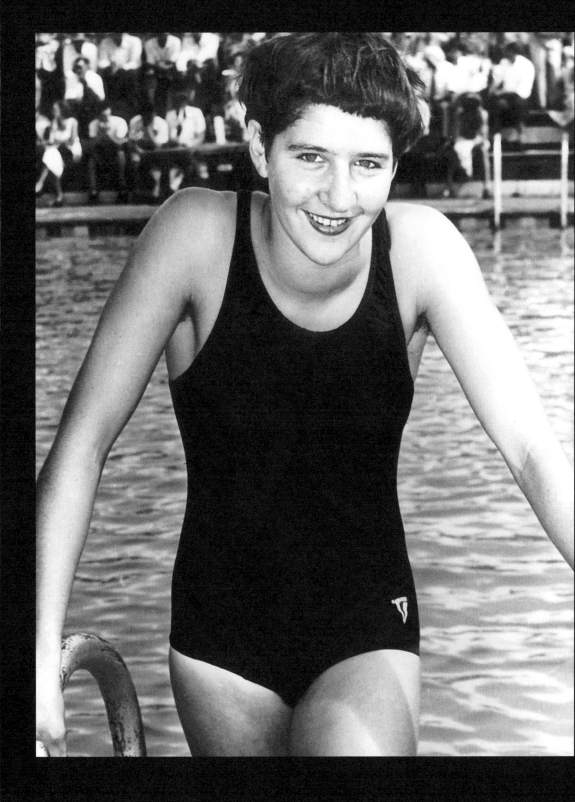

Two decades later, the Elkington Park Baths were renamed Dawn Fraser Pool after the little girl who became, what many people believe, the greatest female swimmer of all time.

Dawn Fraser's favourite movie is *My Fair Lady*. And like Eliza Doolittle, the spunky cockney flower girl, Dawn was transformed and catapulted from humble working-class beginnings into the highest ranks of world sports and social notoriety. At the 1996 Atlanta Olympics, she was honoured as one of the greatest Olympic champions of all time, along with such legends as track and field champ Carl Lewis, diver Greg Louganis, and gymnast Nadia Comăneci. Her place on that podium was secured with twenty-seven individual world records in swimming, twelve relay records and eight Olympic medals. However, none of these accomplishments were more meaningful than the 59.9 seconds she clocked for the 100 meter freestyle in October of 1962. Dawn Fraser was the first woman to break the one-minute barrier.

Dawn's occasional mischievous behaviour, and her penchant for upsetting sporting officials, led to an involuntary retirement. However, to this day she remains active in the sports arena through her personal appearances and her myriad charities, such as the Cerebral Palsy Sports Association and the Wheelchair Sports Association. Dawn Fraser has spent most of her life swimming in the fast lane, oftentimes against the current, always to victory.

From the dust of coal and the ashes of adversity

Dawn Fraser probably inherited her single-mindedness and hoyden character from her father Ken, who immigrated to Australia from Scotland in 1913. A Scottish footballer, the head of the Fraser household worked as a shipwright on the harbour docks near the family's home on Birchgrove Road in Balmain, a suburb of Sydney. The simple family home had a small backyard and one tiny outdoor toilet that somehow managed to serve the needs of Dawn, her seven siblings and her parents.

Dawn came into the world on 4 September 1937, into a loving family of four brothers and three sisters. Dawn recalls that there were no other kids her age in the neighbourhood so she tagged along with her brothers and their friends playing stickball, marbles, jacks and rugby. Mixing it up with the boys inevitably led to teasing. One of the local pastimes was pulling on Dawn's pigtails and shouting, 'Dawn the Prawn!' But she soon learned to give as good as she got. Her childhood experiences led her to believe that she could successfully compete with boys and beat them.

When she stood on the medals podium at the 1956 Olympics in Melbourne she was the epitome of strength and vitality. It would be difficult to believe that a little more than a decade earlier she was a feeble child plagued with asthma. Her respiratory malady grew worse over time. When the ships unloaded coal nearby, the dockside air became polluted with oily soot that clogged Dawn's nose and lungs. However, she learned that swimming relieved her breathing problems and nary a summer day passed when Dawn and her big brother Don did not head for the Balmain public pool.

Don became her first coach, teaching her to float and then to master basic swimming strokes. It quickly became apparent that she had a natural ability. She won her first swimming award at age eight—the Tiny Tot Dog-paddle Championship. As fate would have it, Dawn's cousin, Ray Miranda, was a swimming coach. He began to mold her natural ability into a professional form and enrolled her in the Leichhardt–Balmain Swimming League. Within a couple of years she took the honours at the club's senior women's championship. She was ready to take the next rung on her ladder to success, but her ascent was stopped by a family tragedy.

SARAH 'FANNY' DURACK

(1889–1956), an Australian swimmer, became the first woman to win a gold medal for swimming at the Olympic Games. She won the 100-meter freestyle at the Stockholm Olympics in 1912, the first year women were permitted to compete in swimming events at the Games (tennis and diving were the only other female events). In the late 1910s Durack held every major world women's swimming record, from 100 meters to a mile, breaking twelve world records along the way.

While the entire Fraser clan was supportive, her older brother Don was her biggest fan. He was the first to put a wonderful possibility into Dawn's head. 'You'll be a champ someday, sis', Don would tell her, 'just keep on swimming'. He recognised her physical prowess because he was a consummate footballer. But her brotherly guardian angel would soon fly off. Don contracted a blood disease, and his condition deteriorated until he died of leukemia in the winter of 1951 at the age of twenty-one. Thirteen-year-old Dawn was devastated. She recalls running to the public pool where she and her big brother spent so much time together. It was closed, but she vaulted the fence, huddled in the corner, and cried.

HALINA KONOPACKA

(1900–1989) was a Polish athlete who became the first female recipient of a track and field gold medal at the Olympic Games, coming first in the discus at the 1928 Amsterdam Olympics. The 1928 women's program was limited to five events (the men's had twenty-two), and since then it has been gradually extended to match the men's—the 2008 Olympics held twenty-four events for men and twenty-three for women, with only the 50 kilometre road walk excluded from the women's schedule.

Although still grieving Don, the spring brought new hope, and Dawn began swimming again. She not only competed at the swimming league, but also entered a number of district amateur championships. This would lead to the first of her sports controversies.

Dawn beat the local favourite Lorraine Crapp. Lorraine's coach was furious at the gawky teen who had beaten his 'girl wonder', and he fought to take the win away from her. The claim was that Dawn, as a member of the Leichhardt-Balmain Swimming League, was a professional. While technically true, Dawn was a junior member and had never received cash awards. Nevertheless, the championship was taken away and she was banned from swimming competitively for eighteen months. She had lost her dearest brother a few months before and the thing that now meant most to her—swimming competitively. But 1951 was not over yet.

Later that same year her father and mother were both hospitalised, and Dawn took over the household. Her days became one chore after another. Her schoolwork suffered and her swimming regimen ceased altogether. Dawn admits that she was close to throwing in the towel on swimming when she met Harry, the person who would change her life forever.

The turning point

When things are darkest, the most difficult thing to see is yourself. It takes another person to hold up a light and a mirror. For Dawn, that person was Harry Gallagher. Harry had spotted Dawn training on her own. He was impressed, not only with her raw potential, but with her discipline and tenacity. Knowing her circumstances, he offered to train her for nothing. At about that same time, Harry also took on Jon Hendricks, who would eventually become Dawn's teammate.

Harry was of the breed of coach who demands long gruelling hours of physical conditioning. Dawn and Jon did lap after lap for hours on end until their bodies ached and their eyes burned. One of their most challenging routines involved swimming a half-mile with their ankles tied, dragging a float behind them. Harry used Dawn's competitive instinct by putting Jon in the next lane and telling her to keep pace with her unfettered teammate.

Dawn had power and stamina, so the focus was on smoothing out her technique, learning tactics and conserving power and energy. When the 1954–55 Australian Nationals were held, Dawn was ready. Winning the 220 yard (200 metre) freestyle in the record time of 2 minutes 29.5 seconds put the gangly teenager in the sporting spotlight. Shortly afterward, Harry and his wife moved from Sydney to Adelaide, South Australia to manage a pool.

Dawn in action at the Melbourne Olympic Games.

Eighteen-year-old Dawn left home to be with her coach, and lived with the Gallaghers in their apartment above the pool. She worked in a shop to make ends meet but still managed to put in three training sessions a day—which began with a three-hour session at 4.30 in the morning. She and her teammates spent so much time in the water they earned the nickname 'water babies'. Within a short six months this young woman was in the best shape of her life—just in time for the 1956 Nationals in Sydney and a chance for the Olympics.

Dawn not only defeated all comers in the Nationals, but also broke records in the 110 yard (100 metre) and 220 yard (200 metre) freestyle. She was now part of the Olympic team and months away from representing her country as Australia hosted the Summer Olympics for the first time ever.

Ups and downs on the road to greatness

Ron Clarke ran the torch into the stadium and lit the cauldron—and the 1956 Melbourne Olympic Games began. Dawn was awed by the sheer spectacle but stayed focused on the job at hand. She had logged thousands of hours of training for an event that would take about a minute—the 100 meter freestyle. A large Australian contingent was riveted on Dawn as she stepped onto the starting block. 'Bring it home, love', her mother and father shouted.

At the ready mark, all of Dawn's attention and energy focused on the narrow lane of water that lay in front of her. The pistol shot rang out and her body instinctively leaped into the water. When the clock stopped on sixty-two seconds even, a new world record, and a personal best, for the 100 meter freestyle went into the books.

The deep emotion we have come to expect from Olympians standing on the medals podium ran even deeper for Dawn the day she won her first gold medal. As she told her mother, 'This was Don's race, Mum. I won it for him'. She wrapped up her first Olympics with two more medals—silver in the 400 meter

---

NORMA ENRIQUETA BASILIO DE SOTELO

(1948–) is a Mexican hurdles champion who, at the age of twenty, became the first woman ever to light the Olympic Flame, in the opening ceremony of the 1968 Summer Olympics in Mexico City; it was a precedent that would be matched most famously at the Sydney 2000 Olympics by pioneering Aboriginal Australian champion Cathy Freeman (1973–), who won gold in the 400 meter sprint in the Sydney Games.

freestyle, and gold in the 100 meter relay. She had done her country, her family, and herself proud. Two years later, at the 1958 Cardiff Commonwealth Games, two more gold medals were in her cards: one for the 110 yards (100 metre) freestyle, and one for the 4 x 110 yards (4 x 100 metre) freestyle relay. And two years after that, Dawn would head off to the 1960 Olympics.

Just before departing for the Rome Olympic Games, Dawn pulled a stomach muscle during a butterfly workout. Her bad luck didn't end there. During the flight to Italy, she and her teammates got food poisoning. When they arrived in Rome the Australian swim team was in bad shape. Despite these setbacks, Dawn, who was now the oldest member of the squad, prevailed, winning yet another Olympic gold. 'Granny', as her teammates affectionately called her, took the gold in the 100 meter freestyle event. But it wasn't only her fine performance in the 100 meter freestyle event that would call attention to her in Rome.

From whoopee to whoops!

Dawn's twenty-third birthday fell during the Rome Olympics and she had been out celebrating the night before. That's one possible explanation for why she pulled up halfway through the 200 meter freestyle event, thinking she had won. She had upset teammates the day before when she refused to swim a leg in the 400 meter relay for fear of aggravating her torn stomach muscle. And if that were not enough, she was accused of offering 'an unauthorised swimming exhibition' when she allowed a group of schoolchildren to watch her work out. And while Dawn and her teammates were able to get beyond these upsets, trouble was brewing back in Australia.

Five months after her return from Rome, the manager of the Australian swimming team declared that she had embarrassed the team, and the Australian Swimming Union concurred. She was dropped from the team. This low point in her life was further compounded by the death of her father. But, as she had done in times before, she let the water offer solace.

She continued to train, but now she was competing with the clock. And, at the 1962 Commonwealth Games, she broke the barrier that had taunted her for so long. Dawn Fraser swam the 100 meter freestyle in under a minute in three heats, her best time being 59.3 seconds. It would seem she was back on track, but once again she was headed for another colossal dip in the road.

The Fraser cocktail: tragedy and victory with a dash of controversy

Months before her third Olympic Games, Dawn was driving late at night when her car collided with a truck. Her mother, a passenger in the car, died instantly. Dawn was battered and bruised and spent the next week hospitalised, being treated for neck injuries and depression. But eventually that special something in Dawn kicked in again. The press called it 'tenacity, spunk, and gumption', but it was a spirit that defied words.

Dawn looked forward to marching in the opening ceremony in Tokyo. It would likely be her last Olympics. But her events came early in the week, and the team

Dawn became a third-time gold medalist in the 100 meters freestyle at the 1964 Olympic Games in Tokyo.

BILLIE JEAN KING

(1943–) is an American tennis champion with a long and impressive career of firsts. In 1961 she won her first Wimbledon title, the first of thirty-two Grand Slam titles, including nine singles championships. In 1971, she became the first woman athlete to win more than US$100,000 in any sport in a single season. A keen advocate of equal pay for female athletes, King founded the women's tennis union—the Women's Tennis Association—and helped establish the women's pro tour. In 1973, the US Open became the first major tournament to offer equal prize money for men and women, largely due to her efforts.

rule was that any swimmer competing within three days of the opening ceremony could not march. But the kid who had defiantly jumped over the swimming pool fence twenty-one years before reared her head again, and Dawn paraded into the stadium with her teammates on 10 October 10 1964.

When Dawn took her place on the starting line two days later she was twenty-seven years old—ancient by swimming standards—but she was still a crowd favourite. The natatorium erupted in cheers when the finishing buzzer sounded and the announcer declared that *two* Olympic records had just been smashed: the 59.5 second record for the 100 meter freestyle, and the first athlete to win the same event in three consecutive Olympic Games.

As the world watched Dawn carry her country's flag in the closing ceremony, her slight limp may not have been noticed. Few people knew that she had sprained her ankle participating in a prank the evening before.

As the Games of the XVIII Olympiad were concluding, Dawn had been celebrating with the Australian men's hockey team. After a few beers the unwinding athletes went looking for an appropriate souvenir. They found it on top of the flagpole outside the Japanese Emperor's palace. But before anyone from the hockey team was able to grab it, police whistles sounded and the athletes scattered. Dawn grabbed a nearby police bicycle and took off. She would have made it too, if it weren't for a brick wall. The next morning, however, all was forgiven and the police captain graciously presented Dawn with the flag they were after.

On her return home Dawn was treated like royalty—probably better. She rode in parades, appeared on TV, and was honoured as the 'Australian of the Year'. But she was still an embarrassment as far as swimming officials were concerned. The Australian Swimming Union banned Dawn from competitive swimming for ten years. This pronouncement created an uproar across the country, for Dawn was universally loved, but the ban was not immediately lifted.

As she embarked on retirement, Dawn briefly entered the political arena and remains a celebrity to this day—attending premieres, opening sporting events, and speaking. She uses her notoriety for the good, continually raising money for a wide range of charities. Helping disabled athletes is a cause especially close to her heart.

———◦◦◦———

As Dawn Fraser said in the title of her autobiography, she's had 'one hell of a life'. She held thirty-nine world records, was a gold medalist in three consecutive Olympic Games, and in 1999 was proclaimed 'World Athlete of the Century' at the World Sports Awards in Vienna. However, the story of one of the greatest athletes of all time cannot be reduced to trophies, awards, and records. Dawn Fraser's story is not so much about swimming, or even about women. 'The first woman to …' rings hollow because her victories were about the triumph of the human spirit.

The unbridled energy and resolve that made her a champion also created controversy. The laws, rules, and regulations meant to help and protect, also bind and limit; and Dawn is a woman who tested all limits—physical, emotional, social, and spiritual.

The autobiography of Dawn Fraser is a ride on a wild rollercoaster. The soaring highs seem so much bigger because of the unfathomable lows. Each victory was tempered with a personal loss or a professional setback. However, in her story we seem to have stumbled upon the blueprint for greatness: irrepressible desire, unyielding perseverance, and monumental adversity. And, the most amazing thing may be that her story has not yet ended.

Right: Romania's 'teenage pixie' stunned audiences at the 1976 Montreal Olympic Games.

NADIA COMĂNECI
(1961–)

*Perfect performance in a
less than perfect world*

The Summer Olympics is often politicised and tangled in nationalist fervour. But, there are a few moments in Olympic history when the world comes together to pay tribute to a person whose athletic performance represents what is best in all of us. One of those moments was 19 July, 1976. The athlete was Nadia Comăneci—the first women to score a perfect '10' in any Olympic gymnastics event. What is even more remarkable, she did it at the age of fourteen. Her flawless performances and the difficulty of her routines resulted in a redefinition of the sport forever and the judges' expectations of women gymnasts.

Nadia Comăneci was born on 12 November 1961 in Onesti, a town of 50,000 built around huge petroleum refineries in the mountains of Romania. Her mother named her Nadia, the diminutive of Nadyezhda, which means 'hope', after a Russian movie heroine. From an early age, Nadia clung to the hope for a better life. Today she gives hope to millions.

Nadia began gymnastics at age five. Two athletic coaches at her school noticed Nadia tumbling in kindergarten and enrolled her into a young team called Flame. The following year Béla Károlyi, a gymnastics coach from the Onesti Sports School, visited Nadia's school. He noticed two girls in the playground pretending to be gymnasts—tumbling, prancing and bowing to imagined applause. Before he could get into the playground the recess bell rang. He lost the girls as they disappeared beyond the school doors. Béla went from classroom to classroom, 'Who wants to be a gymnast?' he asked. In the third room two girls jumped up and shrieked, 'We do, we do!' He had found them.

Nadia was the perfect student. 'She knows no fear', Béla would say. At age six her energy seemed endless, but her growing body took a beating. She trained and practised for four hours every day, six days a week, in addition to attending school.

Nadia's first competition was the Romanian National Junior Gymnastics Championship. She came in at thirteenth. Béla gave her a doll for her victory and told her she would never finish thirteenth again. He was right.

She won the Romanian National Championship a year later. That was Nadia's ticket to the Romanian National Gymnastics team. In competition after competition at home and internationally, medals, awards and honours began *pouring in. In most cases Nadia not only won, but also had the distinction of being the youngest person to ever win. By the time she went to the 1976 Olympics in Montreal she had over 200 'victory dolls' in her collection.*

Nadia stood motionless on the gray mat, arms in a perfect V above her head. The eighty-six pound pixie had awed the entire auditorium during her 30 second uneven parallel bar routine. Heads and eyes flashed to the scoreboard. The scoreboard lit up with a 1.00. The spectators were momentarily stunned. The ABC-TV announcers squinted in disbelief. How could this talented fourteen-year-old girl only score one point? Then, suddenly, shouts rang out from the crowd, 'Oh my God! It's a 10 ... a perfect score!' The individual cheers of spectators suddenly erupted into one gigantic roar that shook the huge auditorium. The scoreboard was not built for this unexpected happening, but Nadia had been relentlessly moving to this moment for the previous eight years.

Nadia was the undisputed star of the 1976 Summer Olympics in Montreal, Canada. She nailed a perfect 10 in her first performance on the uneven parallel bars, scored seven more 10s, and walked away from Montreal with three gold medals, one silver and one bronze. The world was in love. Reporter Robert Rigor, from ABC's Wide World of Sports, *produced a slow-motion montage of Nadia's performances set to the theme song for a popular soap opera. It played over and over on television, with the theme song eventually becoming a top ten hit in 1976 and composer Barry De Vorzon renaming it 'Nadia's Theme'. Back home Nadia was awarded the Hero of Socialist Labour, the highest award in Romania; but this honour, and her phenomenal Olympic win, made her not so much a star as the property of the Romanian government.*

Fearing Nadia might defect, the government had her watched twenty-four hours a day, and she was sent to the 23 August Sports Complex in Bucharest. The change was not good for Comăneci. Separated from her familiar coach and her parents, she became depressed, overweight and out of shape, and it showed at the 1978 World Championships where she came in fourth. Fearing a further downhill slide in her performance, Nadia was sent back to her old coach Béla Károlyi. She regained her confidence and form and performed much better in the 1979 World Championships and the 1980 Olympics in Moscow, winning two gold and two silver medals. It seemed her career was back on track when Béla and his wife defected to the United States. Security around her increased once again.

She remained with the Romanian gymnastics team, eventually becoming a coach. She almost faded into the history books when, in 1989, just months before the revolution, she defected with a group of other young Romanians. It was part of a larger plan that a new acquaintance, people smuggler Constantin Panait, had worked out. Nadia paid him $5000 for his help. He met her at the border and escorted her via Vienna to the United States. However, his assistance was motivated not by generosity, but rather avarice.

Nadia Comăneci celebrates as the scoreboard shows her perfect 10 on 19 July 1976.

They travelled the United States together by car. She stayed with him in motel after motel as she performed in exhibitions, did commercials and made television appearances. A New York Times *headline captured the sentiments of the press and public at the time: 'Scorn Gives Comăneci a Lesson in Image'. She was portrayed as a home wrecker and party girl. But this was a story concocted by Panait and his wife as a way to get press attention and notoriety. She was not his heart-throb, but a hostage, convinced Panait could send her back to Romania with a snap of his fingers. Fortunately, there was someone who knew these headlines could not be right—her old coach Béla Károlyi.*

Béla and his friend Alexandru Stefu lured them to Montreal by dangling a lucrative contract in front of Panait's nose. At the meeting Stefu managed to get Nadia alone. 'I have a problem', Nadia told him in her broken English. 'This guy is bad. Can you help me?' Panait came back into the room and realised that his cover was blown. He left the next day.

Stefu and his family took Nadia in until she was able to get her own place in Montreal, where she met up again with Bart Conner, whom she had first met at the 1976 American Cup, where he had won the men's title, and she the women's title. The relationship flourished and he invited her to his hometown of Norman, Oklahoma. They became engaged in 1994 and married in Bucharest in 1996 at the former Presidential Palace. In 2006 they had a son—Dylan Paul Conner.

In addition to running a gymnastics school with her husband, Nadia is active in many charities and on the Board of Directors for both the International Special Olympics and the Muscular Dystrophy Association. She has personally funded and built the Nadia Comăneci Children's Clinic in Bucharest, which provides free and low-cost medical care to Romanian children.

Nadia's colossal contributions to the sport of gymnastics were recognised when she received the Olympic Order, the highest award given by the International Olympic Committee, in both 1984 and 2004. She remains the only person to receive this award twice; and is the youngest recipient as well. The only *and the* youngest *are the two accolades that have always set Nadia apart in the past; and those distinctions enable her today to serve as an inspiration for countless little girls, in playgrounds all over the globe, who dream of being the best.*

INDIRA GANDHI (1917–1984)

The enigmatic 'midwife' of modern India

The Congress Party headquarters was awash in blue-green neon light. In a far back corner a small group of people huddled around a flickering black and white television set awaiting the final election tally. Cigarette smoke engulfed the watchers in a dull haze.

A woman, an orange shawl wrapped around her shoulders, sat alone off to one side staring thoughtfully. A reporter, fishing for quotes, cautiously approached her.

'What is your assessment of the situation?' the reporter asked. The woman did not look up. 'Too early. I cannot say.'

The reporter pressed on, 'Will the next Prime Minister be man or woman?' Without any hint of emotion the answer came back, 'That is not important, but rather who is contending'.

Still in provocative mode, the reporter asked, 'What will you do if you lose?'

The candidate, Indira Gandhi, looked up into the eyes of the reporter who instinctively pulled back. 'I am not afraid of winning, and I am not afraid of losing.'

Indira put her fate to the people of India. If the truth were known, part of her yearned for the freedom that losing the election would offer. At the same time, she could already feel the embrace of destiny. She would soon be the first woman Prime Minister of India.

Indira Ghandi was elected the first woman
Prime Minister of India in 1966.

The pedagogy of political games

While born to a family of privilege, Indira Gandhi came into the world seemingly without one of life's most important gifts—personal choice. Born on 19 November 1917, she was the only child of Jawaharlal Nehru and Kamala Nehru.

Her grandfather Motilal Nehru was a prominent member of the Indian National Congress in pre-Gandhi times, and her father was a popular leader of the Indian Independence Movement created by Mahatma Gandhi. Since Indira's father threatened British supremacy and rule, the family lived in a constant state of fear of siege. They never knew when soldiers would come to search their home, confiscate furniture to pay some sort of fine, or cart Jawaharlal off to jail. Indeed, her father spent much of his time in prison when she was young. Their early relationship was played out in the countless letters they sent to each other.

With her father frequently incarcerated, Indira was often alone as a child, for her sickly mother spent much of her time out of the country, in Switzerland, battling the tuberculosis to which she succumbed in 1936. Indira noted that her first great speeches were made atop the dining-room table to servants as they scurried about. 'All my games were political games', she recalled, 'I was like Joan of Arc, perpetually being burned at the stake'.

Life improved when Indira went to Oxford University in England. There she met a young man, Feroze Gandhi (no relation to Mahatma Gandhi), and they fell in love. She returned to India with him, and shocked her family when she announced their plans to marry. Feroze was a Parsi and Indira was a Hindu, which essentially meant the whole of India disapproved. But despite family and cultural resistance, Indira and Feroze were married in March 1942 in a traditional Hindu wedding.

SIRIMAVO BANDARANAIKE

(1916–2000) was the first woman in the world to serve as a nation's Prime Minister, when she became Prime Minister of Ceylon (now Sri Lanka) in 1960. The widow of Prime Minister Solomon Bandaranaike, who was assassinated by a Buddhist monk in 1959, she took over his party, the Sri Lanka Freedom Party, and won a resounding victory in the general election in 1960. She would go on to lead the party for the next forty years, and was re-elected twice, in 1970 and 1994, when her daughter, Chandrika Kumaratunga, became Sri Lanka's first and only female president.

꧁ꕥ꧂

In her father's footsteps

After their wedding, Indira and her husband devoted their energy to their country's struggle for independence from Britain. And Independence Day finally came in 1947, with Jawaharlal Nehru becoming the country's first Prime Minister. Since her mother had died some years earlier, Indira acted as her father's political attaché, confidant, and hostess. She often travelled with him and made the acquaintance of many national and international political leaders.

During her father's tenure, Indira also took her first steps toward national stature when she was elected to the twenty-one-member Congress Party working committee. Within four years she became president of the party. During the eleven months Indira served as president she displayed a toughness and political savvy that would become her hallmark. It seemed Indira Gandhi's destiny, and that of her country, were becoming completely enmeshed. However, for a brief moment at least, she dreamed about breaking away.

In 1963, when the notion of succeeding her father was gaining popular traction, Indira confided to her friend in England, Dorothy Norman, her desire to break away and start a new life in London. She had even identified the house she intended to buy and her plan for making a living by renting rooms to Indian students. However, Dorothy noted, 'She knew that politics was something she could not escape'. And that reality took hold when Jawaharlal Nehru died suddenly of a stroke in May 1964.

The fast track to posterity

Lal Bahadur Shastri succeeded Nehru as Prime Minister, and not long afterward appointed Indira to a cabinet post—Minister of Information and Broadcasting. Right away, since the majority of the Indian population was illiterate, Minister Gandhi embarked on a program to produce and distribute inexpensive radios nationwide, and instituted several educational radio programs sponsored by the government. She also quite frequently operated outside the realm of her official duties where she saw the need.

One notable early example of Indira's leadership-outside-the-box occurred during her 1964 trip to Madras (now Chennai), the capital of the non-Hindi-speaking southern state of Tamil Nadu, where riots had broken out when Hindi was declared the national language. She engaged community leaders, spoke to governmental officials and, later, supervised the reconstruction of the strife-ridden area. Respect for Indira quickly grew within her party and among the people, and was peaking when, unexpectedly, Prime Minister Shastri died of a heart attack. Indira's party elected her to the post of interim Prime Minister until elections could be held.

Boldness with genius in it

Indira's political savvy came to the fore when she out-manoeuvred her party's elite—K. Kamaraj, Morarji Desai and others—to become the Congress Party's prime ministerial candidate in the 1966 elections. Deeply divided around which candidate should be placed in the race and unable to reach a majority decision, the party leadership, led by Kamaraj, settled on Indira, convinced that she, as a mere woman, could be controlled by them. The party elite were so paternalistic that they sometimes referred to Indira as *gungi gudiya*, or 'dumb doll'. But Indira turned the tables on the strategy. The 'dumb doll' spoke, and the entire country listened and liked what they heard and saw.

CORY AQUINO

(1933–2009), born Maria Corazon Sumulong Cojuangco, was the eleventh President of the Philippines, serving from 1986 to 1992. She was the first female President of the Philippines, as well as Asia's first female president (excepting Soong Ching-ling, head of state of the People's Republic of China for twelve days in 1981). Cory Aquino was a world-renowned advocate of democracy, peace, women's empowerment, and religious piety.

Indira Gandhi was an expert at manipulating the media, which she courted to gain broad-based, nationwide recognition. Her popularity initially shielded her from retribution from the party leadership and, in the end, the candidate became less important than winning the election.

She was a shrewd campaigner. She spoke in broad, general terms that made it difficult to pin her down on any particular issue, and she was able to form alliances with minority political groups. Most importantly, she knew what to do, and what to say, to ensure that she would show up in the headlines. Her party won, but this time only by a narrow margin. She had become India's first woman Prime Minister.

The country was in a deep recession when Indira took the reins. The monsoons had not come for two years in a row. Because only forty per cent of India's farmland is irrigated, without these annual rains the food supply had been decimated. Hundreds of millions of people were at risk of starvation. Indira designed a ten-point program to bring about economic stability. But because the Congress Party held only 297 of the 545 seats in the Lok Sabha, India's parliamentary body, and her own party was divided, Indira enlisted the support of the Socialist and Communist parties to launch her new domestic initiatives. Her focus from the beginning was on domestic issues, but soon other events would thrust her and her country into the world arena.

In marked contrast to her father's lifelong opposition to nuclear weapons, Indira set her country on the path toward its first underground nuclear test. The nuclear program had actually begun soon after World War II, initially focused on energy production. The planned testing program was not only condoned, but also materially supported, by the United States. Recent nuclear tests by the People's Republic of China had alarmed America, which was anxious to establish an ally in the region. Since India relied on America for ongoing shipments of wheat, Indira felt that aligning with the West at this time was politically expedient. But fearing that the United States would exploit India's dependency further, she launched the Intense Agricultural District Program, 'The Green Revolution'.

VIGDÍS FINNBOGADÓTTIR

(1930–) is Iceland's first and, so far, only female president and head of state. As the fourth president of Iceland, serving from 1980 to 1996, she became the world's first elected female President (not including prime ministers, or non-elected leaders). In a country of political firsts, in 2009 Jóhanna Sigurdardóttir (1942–) became Iceland's first female Prime Minister and the world's first openly gay head of government.

❧

The Green Revolution diversified crops and modernised farming techniques. Within a few years India moved from a place of food shortages to a production surplus of wheat, rice, cotton, and milk. This highly successful program made Indira a favourite of the people and would help ensure her reelection, although international events demanded most of her time near the end of her first term.

In early 1971 army forces from West Pakistan conducted widespread incursions and atrocities against civilian populations in East Pakistan. Ten million refugees flooded into India, creating financial hardship and threatening political stability, and in March East Pakistan declared itself the independent nation of Bangladesh. Understanding that

Following pages: Campaigning in 1979, Indira Gandhi waves to an enthusiastic crowd in Kerala.

this was a turning point for her country, as well as for herself as a world leader, Indira Gandhi declared war on West Pakistan. She may have been bolstered by the words her father had once written to her, 'Be bold. All matters take care of themselves if you are bold. You will be able to do anything. Nothing will stand in your way'. His advice proved right in this instance. Indian troops were victorious against West Pakistani forces, which surrendered, and the separate nation of Pakistan came into being in December 1971.

Bright future overshadowed by dark times

'Garibi Hatao' ('Stop Poverty') was the slogan and banner that Indira Gandhi ran under in the 1971 election. She was able to maintain her popularity with the urban commercial population while, at the same time, bringing the huge poor and rural population under her umbrella. She gave the voiceless poor political weight that they had never before known. Her strategy worked and she emerged from the forty-three-day campaign with a parliamentary victory reminiscent of those her famous father enjoyed. However, in moving to the people for her power, she became a threat to the old guard, who were feeling increasingly powerless. In an attempt to get her to walk in step with the party, she was accused of 'grave acts of indiscipline'. At the same time, a faltering economy, continued droughts, inflation, and huge oil price increases came together to make daily life almost unbearable for the Indian people. Not surprisingly, her popularity began to plummet and her political adversaries took advantage of her vulnerability.

Political opponents conspired and eventually convicted her of electoral corruption. In reality, Indira's 'corruption' amounted to employing the aid of a governmental official during her campaign, and utilising a government-owned rostrum at some of her rallies, but the charges were enough to generate calls for her resignation. Her opponents, however, underestimated her will and tenacity. Instead of resigning, in 1975 Indira declared a state of emergency, and had the main conspirators arrested, along with

> ## ELLEN JOHNSON-SIRLEAF
>
> (1938–) is Africa's first elected woman head of state. In 2006, 159 years after the first modern nation in Africa was established by freed American slaves, Ellen Johnson-Sirleaf was inaugurated as its first woman president. Fondly called the 'Iron Lady' by her supporters, she is the current President of Liberia.

thousands of their supporters. Her actions would lead to a dark time in Indian history when democracy was at risk.

Resurrecting an old British law, the *Maintenance of Internal Security Act*, Indira imprisoned thousands of people, including twenty-one members of Parliament, suspended India's equivalent of the Bill of Rights, and censored the media. This only served to escalate the political turmoil. Demonstrators took to the streets chanting for her resignation. Strikes were organised. The entire country was paralysed. Public discontent grew to unprecedented levels. The foreign press and observers proclaimed that democracy was dead in India. Indira rebuffed the accusations: 'In India democracy has given too much licence to people'. Less than two months after Indira Gandhi assumed her new powers, more than 50,000 opponents were behind bars. The people called it 'the era of darkness'.

The prime minister was ruling by decree. For the first time in her life, Indira was out of touch with the people; she called for elections believing she still had broad support. She lost the 1977 elections, and her old adversary Morarji Desai became Prime Minister. Indira Gandhi was down … but not beaten.

Rising from the ashes

Winning the election was evidently not good enough for her opponents. In retribution, the new Janata Party government ordered her arrest on several charges, none of which could be proved in court. Their strategy was not to seek conviction, but rather to remove her from the political arena in India, once and for all. But, once again, Indira Gandhi demonstrated her political genius.

Mirroring Mahatma Gandhi's tactics, Indira insisted on being arrested in the Parliament. She waited almost three hours for the arresting officer to arrive; that entire time people began to gather in the street outside the Lok Sabha wondering how the standoff would end. As the officer entered the chamber and approached, Indira stood, stepped onto her chair and up on a table. She folded her hands together in front of her chest and, and with a slight bow of the head offered the traditional Hindu salutation— 'Namaste'. The news photographers' flashbulbs lit up the room. Even as her detractors watched her being led away to jail, it was clear their plan had backfired.

Her arrest on trumped-up charges gained her new sympathy from the people. Crowds began to fill the streets—this time in support of Indira. Citizens who, just two years earlier, feared she had become a dictator, were now asking her to once more lead them. The ruling party, crippled by their vendetta, began infighting. Within a few months the government was dissolved and elections were called for the following year.

Trouble in the north country

A tireless campaigner, Indira once again marched across India to rally popular support, and forge new political alliances. She won the 1980 election taking two-thirds of the seats in Parliament.

India's old ghosts—poverty and overpopulation—continued to haunt the country, compounded by a forty per cent fall in the value of the Indian rupee. And things were not much better on the international front. During her last term, Indira had been forced to deal with the Soviet intervention in Afghanistan. Her position changed several times— seemingly from day to day. It is unclear as to whether this was a shrewd strategy or out-of-character insecurity. The people, however, felt secure in Indira's leadership and her popularity rose to new heights. As a result, she could count on support from eighteen of India's twenty-two state governments. But there was trouble brewing in the northern state of Punjab, where Sikh separatists had sparked a bloody rebellion.

In June of 1984, the leader of the rebellion, Jarnail Singh Bhindranwale, began amassing weapons and supplies inside the Golden Temple, Sikhism's holiest shrine. Indira's response was quick and swift. She authorised Operation Blue Star, sending in army troops despite the presence of thousands of civilians within the temple complex. The operation was a technical success, but the toll on human life was enormous.

Government and independent accounts differ wildly on the number of casualties. Government estimates were eighty-three members of the army and 492 Sikhs. Independent accounts suggest that more than 500 troops

HILLARY RODHAM CLINTON

(1947–) is the first American First Lady ever to be elected to national office, being elected to the Senate in 2000. In 2008, she won the New Hampshire Democratic presidential primary, becoming the first woman in US history to win a presidential primary contest. In early 2009 Clinton became the US Secretary of State, a role that women have dominated in recent years, with three of the last four posts being held by women— Madeleine Albright (1937–), who became the first female Secretary of State in 1996, and Condoleezza Rice (1954–) who became the first African American woman to hold the office in 2005, are the other two.

and over 3000 Sikhs were killed, including women and children caught up in the conflict. While the Prime Minister was widely condemned internationally for this brutal action, overall India's people approved. The national magazine *Illustrated Weekly* conducted a poll a few months after the attack on the Golden Temple, and ninety-four per cent of those polled rated Indira Gandhi an able leader. However, there would soon be one more person added to the death toll for Operation Blue Star.

On 31 October 1984, Indira Gandhi was assassinated in the garden of her private residence in New Delhi. On her way to an interview with actor Peter Ustinov, to be aired on Irish television, she passed through a gate guarded by two of her bodyguards, Satwant Singh and Beant Singh, both Sikhs, who opened fire on her. She died on the way to hospital from multiple gunshot wounds.

From her birth to her death, Indira Gandhi's beloved country was in an almost constant state of turbulence. Nevertheless, this enigmatic woman was able to shepherd the nation through the critical transition from struggling provincial country to independent world power.

Mahatma Gandhi's humanism planted the seeds of India's independence, but a gritty, pragmatic politician was needed to protect and grow that seed until it blossomed. That was Indira Gandhi's destiny. With her leadership, India was able to span the gap between ancient heritage and modernity. She took on the monumental problems of poverty, starvation, and overpopulation, and on the international front positioned India as a major world power.

Biographers and historians struggle to reconcile what appears to be a duality in her character and choices. At times she sought a loving, nurturing, and peaceful path; at other times a cold, politically ambitious, and bellicose one. It may be impossible to penetrate the shell of this enigmatic woman because no one saw the world the way she did, although her own words offer an insight into how she saw her role. 'The task of building the new generation', she said, 'lies on the shoulders of women as men could never do, no matter how much they talk about it'. Her words seem to beckon to billions of women around the world. If we are to have a better world, it will be women who will lead the way. Indira Gandhi graciously accepted and met her responsibility as an Indian woman. And today, the 'new generation' Indira Gandhi dreamed about is manifesting in her beloved country and beyond.

MARGARET THATCHER

(1925–)

Towering figure of the
twentieth century

'I have changed everything', Margaret Thatcher said shortly after being elected leader of the British Conservative Party in February 1975, becoming the party's first woman leader. And thus began a fifteen-year ascendancy that would change the face of the nation.

Following the 1979 general election, Mrs Thatcher became the first female Prime Minister of the United Kingdom. She was the only British Prime Minister in the twentieth century to win three consecutive terms and, at the time of her resignation, Britain's longest continuously serving Prime Minister since 1827. But her significance goes far deeper than this. More than any of her peacetime predecessors, she carved her name on the country. By personality as much as achievement, she is considered the most renowned British political leader since Winston Churchill.

The daughter of Alfred Roberts, a strict Methodist, small-town grocer and alderman, and Beatrice Stephenson, Margaret was raised in the town of Grantham in Lincolnshire, England. Later, she received her Bachelor of Arts and Master of Arts degrees at Somerville College, Oxford. In her early twenties she became active in the Conservative Party in Kent and, at twenty-five, ran for election as a Member of Parliament; she was, at the time, the youngest ever female Conservative candidate, and her campaign attracted a wave of media attention. She lost the election but found Denis Thatcher, a wealthy businessman, whom she married in 1951.

She rose steadily through the Conservative Party, serving in a number of positions over the next three decades. As Secretary of State for Education and Science (1970–74), in the Cabinet of Edward Heath (she was only the second woman to hold a Cabinet portfolio in a Conservative government), she eliminated a program that provided free milk to schoolchildren, provoking a storm of controversy and prompting opponents in the Labour Party to taunt her with cries of 'Thatcher the milk snatcher'. She also created more comprehensive schools than any other education minister in history, although they were undermined during her tenure as Prime Minister.

It's been noted that Margaret Thatcher's brand of conservatism was rooted in the English provinces, and the English class system: 'My policies', she once said, 'are not based on some economic theory but on things I and millions like

---

Left: Margaret Thatcher, always immaculate, making a point in Parliament.

me were brought up with: an honest day's work for an honest day's pay; live within your means; put a nest egg by for a rainy day; pay your bills on time; support the police'. To reporter Douglas Keay, for Woman's Own *magazine on 23 September 1987, Mrs Thatcher remarked: 'I think we have gone through a period when too many children and people have been given to understand "I have a problem, it is the Government's job to cope with it!" ... and so they are casting their problems on society and who is society? There is no such thing!'*

Her political philosophy and economic policies advocated reduced state intervention, free markets, entrepreneurialism, privatisation of state-owned enterprises and the sale of public housing to tenants, as well as a cut in funding for social services and education. (In 1985, as a deliberate snub, the University of Oxford voted to refuse her an honourary degree.) While she was in office, the term 'Thatcherism' came to refer not just to these policies but also to certain aspects of her outlook and character, namely moral absolutism, fierce nationalism, a zealous regard for the interests of the individual, and a combative, uncompromising approach to achieving political goals.

Before Margaret Thatcher came to office, the United Kingdom appeared to be in terminal decline—ungovernable and an economic train-wreck. It was saddled with an empire, albeit a shrinking one, and ex-imperial attitudes still harder to shake off. At the same time, its industries were stuck, starved of investment, and wracked by awful labour relations. In her foreword to the 1979 Conservative Manifesto, she wrote of 'a feeling of helplessness, that a once great nation has somehow fallen behind'. She entered 10 Downing Street determined to challenge the old establishment. The next ten years would see her endlessly battling its members. Mr Julian Critchley, an irreverent Conservative backbench member of Parliament, would say, 'She cannot see an institution without hitting it with her handbag'. Others would say it was more like she took a sledgehammer to the Old Guard, as she doggedly worked to move the country to a global free-market economy.

Mrs Thatcher embarked on an ambitious program of privatisation of state-owned industries and public services, including aerospace, television and radio, the utilities, transportation, and British Steel. She lowered income tax and, ignoring words of caution from over 350 leading economists, raised indirect taxes. In 1981, unemployment soared and the Prime Minister's popularity correspondingly plummeted. The next year, when the impact of her economic rigour threatened to lose her the next election, Argentina's invasion of a British overseas territory, the Falkland Islands, brought a wave of patriotic enthusiasm and offered her a stunning way to reassert herself. In 1983, Mrs Thatcher won election to a second term in a landslide victory—the biggest victory since Labour's great success in 1945.

The Falklands War spotlighted her most significant international relationship, with US President Ronald Reagan (1981–89). The Prime Minister and the President, who together made the 1980s the decade of conservatism, shared a vision of the world in which the Soviet Union was an evil enemy. But Mrs Thatcher lacked the sunny charm that Reagan brought to his most controversial policies, and her 1976 speech condemning Communism earned her the nickname 'Iron Lady' in the Soviet press.

During her second term, she continued to make the kind of unequivocal decisions that had eluded a generation of British politicians. Most prominently, she took on the trade unions. The miners' strike in the spring of 1984 was the climax

Margaret Thatcher faces the press as leader of the winning Conservative Party, and therefore Prime Minister, on 20 February 1975.

of confrontation. For an entire year, she staunchly refused to meet the demands of the National Union of Mineworkers, who staged a nationwide strike to prevent the closure of twenty coal mines that the government claimed were unproductive. In the end she won; the miners returned to work without winning a single concession. The eventual closure of 150 collieries devastated entire communities. By the end of her second term, few aspects of British life had escaped the most sweeping transformation since the postwar reforms of the Labour Party.

The second half of Margaret Thatcher's tenure illuminated her hard-line attitude even more. She put pressure on US President George H.W. Bush to deploy troops to the Middle East to drive the Iraqi army out of Kuwait. Bush was somewhat apprehensive about the plan, so she remarked to him during a telephone conversation, 'This was no time to go wobbly!'

This later half of her premiership was also marked by an inexhaustible face-off with her traditionally pro-European party, when she adopted a hostile stance toward unifying with the European Community and resisting the Continental trend toward a single currency; a string of senior ministers left the Cabinet over the issue. She did not fare so well with the public, either. The implementation of a poll tax in 1989 produced outbreaks of street violence that spurred Conservative members of Parliament to move against her in November 1990. On 22 November, she announced her resignation as Conservative Party leader and Prime Minister.

To some she was ruthless, to others revolutionary. That she was controversial almost goes without saying: on average during her time in power, she had the second-lowest approval rating of any postwar Prime Minister, at forty per cent. Yet to her supporters, Margaret Thatcher remains a revolutionary figure who revitalised Britain's economy, impacted the trade unions, and put the United Kingdom on the path to recovery and long-term growth. No matter how little, or how much, she was supported during her long tenure, after her resignation in 1990, a MORI poll found that fifty-two2 per cent of Britons agreed that 'On balance she had been good for the country'. One thing is certain: the woman who said in 1974, 'It will be years—and not in my time—before a woman will lead the party or become Prime Minister', managed to defy every conventional expectation of women in power, stunning the British public in the process.

Right: 'The only real prison is fear'.

AUNG SAN SUU KYI

(1945–)

*Nobel Peace laureate who's
been denied 'first' status*

Some consider her the most courageous woman alive. Standing her ground at 160 centimetres and a mere 45.5 kilograms, before one of the world's most repressive military regimes, her diminutive appearance belies nerves of steel and an unrelenting devotion to democracy.

The leader of Burma's beleaguered democracy movement, Aung San Suu Kyi earned the right to become Prime Minister when her party won a landslide victory in a democratic election in 1990. The Burmese military junta, which has ruled the country since 1962, refused to turn over power, which would have made Suu Kyi the country's first woman Prime Minister. In 1989, with no specific charge or trial, she was placed under house arrest, where she has spent more than a dozen of the last twenty years. Despite her imprisonment, she has never given up her

Burmese pro-democracy activist holding a portrait of Aung San Suu Kyi during a rally in Tokyo on 24 May 2009.

struggle for social equality, human rights, and conciliation by peaceful means. Yet she was never primed for the life of a dissident.

Once a soft-spoken scholar at Oxford University, this daughter of a military hero who formed the Burma Independence Army (which helped end Japanese occupation and then drove the British out of the country), was only two years old when her father was assassinated—just six months before Burma declared its independence. As fate would have it, Suu Kyi would follow in her father's freedom-fighting footsteps years later. After receiving her education in Rangoon, Delhi, and at Oxford, she worked at the United Nations in New York. For most of the next two decades, she was committed to raising a family in England with her British husband, a dedicated Tibetan scholar. During this time, she cultivated a deep curiosity about her roots and her country's history, and decided to write her father's biography. She was forty-three years old when she returned to Burma to care for her dying mother, and found herself in the midst of an unexpected mass uprising against twenty-six years of repressive rule. On 8 August 1988, the army moved to crush the demonstrations, shooting down thousands of unarmed students, monks and civilians. The killings went on for four days, but the demonstrations continued until the new president finally resigned. It was at this moment that Suu Kyi decided to step forward and take a stand.

On 26 August she mounted a platform beneath Rangoon's imposing Shwedagon Pagoda and, before a crowd 100,000 strong, delivered a speech that would propel her onto the political stage and catapult her to prominence. Amid wild jubilation, the military hero's daughter labelled the national crisis 'the second struggle for national independence', and rallied the people to campaign for a democratic system of government. In no time the army cracked down again, and martial law was declared. The democracy activists promptly formed a new party, the National League for Democracy, with Suu Kyi emerging as their leader in the role of general secretary. In April 1989, she had a bold face-off with regime soldiers during a campaign trip through the villages, which resulted in the soldiers backing down and Suu Kyi being vaulted to iconic status.

The National League for Democracy went on to win more than eighty per cent of the legislative seats in May 1990, in the first free elections held in Burma in nearly thirty years, even though its leader had been put under house arrest in July 1989. After the elections, the junta refused to transfer power to a civilian government as it had promised, annulled the election results, and kept Suu Kyi detained until July 1995. But it would not be the last time she would be placed under house arrest.

Over the last decade and a half, Suu Kyi has spent more time in detention than not. In a rare period of freedom, she was faced with a heart-wrenching choice: leave Burma to join her husband, Michael Aris, who was dying of cancer in England, and risk being refused re-entry into her homeland; or stay put, and risk not being at her husband's death bed. Decades earlier, before agreeing to marry him and make a life in England, she had written in a letter to Michael: 'I only ask one thing, that should my people need me, you would help me to do my duty by them'. The time had come for Michael to make good on his promise. He petitioned the Burmese authorities to allow him to visit his wife one last time, but they refused to grant him a visa. Michael Aris died in London on 27 March 1999. Suu Kyi hadn't seen her husband for over three years, and had been with him only five times since her first house arrest in 1989. She also remains separated from her children, who live in the United Kingdom.

Suu Kyi is the recipient of the 1990 Rafto Human Rights Prize and the 1990 Sakharov Prize for Freedom of Thought. She was awarded the Nobel Peace Prize in 1991, attracting the world's attention to the plight of Burmese dissidents. In 1992, she announced that she would use her $1.3 million Nobel Peace Prize money to establish a health and education trust for the Burmese people.

She was expected to be freed in May 2009, when unexpectedly the military junta filed a new subversion charge. Suu Kyi was accused of violating her house arrest by providing shelter to an American visitor who trespassed on her property on 3 May. Despite her assertions that she didn't know the man, a trial took place at Insean Prison, where she had been held since the incident, which concluded on 11 August with Suu Kyi being sentenced to imprisonment for three years with hard labour, commuted to further house arrest of eighteen months. Her supporters say the trial was a pretext for keeping her detained so she cannot participate in the 2010 general elections.

Yet for all the attempts to silence Aung San Suu Kyii, this prisoner of conscious—who says 'The only real prison is fear'—vows to continue the fight for freedom until it is won. As to the dangers ahead, she says: '[The military regime] has been threatening to annihilate us for years. This is nothing new … We will go on. We believe in hoping for the best and preparing for the worst'.

Bibliography

PHARAOH HATSHEPSUT

Andronik, Catherine M. *Hatshepsut: His Majesty, Herself.* New York: Atheneum Books, 2001.

Cuppy, Will & Steig, William. *The Decline and Fall of Practically Everybody.* New York: Barnes & Noble Books, reprinted 1992 [1950].

The Story of Hatshepsut: http://www.bediz.com/hatshep/story.html.

Tyldesley, Joyce. *Hatchepsut: The Female Pharaoh.* New York: Penguin Books, 1998.

Wilford, John Noble, 'Tooth May Have Solved Mummy Mystery', *New York Times*, 27 June 2007.

LILIUOKALANI

Allen, Helena G. *The Betrayal of Liliuokalani, Last Queen of Hawaii, 1838–1917.* Honolulu: Mutual Publishing, 1991.

Dougherty, Michael. *To Steal a Kingdom: Probing Hawaiian History.* Waimanalo, Hawaii: Island Style Press, 1992.

Liliuokalani. *Hawai'i's Story by Hawai'i's Queen.* Rutland, VT: Charles E. Tuttle Co., 1964.

Office of Women's Affairs, University of Iowa, Queen Lydia Lili'uokalani: www.uic.edu/depts/owa/history/liliuokalani.html.

HYPATIA OF ALEXANDRIA

Deakin, Michael A. *Hypatia of Alexandria: Mathematician and Martyr.* Amherst, NY: Prometheus Books, 2007.

Dzielska, Maria. *Hypatia of Alexandria*, translated by F. Lyra. Cambridge, MA: Harvard University Press, 1995.

Ogilvie, M.B. *Women in Science: Antiquity Through the Nineteenth Century.* Cambridge, MA: MIT Press, 1986.

Whitfield, Bryan J. 'The Beauty of Reasoning: A Reexamination of Hypatia and Alexandria', *The Mathematics Educator* (University of Georgia) 6, Summer 1995, (1): 14–21.

ELENA LUCREZIA CORNARO PISCOPIA

Fusco, Nicolo. *Elena Lucrezia Cornaro Piscopia: 1646–1684.* Pittsburgh: U.S. Comm. for the E.L. Cornaro Piscopia Tercentenary, 1975.

Guernsey, Jane Howard. *The Lady Cornaro: Pride and Prodigy of Venice.* New York: College Avenue Press, 1999.

The Life of Helen Lucretia Cornaro Piscopia, Oblate of the Order of St Benedict and Doctor in the University of Padua. Rome: St Benedict's, 1896.

Thieling, Sarah. 'Elena Lucrezia Cornaro Piscopia'. Paper written for class of 1999. Decatur, GA: Agnes Scott College: www.scottlan.edu/lriddle/women/piscopia.htm.

WU ZETIAN

Clements, Jonathan. *Wu: The Chinese Empress who Schemed, Seduced, and Murdered her Way to become a Living God.* New York: The History Press, 2007.

Rothschild, N. Harry. *Wu Zhao: China's Only Woman Emperor.* New York: Pearson Education, Inc., 2008.

Shu-fang Dien, Dora. *Empress Wu Zetian in Fiction and in History: Female Defiance in Confucian China.* New York, Nova Science Publishing, 2003.

Yutang, Lin. *Lady Wu: A True Story*, London: William Heinemann, 1957.

POPE JOAN

Kelly, J.N.D. *Oxford Dictionary of Popes.* Oxford University Press, 1986.

Rustici, Craig M. *The Afterlife of Pope Joan: Deploying the Popess Legend in Early Modern England.* Ann Arbor: University of Michigan Press, 2006.

RAZIA SULTAN

Brijbhushan, J. *Sultan Raziya, Her Life and Times: A Reappraisal.* South Asia Books, 1990.

Dasgupta, Shahana. *Razia, The People's Queen.* Delhi: Rupa & Co., 2002.

The Delhi Sultanate: www.historytoday.com.

Hansen, Kathryn. 'The Virangana in North Indian History', *Economic and Political Weekly*, April 30, 1988.

Olsen, Kirsten. *Chronology of Women's History.* Westport, CT: Greenwood Press, 1994.

Satish, Chanda. *History of Medieval India (800–1700).* New Delhi: Orient Longman Private, 2007.

Zakaria, Rafiq. *Razia, Warrior Queen of India.* New York: Oxford University Press, 1966.

SHAGRAT AL-DURR

All Empires History Community: www.allempires.net/topic15135_post278637.html.

Gould, Vivian. *Daughters of Time: 2000 Notable Women: Antiquity to 1800.* BookSurge Publishing, 2006.

Time Magazine: Woman of the Millennium: www.bio.net/bionet/mm/neur-sci/1998-October/033806.html.

CHRISTINE DE PISAN

De Pisan, Christine. *The Book of the City of Ladies*, ed. Earl Jeffrey Richards, New York: Persea Books, 1998.

Hopkins, Andrea. *Most Wise and Valiant Ladies: Remarkable Lives*, London: Collins & Brown Ltd, 1997.

SparkNotes: *The Book of the City of Ladies: Character List*:

www.sparknotes.com/lit/cityladies/characters.html.

Ulrich, Laurel Thatcher. *Well-Behaved Women Seldom Make History*, New York: Vintage Books (A Division of Random House, Inc.), 2007.

Willard, Charity Cannon. *Christine de Pisan: Her Life and Works*, New York: Persea Press, 1984.

∞   LADY MURASAKI SHIKIBU

Dalby, Liza. *The Tale of Murasaki: A Novel*. New York: Vintage Anchor, 2001.

Nimura, Janice P. Review of *The Tale of the Genji*, translated by Royall Tyler (New York: Viking Press), *New York Times Review of Books*, 2 December 2001.

HILDEGARD OF BINGEN

Bennett, Judith M. & Hollister, C. Warren. *Medieval Europe: A Short History*. New York: McGraw-Hill, 2006.

Hopkins, Andrea. *Most Wise and Valiant Ladies: Remarkable Lives: Women of the Middle Ages*. New York: Welcome Rain, 1997.

Maddocks, Fiona. *Hildegard of Bingen: The Woman of Her Age*. New York: Doubleday, 2001.

Ruether, Rosemary Radford. *Visionary Women*. Minneapolis: Augsburg Fortress, 2002.

∞   JULIAN OF NORWICH

Baker, Denise Nowakowski. *Julian of Norwich's Showings: From Vision to Book*. Princeton, NJ: Princeton University Press, 1997.

Jantzen, Grace. *Julian of Norwich: Mystic and Theologian*. Mahwah, NJ: Paulist Press, 2000.

Julian of Norwich, Encyclopaedia Britannica Profiles. Encyclopaedia Britannica: www.britannica.com/women/article-9044118.

SOFONISBA ANGUISSOLA

Danto, Arthur Coleman. 'Sofonisba Anguissola (painting; Museum of Women in the Arts, Washington, D.C.)'. *The Nation*, 31 July 1995.

Perlingieri, Ilya Sandra. *Sofonisba Anguissola: The First Great Woman Artist of the Renaissance*. New York: Rizzoli, 1992.

Richard, Paul. 'The Lady-No-Longer-In-Waiting; Sofonisba Anguissola Finally Gets Her Due, and More, in "A Renaissance Woman"'. *The Washington Post*, 16 April 1995.

∞   ARTEMISIA GENTILESCHI

Chadwick, Whitney. *Women, Art, and Society*. London: Thames & Hudson, 1983.

Garrard, Mary D. *Artemisia Gentileschi*. Princeton, NJ: Princeton University Press, 1989.

Lapierre, Alexandra, *Artemisia: A Novel*, translated by Liz Heron. New York: Grove Press, 2001.

Mann, Judith (ed.), *Artemisia Gentileschi: Taking Stock*. Turnhout, Belgium: Brepols Publishers, 2006.

Vreeland, Susan. *The Passion of Artemisia*. New York: Penguin, 2002.

LUCY STONE

Blackwell, Alice Stone. *Lucy Stone: Pioneer of Women's Rights*. Boston: Little, Brown & Company, 1930.

Hays, Elinor Rice. *Morning Star: A Biography of Lucy Stone 1818–1893*. New York: Harcourt, Brace & World, 1961.

Kerr, Andrea Moore. *Lucy Stone: Speaking Out for Equality*. New Jersey: Rutgers University Press, 1992.

Lasser, Carol & Merrill, Marlene Deahl, eds. *Friends and Sisters: Letters between Lucy Stone and Antoinette Brown Blackwell, 1846–93*. University of Illinois Press, 1987.

Lunsford, Andrea A. *Reclaiming Rhetorica: Women in the Rhetorical Tradition*. University of Pittsburgh Press, 1995.

∞   CHRISTABEL PANKHURST

Liddington, Jill. *Rebel Girls: How Votes for Women Changed Edwardian Lives*. New York: Virago Press, 2006.

Nelson, Carolyn Christensen. *Literature of the Women's Suffrage Campaign in England*. Calgary: Broadview Press, 2004.

Pugh, Martin. *The Pankhursts*. Harmondsworth, London: Penguin Books, 2002.

ELIZABETH BLACKWELL

Baker, Rachel. *The First Woman Doctor: The Story of Elizabeth Blackwell, M.D.* New York: Simon & Schuster, 1973.

Blackwell, Elizabeth. *Pioneer Work in Opening the Medical Profession to Women*, Introduction by Amy Sue Bix. New York: Humanity Books, 2005

Boyd, Julia, *The Excellent Doctor Blackwell: The Life of the First Female Physician*. Stroud, UK: The History Press, 2006.

Fancourt, M. St. J. *They Dared to be Doctors: Elizabeth Blackwell and Elizabeth Garrett Anderson*. London: Longmans, 1965.

Hays, Elinor Rice. *Those Extraordinary Blackwells: The Story of a Journey to a Better World*. New York: Harcourt, Brace & World, 1967.

Kline, Nancy, *Elizabeth Blackwell: A Doctor's Triumph*. Berkeley CA: Conari Press, 1997.

∞   DR. JAMES MIRANDA BARRY

Brandon, Sydney: 'Barry, James (c. 1799–1865)', *Oxford Dictionary of National Biography*, Oxford University Press, Sept. 2004; online edn, Jan. 2008.

Holmes, Rachel. *Scanty Particulars: The Life of Dr. James Barry*. Harmondsworth: Penguin Books, 2003.

Holmes, Rachel. *The Secret Life of Dr James Barry: Victorian England's Most Eminent Surgeon*. Port Stroud, Gloucestershire: The History Press/Tempus, 2007.

Rose, June. *The Perfect Gentleman*. Hutchinson, 1977.

MARY SURRATT

Hartranft, John F. *The Lincoln Assassination Conspirators, Their Confinement and Execution, as Recorded in the Letterbook of John Frederick Hartranft*, edited by Edward Steers Jr. and Harold Holzer. Louisiana State University Press, 2009.

Larson, Kate Clifford. *The Assassin's Accomplice: Mary Surratt and the Plot to Kill Abraham Lincoln*. New York: Basic Books, 2008.

Swanson, James L. *Manhunt: The 12-Day Chase for Lincoln's Killer*. New York: HarperCollins, 2007.

Trindal, Elizabeth Steger. *Mary Surratt: An American Tragedy*. Gretna, LA. Pelican Publishing Company, 1996.

PEARL HART

Alward, Mary M. Pearl Hart: The Arizona Bandit; Women in History: www.suite101.com/article.cfm/historys_wild_women/113805/1.

Coleman, Jane Candia. *I, Pearl Hart*, New York: Leisure Books, 2000.

Legends of America: A Travel Site for the Nostalgic & Historic Minded. Pearl Hart – Lady Bandit of Arizona: www.legendsofamerica.com/WE-PearlHart.html

Metz, Leon Claire. *The Shooters*. New York: Berkley Trade, 1996.

ISABELLA BIRD

Barr, Pat. *A Curious Life for a Lady: The Story of Isabella Bird, a Remarkable Victorian Traveller*. New York: Doubleday, 1970.

Bird, Isabella L. *The Englishwoman in America* [1856]. Lenox, MA: Hard Press Editions, 2006.

Bird, Isabella L. *Among the Tibetans* [1894]. Lenox, MA: Hard Press Editions, 2006.

Kaye, Evelyn, *Amazing Traveler Isabella Bird*, Boulder, CO: Blue Panda Publications, 1994.

Stoddart, Anna M. *The Life of Isabella Bird (Mrs. Bishop)*. New York: E.P. Dutton & Co, 1907.

ALEXANDRA DAVID-NÉEL

Duncan, Joyce. *Ahead of Their Time: A Biographical Dictionary of Risk-Taking Women*. Westport, CT: Greenwood, 2002.

Foster, Barbara & Foster, Michael. *Forbidden Journey: The Life of Alexandra David-Néel*. New York: Harper & Row, 1987.

Foster, Barbara and Foster, Michael. *The Secret Lives of Alexandra David-Néel: A Biography of the Explorer of Tibet and its Forbidden Practices*. New York: Overlook Press, 1997.

Middleton, Ruth. *Alexandra David-Néel: Portrait of an Adventurer*. Boston, MA: Shambhala, 1989.

MARIE CURIE

Curie Labouisse, Eve. *Madame Curie: A Biography*. Reading, MA: Da Capo Press, 2001.

Pflaum, Rosalynd. *Grand Obsession: Madame Curie and her World*. New York: Doubleday, 1989.

Quinn, Susan. *Marie Curie: A Life* (Radcliffe Biography Series). Reading, MA: Da Capo Press, 1996.

Reid, Robert. *Marie Curie*. New York: Signet Books, 1978.

BERTHA VON SUTTNER

Abrams, Irwin. Alfred Nobel, Bertha von Suttner and the Nobel Peace Prize; published as 'The Odd Couple' in Scanorama 23, no. 11 (November 1993): 52–56: www.irwinabrams.com/articles/oddcouple.html.

DOROTHY LEVITT

BBC Television. *Penelope Keith and the Fast Lady*, 19 February 2009.

Barrett, J. Lee. *Speedboat Kings: 25 Years of International Speedboating*. Detroit: Arnold-Powers Inc., 1939.

Levitt, Dorothy. *The Woman and the Car: A Chatty Little Hand Book for All Women Who Motor or Who Want to Motor*. New York, London: John Lane Co., 1909.

Historic Racing: A View of 1903 Court Cases: www.historicracing.com.

Spooner, Stanley. *The Auto Motor Journal 27*, vol. XI, July 7, 1906.

Wosk, Julie. *Women and Machines*. Baltimore: Johns Hopkins University Press, 2002.

BERTHA BENZ

Bertha Benz Memorial Route: www.bertha-benz.de/indexen.php?inhalt=home.

Bertha Benz Monument: www.zercustoms.com/news/Bertha-Benz-Monument.html.

Bingham, Mindy. *Berta Benz and the Motorwagen: The Story of the First Automobile Journey*. Santa Barbara, CA: Advocacy Press, 1989.

AVIS AND EFFIE HOTCHKISS

Ferrar, Ann. *Hear Me Roar: Women, Motorcycles and the Rapture of the Road*. Center Conway, NH: Whitehorse Press, 2001.

Spoke To Spoke. Women in Motorcycle History: Effie Hotchkiss: www.cycleconnections.com/articledetail.asp?TypeID=8&ID=1866.

www.bikerlady.com/bikerladyweb/effie!.htm.
www.harley-davidson.com/wcm/Content/Pages/Women/
women_history_2.jsp?locale=en_US.

AMELIA EARHART
Butler, Susan. *East to the Dawn: The Life of Amelia Earhart*.
New York: Da Capo Press, 1999.
Haugen, Brenda. *Amelia Earhart: Legendary Aviator* (Signature
Lives). Minneapolis, MN: Compass Point Books, 2007.
Pflueger, Lynda. *Amelia Earhart: Legend of Flight* (Historical
American Biographies). Berkeley Heights, NJ: Enslow
Publishers, 2003.
Shore, Nancy. *Amelia Earhart*. New York: Chelsea House
Publishers, 1987.

RAYMONDE DE LAROCHE
Baroness de Laroche biography: http://earlyaviators.com/
edelaroc.htm.
Harper, Harry. 'The Brave Baroness: First Licensed
Ladybird', *Air Trails*, July 1953.
Lebow, E.F. *Before Amelia*. Washington, DC: Brassey's Inc.,
2002.
Museum of Women Pilots: www.museumofwomenpilots.
com/index.html.

BESSIE COLEMAN
Fisher, Lillian. *Brave Bessie: Flying Free*. Houston, TX:
Hendrick-Long Publishing Company, 1995.
Hart, Philip S. *Up in the Air: The Story of Bessie Coleman*
(Trailblazer Biographies). Minneapolis, MN:
Carolrhoda Books, 1996.
Rich, Doris L. *Queen Bess: Daredevil Aviator*. Washington,
DC: Smithsonian Books, 1993.

VALENTINA TERESHKOVA
Lothian, A. *Valentina: First Woman in Space*. Edinburgh:
Pentland Press, 1993.
Oberg, James E. *Red Star in Orbit: The Inside Story of Soviet
Triumphs and Failures in Space*. New York: Random House,
1981.
O'Neill, Lois Decker. 'Farthest out of all: The first
woman in space', in *Women's Book of World Records and
Achievements*. Garden City, NY: Doubleday/Anchor
Press, 1979.
Sharpe, Mitchell R. *It Is I, Sea Gull: Valentina Tereshkova, First
Woman in Space*. New York: Crowell, 1975.

SALLY K. RIDE
Camp, Carol Ann. *Sally Ride: First American Woman in
Space (People to Know)*. Berkeley Heights, NJ: Enslow
Publishers, 1997.

Hopping, Lorraine Jean. *Sally Ride: Space Pioneer*. New York:
McGraw-Hill, 2000.
Hurwitz, Sue. *Sally Ride: Shooting for the Stars* (Great Lives
Series). New York: Ballantine Books, 1989.
Kramer, Barbara. *Sally Ride: A Space Biography*. Berkeley
Heights, NJ: Enslow Publishers, 1998.
NASA. Biographical Data: Sally K. Ride, PhD.: www.jsc.
nasa.gov/Bios/htmlbios/ride-sk.html.

PEGGY WHITSON
Internet Broadcasting Systems, Inc. (2007). History in
Space: 2 Women Commanders; Local6.com Internet
Broadcasting Systems, Inc.: www.local6.com/
nejws/14290968/detail.html?rss=orlpn&psp=news
National Aeronautics and Space Administration,
International Space Station. Preflight Interview:
Peggy Whitson: www.nasa.gov/mission_pages/station/
expeditions/expedition16/exp16_interview_whitson.
html
National Aeronautics and Space Administration: www.jsc.
nasa.gov/Bios/htmlbios/whitson.html.

DAWN FRASER
Brasch, Nicolas. *Great Australian Women in Sports*.
Melbourne: Heinemann, 1997.
Dawn Fraser Biography: www.biggeststars.com.
Dawn's Own Website: www.dawnfraser.com.
Fraser, Dawn. *One Hell of a Life: Dawn Fraser*. Sydney:
Hodder Headline Australia, 2001.
Yadav, Kartik. The Life of Dawn Fraser: www.bookrags.
com/essay-2005/3/26/01546/3097.

NADIA COMĂNECI
After Escaping: www.nadiaComăneci.com.
'Gymnasts', *The Columbia Electronic Encyclopedia*, 6th edn.
New York: Columbia University Press, 2007.
Nadia Comăneci: www.romanian-gymnasts.com.
Nadia Comăneci: www.pocanticohills.org.
Nadia Comăneci: www.en.wikipedia.org.
'Scorn Gives Comăneci a Lesson in Image', *New York Times*,
December 13, 1989.

INDIRA GANDHI
Ashby, Ruth & Ohrn, Deborah Gore, eds. *Herstory*. New
York: Viking, 1995.
Bhatia, Krishan. *Indira: A Biography of Prime Minister Gandhi*.
New York: Praiger, 1974.
Frank, Katherine. *The Life of Indira Nehru Gandhi*. London:
HarperCollins, 2001.
Indira Gandhi: www.cncw.com/india/indira.htm.
Indira Gandhi: www.netsrq.com/.

ᔕ AUNG SAN SUU KYI

Aung San Suu Kyi. *Letters from Burma*. Penguin Group, 1997.

Clements, Alan. *The Voice of Hope: Aung San Suu Kyi Conversations with Alan Clements*. New York: Seven Stories Press, 2008.

Stewart, Whitney. *Aung San Suu Kyi: Fearless Voice of Burma*. New York: Twenty-First Century Books, 1997.

Online Burma/Myanmar Library: Aung San Suu Kyi: http://burmalibrary.org/show.php?cat=7&lo=d&sl=0

The Nobel Peace Prize 1991: Aung San Suu Kyi: http://nobelprize.org/nobel_prizes/peace/laureates/1991/ www.freeburma.org/

ᔕ MARGARET THATCHER

Berlinski, Claire. *'There Is No Alternative': Why Margaret Thatcher Matters*. New York: Basic Books, 2008.

Hughes, Libby. *Madam Prime Minister: A Biography of Margaret Thatcher*. Minneapolis, MN: Dillon Press, 1998.

Margaret Thatcher, *Encyclopaedia Britannica*: www.britannica.com/EBchecked/topic/590098/Margaret-Thatcher.

Ridley, Matt, 'Et tu, Heseltine? Unpopularity was a Grievous Fault, and Thatcher hath Answered for it', *Washington Post*, 25 November 1990.

Watching the pits disappear, BBC, 5 March 2004: http://news.bbc.co.uk/2/hi/uk_news/3514549.stm.

Acknowledgments

I would like to thank Diana Hill at Murdoch Books, for her encouragement, unerring attention to detail, and unfailing comic relief throughout the writing of this book. I am grateful to the staff at Clearfield Public Library, for honouring my countless requests and providing me with a cozy corner in which to work; and to my son, Theo, and my daughter, Luella, whose infectious enthusiasm kept me on track. And finally, thanks to my parents, Dolores and Thomas Santa Lucia, for their invaluable support and without whom this book could not have been written at all.

Picture credits

AKG Images: pages 33, 38, 77, 197, 209, 232

Australpress: pages 139, 147, 156-157, 160

Corbis: pages 22, 69, 80, 82-83, 88, 111, 131, 222–223, 226, 229, 235, 236, 239, 245, 255, 282–283, 288, 293, 294

Getty: pages 9, 25, 55, 126, 151, 181, 186, 194, 217, 241, 252, 256, 261, 265, 268, 271, 274, 277

Mercedes-Benz Archive & Sammlung: page 210

Photolibrary: pages 12, 16–17, 21, 27, 34, 40, 43, 47, 53, 57, 61, 67, 71, 85, 95, 99, 102–103, 107, 114, 129, 142, 165, 174, 176, 179, 191, 199, 204–-05, 248, 258, 291

Picture Desk/The Art Archive: pages 117, 163

Index